Also available at all good book stores

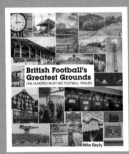

9781785316470

9781785313929

9781801500630

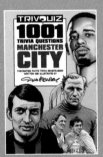

9781801500173

9781785319853

9781785316678

9781785316692

9781785315633

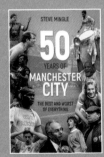

9781785313288

FEELING BLUE

Dickie Denton

A TRUE STORY OF LOVE, LIFE AND BELONGING

FEELING BLUE

FOREWORD BY PETER DRURY

First published by Pitch Publishing, 2022

Pitch Publishing
A2 Yeoman Gate
Yeoman Way
Worthing
Sussex
BN13 3QZ
www.pitchpublishing.co.uk
info@pitchpublishing.co.uk

ISBN 978 1 80150 076 0

Typesetting and origination by Pitch Publishing
Printed and bound in India by Replika Press Pvt. Ltd.

Contents

'Everything I know about morality and the obligations of men, I owe it to football.'

Albert Camus

Foreword

by Peter Drury

IT FEELS ridiculous to admit this now, but the funny thing, in hindsight, about the morning of Sunday, 13 May 2012 was that it felt so calm. To the dispassionate (neither blue nor red), it seemed so obvious. Clearly, Manchester City would beat QPR. The stakes were unquestionably high; the jeopardy less so. City were simply a much, much better team. (Nobody told Jamie Mackie!)

With a naivety bordering on dereliction of duty, I assumed (in fact, I *knew*), on the northbound train that morning, that City would become champions. This would be a 'routine' coronation.

Of course, the briefest reflection on City's fabled (sometimes comedic) historical narrative should have shaken me from that misguided mindset. Had this book been my companion between London and Manchester Piccadilly that Sunday, I would have remembered to panic. City's story is NEVER routine.

Being present to witness those crazy events counts as one of the greatest blessings of my professional life. To an extent,

I feel guilty about it. I had no 'entitlement' to that blessing. I hadn't earned the right, suffered for the cause or endured decades of sniggering disdain. Your author had ... and he was thousands of miles away on another continent. He deserved to be there, not me!

There are relatively few moments in a commentator's career when he is utterly set free. The 'Aguero moment' was one of those rare and precious instances. No amount of preparation, no statistical data, no biographical or historical recall could enhance that raw event. It just happened; and all of us who were fortunate enough to be holding a microphone at the time were carried along for the ride.

Only the foolishly vain amongst the broadcasting fraternity would ever claim a goal for themselves. No commentator ever scored; he was just lucky to be there when someone else did. Nevertheless, these moments can attach themselves.

Some years after the event, I happened to be on a packed train home from a City game with Martin Tyler whose articulation of that title-winning moment (for Sky Sports in the UK) was utterly brilliant. We both had to get off at the same stop and – as we picked our way between weary, beer-soaked fans – one of them spotted him. 'Hey, Martin,' he slurred, 'Thanks so much for that Aguero goal!'

Once on the platform and away from the crowd, I exclaimed to Martin that 'they have reached the point of believing you were actually responsible for that goal! The Premier League should take the assist away from Balotelli!'

From somewhere, on that frenzied evening, my subconscious lexicon came up with the word 'Staggering'.

I guess it was as apt a word as any but – in the immediate aftermath – I thought little of it. In the decade since, that unremarkable adjective has followed me all over the world. And now it's the heading for a chapter. Thanks Kun!

It's a massive privilege to have been a tiny, tangential part of that day, particularly in the context of the very personal story you are preparing to read here.

'Aguero day' was defining in so many personal histories. Thousands (millions even) intertwine their 'real' lives and relationships with the complex, irrational, inexplicable bond they feel with a football club. Not much of it makes any sense. It doesn't have to.

Football (and sport in general) is about human beings. This is a beautifully told human story, wrapped in a social history of the late twentieth century and beyond. Manchester City – a larger-than-life club (even when times were bleak) which has always been a glorious 'caricature of itself' – provides the ideal backdrop … and, of course, the unimaginably happy ending. Enjoy!

Introduction

I SET out to tell a football story. Somewhere along the way it became a story of identity and belonging (and some football). But it was football that first gave me my voice and that is why I will always love the game.

There is an acknowledged truth that we all have, within ourselves, a book; a story to tell. I believe it is just a matter of finding the right one. Consequently, I have searched among the hobbits, heroes, boardrooms, and bedrooms of life and literature but found nothing that gave me the inspiration to create a story. Maybe I just lack imagination in that respect. I am therefore taking the easy way out. I am not going to invent a story. Why would I when I have my own to tell? Like many tales that have gone before, it is one of hope overcoming despair. It is about faith, family, and football, but most of all, it is a story of love. Its themes and challenges are not unique to me; how could they be, when they are so universal?

At approximately 5.44pm on 13 May 2012 an Argentine footballer named Sergio Agüero scored the most celebrated goal in Premier League history. With due deference to Geoff Hurst and Michael Thomas, it is possibly the most famous goal in English football's glorious past. Worldwide media and the global phenomenon of the Premier League have certainly made it the most viewed.

On that sunny Manchester afternoon, as Agüero wheeled away in triumph, football watchers across the globe let out a collective gasp. Thousands of Manchester City supporters in locations all over the world celebrated like never before. For many it felt like the end of a journey. For some it had lasted for ten years, for others 20. My journey lasted for nearly 40 years. For many more it was even longer. There is only one version of this journey's joyful end; television has recorded it, and the Agüero moment will forever unite the weary travellers. However, the winding paths that took so many people to that happy place are diverse and varied. This is my version, my journey, my life, and my faith.

It is a story told from memory, each event and occurrence an indelible impression in my mind. The only research has been to verify dates here and there. Some names have been changed out of respect, but otherwise each word of it is my true and honest recollection. I did wonder if I would ever finish it as, like Manchester City, I often start off with bright ambition only to disappoint. Remarkably, I did, and I can only hope that you enjoy it.

Prologue

Sunday, 13 May 2012
1 Newton Road, Singapore – 8pm

DESPERATE TO kill time, I picked up my phone and sent a text message to my friend Nick in the UK, 'No more sleeps.' Like a five-year-old waiting for Christmas, I had been counting down the days and nights of the preceding week.

The previous Sunday's win at Newcastle had left City with just one game left to play and one tentative hand on the Premier League trophy. Upon hearing the final whistle, the commentator had lyrically proclaimed, 'Start preparing the ribbons ... and those ribbons are sky blue.' Nick, a Newcastle fan, had been at St James' Park. He had reported back that City were deserved winners and would be worthy champions. Only Queens Park Rangers now stood between City and the title.

Until the last plane for Manchester had departed Singapore's Changi airport, I was still desperately trying to get a ticket for the game. During the last week frantic emails had been sent to my usual contacts, and then anyone and everyone who came to mind. But this was something incredibly special and each avenue I went down was a dead end. With a heavy heart, the flight reservations, made in hope rather than expectation, had been cancelled.

Singapore was starting to feel like home anyway. Work had taken me there and in the past three years I had developed a great attachment to the city, its culture, and the people. The only question that therefore remained was where to watch the match. At home or in public? The sanctity and security of my Newton Road apartment was the safe option. Not safety from any physical danger, as that simply does not exist in Singapore, but refuge from ridicule. After 37 years of loyal support, ridicule was nothing new, especially from Manchester United fans. United were the 'pride of Singapore' and if we were to fail, I would be surrounded.

Just thinking about it made me feel nauseous. Wherever we went in Singapore we would be outnumbered. Only United could win the title if City stumbled, and if that were to happen, I did not want to drown in a sea of red celebration. On the other hand, should we win then where better to be than out and among them all? Proud, sky blue champions. The big fat silver Premier League trophy, the one that defines United, would be ours for all to see. Choosing where to watch was a tough, albeit very much a First World problem.

Finally, we decided: fellow City fan Ryan and I, plus a select group of friends, would meet in front of the big screen in Robertson Quay. Al fresco glory beckoned on a balmy Singapore night, 7,000 miles away from Manchester's late spring afternoon.

Watching football in the island state of Singapore entails a lot of long evenings. Even the UK's lunchtime games become late affairs. With a seven- or eight-hour time difference the matches straddle the hours either side of midnight. For a single man, lubricated by free-flowing towers of Tiger beer, it makes for an exceptionally good Saturday night. In the case of a Sunday fixture, it can mean an agonisingly long weekend, during which nerves build, hope becomes fear, and belief becomes doubt.

The kick-off would be at 10pm local time. As a technical director for the world's largest adult drinks company, I should have been preparing for the week ahead, but for now this transcended the real world of work. Anxious that someone might usurp the seats that were reserved, I allowed two hours for the 15-minute taxi journey. Cautious about the public humiliation that might ensue if things did not go to plan, I wore no colours. I stepped into the elevator on the 26th floor and looked back through the glass doors into my apartment. In a few hours I would return with a lifetime's faith and loyalty repaid, or alternatively as a broken man. There was no middle ground. I had woken up on that Sunday morning full of joyful anticipation. Now all I could feel were the all-too-familiar butterflies. My stomach tightened as the elevator doors closed and the descent commenced. There was no turning back.

1

Baptism

I CAN still remember so vividly when and where it all started. Sometimes, when a sterile Premier League game feels like the product of a corporate marketing department, I wish I could go back and relive it. I wish it even more so during lockdown. I wish it for my nephews and nieces and for the generation of football followers yet to come, but especially I wish it for those of my generation. For those boys, now middle-aged men, who once they had experienced it, were hooked for life. I wish to relive it apart from one small detail, and that I will come to later.

The date was 30 November 1974. The venue: West Didsbury, Manchester.

For days I had been begging my father to take me to the match. I am sure we called it 'mithering' back then. He had promised to take my two brothers but, my eight and a half years were deemed to be too young. At nine and ten, my brothers were not much older, but I suppose that he thought that being responsible for all three young Denton boys might be too much of a handful. He was not a football man, my father; in fact, nobody in the family was.

Michael James Denton was born in Northampton, of lower middle-class stock. He failed his 11-plus examination but was the first member of his family to win a place at university. After graduating in physics he went on to become a textile scientist. A late convert to Catholicism, he met my mother, Anne, via Manchester University's Catholic Society. He never returned to live in Northampton because my mother was south Manchester through and through. At the age of 25, her father, Walter, had been appointed as the city's youngest ever headmaster at St Cuthbert's Catholic Primary School in Withington. He remained in that position for some 40 years until he retired in 1969.

My mother, the youngest of Walter and Annie's three children, attended St Cuthbert's and then Loreto College. When she met my father, she was studying for a degree that serious illness prevented her completing. In 2009, two days after my parents' 50th wedding anniversary, I took my mother back to Manchester to revisit some of her childhood memories. We stopped the car outside St Cuthbert's and decided to ask if we could enter. Fully expecting, in these days of high security, to be asked to leave the moment the CCTV captured us at the gate, we tried the intercom and explained to the receptionist my grandfather's past status in the school.

'Oh, you mean Mr Clift,' she said, as if he were still the incumbent headmaster.

It had been 40 years since his retirement and another 20 since his death. The receptionist also happened to be an ex-pupil and welcomed us with genuine warmth as she showed us round the building, my mother seeing memories at every turn. It was a special moment for both of us.

Michael Denton and Anne Clift married, at St Cuthbert's Church of course, in April 1959. Within a few, action-packed years they had fulfilled their devout Catholic duty and brought forth six young Dentons. Born in March 1966, I was the last. To be factually correct they did only bring forth five children biologically; my brother David was adopted prior to my birth. My siblings and I could only see him as our brother, but as I grew up, I became increasingly aware that those around us often saw him differently. I do not know a lot about my brother David's parentage and birth other than that he was born in London of an Asian mother and adopted by my parents before his second birthday via a Manchester-based Catholic adoption society. I do not believe that David knows any more himself.

So, we were a family of eight: my parents, followed by my three sisters Elizabeth, Katherine, and Rachel and my two brothers Alban and David. Like all my siblings, I was delivered into the good care of the nurses at Withington Hospital, where on a good day and with a fair wind you could hear the roar from the Maine Road crowd. At least that is what I like to think. We lived initially in Heaton Mersey, Stockport, in a three-bedroom, semi-detached house so typical of 1930s suburban development. Eight was a squeeze, but that soon became nine when my paternal grandfather Arthur, or Poppa as he was known to us, moved in following the death of my grandmother. The rapid expansion of the Denton family necessitated a bigger house and in 1973 we moved to 1 Winster Avenue, West Didsbury.

With six hungry mouths to feed, bodies to clothe and minds to stimulate, my parents were kept busy. We were not poor in the Dickensian sense, but each penny had to be counted. My mother's two elder siblings had produced offspring with similar ruthless efficiency which meant that we were never short of hand-me-downs from our many cousins. Football, though very much a working man's game in 1974, was a luxury to the Dentons, an unnecessary financial indulgence and an unwelcome disruption. Six children between the ages of eight and 14 required routine, structure, and order. Football, with its chaos and unpredictability, was the antithesis of that. Not surprisingly, my exposure to football had therefore been sparse. I am not even sure why I wanted to go to the match. No doubt a youngest sibling's natural fear of missing out was a big part of it. There was a lot of that about when there were six of you separated by seven years.

My interest in football was not particularly strong. I recall redeeming several Typhoo Tea vouchers in exchange for a picture of Gordon Banks, and my brother Alban had a picture of George Best on our shared bedroom wall. We had an outdated *Shoot!* album, bought from a jumble sale or church Christmas fayre, but it was rarely looked at with any interest. The battered Subbuteo set, so old that the figures were made from card and not plastic, had been donated by a kindly neighbour but it rarely saw the light of day. Despite this tepid interest I desperately wanted to go.

The haranguing of my father continued through the morning and up to lunchtime, with no quarter given on either side. I remember my father finally ordering, 'Right everyone who wants to go to the match had better get ready – coats, hats, scarves.' I needed no further encouragement.

I was 'everyone'. Before my brothers could locate and don their anoraks, I stood ready and waiting by the front door. Coated, hatted, and scarfed to the eyeballs, probably also with wellington boots. I still half expected to be left behind, to be told that my father had not intended to include me. It did not happen and I would be going to the football. I looked like Paddington Bear but I felt like Cinderella.

I am sure that everyone has had just one or two moments in their life where the direction of it, either through conscious decision or twist of fate, is set in stone. Life-defining moments. Mine was the first time I walked into a football stadium on that fateful November day – a typical, grey, Manchester afternoon. From that moment my life changed forever.

There was the pulsating noise and the hypnotic movement of the crowd, singing and swaying in unison; 60,000 eager and expectant voices. I could almost reach out and touch the atmosphere, so dense was it with the essence of real lives and working men at leisure. My nostrils were drawn to the sweet warm stench of cigarette and pipe smoke, the smouldering pies, the stale beer, and the meaty Bovril that drifted up the terraces. At pitch level it mingled with the earthy smell from the steaming grass and the human odour circling around me. I could taste it on my tongue.

Led by Dad, we worked our way through the thick forest of Manchester's masses to the front of the terrace. I had never been exposed to the physical proximity of so many bodies. Totally absorbed and oblivious to any potential danger around me, I felt not fear from the crush of the crowd but the caress of a community. I could see the Wagon Wheels, the crisps, and the pies as I watched the refreshment sellers' parade around the pitch, trays in front of them, white straps across the chest like Christmas drummer boys. There was no chance that I would get my hands on any of their wares – the Dentons did not buy snacks, but like Charlie Bucket salivating over a scrumdiddlyumptious candy bar, the vicarious thrill was enough for me. That was because by now I had more glorious things to be concerned with. I had seen football pitches on television, and even played on them at Wythenshawe Park, but nothing could have prepared me for the sight I now beheld.

Before me lay the most beautiful thing I had ever seen in my short life. The greenest green there ever could be, a shimmering grass carpet, framed with crisp white lines. Under the bright floodlights that pierced the fading Manchester afternoon it glistened and gently breathed. Not so much a piece of grass but a stage for life's drama. Little did I know that it would become the unbidden stage for much of my own life's drama.

Despite being totally enthralled with the surroundings and the occasion, something intuitively told me all was not right. This one minor detail was confirmed when the crescendo of noise signalled the teams' entrance on to the pitch. There was no piped anthem or orchestrated handshakes in 1974. I arched my neck and stuck my head through the bigger bodies in front of me, trying to get a glimpse of the players as they emerged from the tunnel in the opposite stand. And then I saw those red shirts run on to the pitch. To my right, the roar 'U-NI-TED, U-NI-TED' went up from the Stretford End. I was at Old Trafford, the home of Manchester United.

The match itself was something of a classic and features on the BBC's *Best of Match of Day* compilation DVD. The Denton boys and their father were just four bodies among the 60,324 there to watch United beat Sunderland 3-2, during their one season of Second Division purdah. We were stood on the paddock that is known today as the Sir Alex Ferguson Stand. My memories of the game itself are a bit of a blur. I recall Stuart Pearson scoring the first goal and then the feeling of outrage and injustice as Sunderland hit back twice in quick succession. The crowd sang Willie Morgan's name after he scored in the second half and generally did everything expected of a 1970s winger – nice hair, shame about the end product. The Stretford End taunted the Sunderland fans with cries of 'Geordies, Geordies', and when I asked Dad why, he, ever the stickler for detail, asserted they were not Geordies, as they came not from Newcastle, but were in fact Wearsiders. My father was never one to miss an educational opportunity regardless of the occasion.

Ninety minutes had never flown by so quickly and once the final whistle had sounded, the rush, push, and crush to squeeze the mass of impatient bodies through the narrow exits began. I must have been scared but mostly I recall the exhilaration and adrenaline being stronger than the fear. I felt pride that I did not cry, unlike my brother David, as we got engulfed by the swarming bodies and momentarily lost contact with Dad. Outside the ground the scene really did resemble a Lowry painting as we started to make our way home. The floodlit stadium behind us was glowing in the autumn night sky; the last of Salford's industry was churning out its smoke, and the residential chimneys of the terrace houses betokened the warm hearths and homes that lay beneath. Thousands of cloth-capped, duffel-coated match stalk men dispersed in all directions. At least, that is how I remember it. The likelihood is that it was all parkas, scarves tied around wrists, flared trousers, and Doc Marten boots.

We walked home through the navy-blue Manchester evening, the drizzle dancing like fireflies in the headlights of the cars that slowly filed away from the stadium. The distance was about three miles, but we were used to it. We had a family car, in fact we had a camper van, but walking was a good and wholesome activity. I watched orange bus after orange bus pass us by, both decks illuminated in the darkness, standing room only. The dear old ladies, out for their afternoon visits or shopping trips, laden bags resting on knees, were unexpectedly swamped by the celebrating hordes with their red-white-and-black scarves. As we got further from the ground the buses dispersed in multiple directions across the city and towards the centre.

If the Saturday night TV dinner had become a widely adopted convention by 1974, it had yet to make any impression on the Denton household. Breaks with tradition generally arrived under my parents' suspicious gaze quite some time after the rest of society had embraced them. Consequently, dinner was a formal occasion with nine of us around the large wooden kitchen table, the only external interference being from Radio 4, or Radio 2 – the BBC of course. ITV and commercial radio came into the 'questionable and not to be trusted' category. While we were having dinner – or tea as we Manchester folk called it – Dad called for quiet. Something on the radio had captured his attention and within seconds it also held me captivated. He was listening to a report from a football match – but not just any one. It was *the* match report from Old Trafford. Not only had I enjoyed the most exhilarating afternoon of my life, but the BBC were now talking about it on national radio. I had taken part in a newsworthy event. The action I had witnessed in person was now being described to the millions of people out there. Being a part of the nation's news – how cool was that?

There remained one final act on this defining day. As I had watched the game, trying my best to absorb all that was happening around me, I noticed around the touchline a few red-tracksuited boys who were older than me. They were throwing the ball back to the players whenever it left the pitch. 'I could do that,' I thought to myself. I asked Dad how I could get this job. He said he did not know but he knew of a man who might be able to help. 'You should write a letter to the club secretary,' he told me. That same night, I did. Sat in my pyjamas, at the dining room table, I set the Woolworths writing pad in front of me, and with the neatest, most grown-up handwriting I could muster I laid out my credentials as to why I should be appointed to the position of ball boy at Manchester United Football Club. Dad looked up the address from the phone book and posted my letter. I fully expected a reply before the end of the weekend, acknowledging my kind offer and inviting me to report for duty the following week. I waited but the response never came. It was a disappointment, but one that was soon forgotten, because football had irrevocably hooked me. The only question now was which team?

There are many ways by which an impressionable boy can choose his football team. To some people it is a decision of little importance that can be reversed at any time if a mistake has been made, the stark reality of youthful impetuousness exposed as the trophy cabinet lies perennially bare. For others, it is a life-defining and irreversible decision. If you allow it, one that will shape the person you become and your attitude to life. It can influence how you view others and how they view you. It can determine your friends, your job, your life partner and where you live. For the most loyal of supporters, it is for better or worse, for richer or poorer, in sickness and in health. Choosing one's football club is, therefore, not an enterprise to be entered into unadvisedly or lightly, but reverently, discreetly, advisedly, soberly; and, if not in the fear of God, then certainly in the fear of ridicule from friends and family. So, if you are about to commit your soul and fortune to this noble pursuit for ages yet to come, your choice had better be the right one. The problem is that nobody tells you any of this at the beginning.

I would expect that the most common influence on shaping this momentous decision comes from within the family. I did not have that sort of guidance; Dad was of little help. When I later insisted that he supported a team he chose Scunthorpe United by virtue of their place at the bottom of the Football League. My brothers had developed a passing interest in the Uniteds of Manchester and Leeds. The only one with any semblance of patronage was my paternal grandfather, Poppa, who frequently extolled the achievements of Northampton Town in the mid-1960s. Remarkably, the Cobblers, as he affectionately referred to them, went up from the Fourth Division to the First and all the way back down again, in successive seasons. Support Northampton Town? I might not have known much but what little I did I know told me that was never going to happen. Not streetwise enough about stylish kits, past trophies, or star players I was unable to base my decision on any of those considerations. Ultimately another great sphere of influence, the school playground, swayed me.

Paul Burns was the cool kid in Mr Donovan's class at St Aidan's Primary School. Well, as cool as an eight-year-old boy who was ridden into school in a seat on the back of his mother's bike could be (even then he had the air of Julius Caesar entering the Colosseum on his horse-drawn chariot). He was just one of those kids to whom others migrated and wherever he went at playtime you followed. I do not recall the conversation as being a particular long or deep one.

'Are we going to play football today, Paul?'

'I don't know, who do you support?'

I knew enough by now to know that there were only two possible answers to this question.

'Ummm. United, I think.'

'They're shit. You should support City, they're better.'

'Okay.'

That was it, done and dusted. A course set and a life long voyage into the unknown begun. The cool kid became my first best friend. Despite my association with Paul, I was never close to being the cool kid.

So all was good in this young man's life. Happy home, happy family, doing quite well at a school I liked, a reasonable number of friends and a football team to follow. There was hardly a 'blue Monday' in sight. What more could a young Manchester lad ask for in those innocent pre-Factory Records, Oasis and Haçienda days?

Life in our West Didsbury house was one of contentment and security. We did not have a life of luxury or indulgence, but it was a good one, protected from pretty much all the hardships of the world. My mother and father, through discipline, thriftiness, and industry, had turned the ramshackle house that they had scraped and saved to purchase into a homely family nest. We had what we needed but not much more. There was a garden big enough to get lost in and with sufficient nooks and crannies to serve any adventure. My siblings and I each had our own allotted vegetable patch; the crowning glory of mine was a 12-foot-high oak sapling that I had grown and nurtured from an acorn. We were surrounded by elderly neighbours who doted on the six young children that would sporadically lean over their fences in the hope of a glass of lemonade or an Uncle Joe's Mint Ball.

Holidays were only once a year, but that was fine. We never went far, but to me North Wales was every bit as exotic as Spain. The restless excitement of all eight of us lying on camp beds in the old barn on Mr and Mrs Cribb's farm near Porthmadog is a genuinely happy memory. I can still smell the paraffin lamp and picture the blue flame that flickered through the long summer nights as we drifted off to sleep.

Television was rationed and censored. BBC good, ITV bad. *Blue Peter* good, *Magpie* bad, *Look North* good, *Granada Reports* bad. Sunday night was a TV treat as Poppa cooked for my parents to give Mum a break. Bathed and in night clothes, we were permitted to crawl under the dining room table and watch *Dad's Army* as the adults ate. A dining table large enough to accommodate six squatters had to be of a certain stature. My father had bought it from his first employers, the Shirley Institute, for about £50 in 1973. When fully extended, with its six additional leaves, it transformed from a round table into an oval some 30 feet long. The only time it has ever been fully extended was on the two occasions it appeared on the BBC's *Antiques Roadshow* where its value was estimated at over £40,000. Not a bad little investment, and one that remained in the family until recently.

My other abiding memory of television was the day we all came home from school to one of Mum's 'announcements': Dad was going to appear on the BBC's early evening news and current affairs magazine programme *Nationwide*. The subject was, not surprisingly, related to the textile industry. We all duly huddled around the TV at six o'clock and listened in wonderment and pride as 'Mike Denton' was introduced. I did not have the first clue what he was talking about.

We had extended family close to us with Mum's siblings and my multitude of cousins. My maternal grandparents, known to us all as Nanna and Gangan, lived a couple of miles away. Visiting their Withington home was a treat that invariably ended with a trip to the local sweet shop that we christened 'Walter's' after my grandfather. My grandmother had a real skill for making the most imaginative and creative cakes featuring hedgehogs made from cocktail sausages and steam trains with liquorice spirals for wheels. She also had the consummate ability to make you feel and believe that you were her only grandchild rather than just one of 24.

In common with many families of the day, the other major institutions in our lives were church and school. Unlike choosing your football team, religion was non-negotiable. My grandparents were Catholics, my parents were Catholics, I was baptised Catholic. I remain a Catholic. Church on Sunday was a must, and we celebrated the big public holidays with religious observance and social significance. Sundays had their own strict ritual with two choices. Dad liked to make the most of his weekends. By fulfilling his Catholic obligation early, he was left with a full day to complete the various gardening or household chores he had set himself and his reluctant sons. He therefore drove into the centre of Manchester to St Augustine's Church on Grosvenor Square where the city's only 6.30am Sunday Mass took place. As the concept of an alcohol-induced lie-in was an experience I had yet to encounter, I usually chose this option. The brevity of the Mass as well as the chance to relieve the boredom by being an altar boy made it a better prospect than the alternative.

That alternative accommodated a more leisurely start to the day with 9am Mass at St Cuthbert's with Mum and my grandparents. The extra couple of hours in bed did not compensate for the length of the Mass, the incessant singing, and the long, incomprehensible sermon. There was also little chance of being an altar boy, despite my grandfather's influence, as they seemed to have dozens of them. The service survived, there was then the ordeal of leaving church. Former teachers, pupils, class-mates of my mother and friends of my grandparents would accost us to say hello, rub my hair, pinch my cheeks, and generally do all those things that an eight-year-old boy despises.

'What do you want to do when you grow up?' I would be asked for the fifth week running. 'The same as last week, Mrs Jones. I want to waste all my youth, energy, money, and romantic intention following a terrible football team around the country until they win something long after you are dead.'

Then again, going to Mass with my grandparents did mean there was a chance that Gangan would reach into his deep pockets and retrieve a ten pence piece to be spent at Walter's on the way home. In the end, 6.30am at St Augustine's just about won the day.

I enjoyed my early school days, progressing steadily if not spectacularly. St Aidan's, Wythenshawe, was a happy school, and I was a happy student. In my innocence I was blind to the fact that its location was in one of the more deprived areas of Manchester. The red-brick buildings were augmented by prefabricated classrooms to cope with the post-war baby boom. After working my way through Miss Binns, Mrs Costello and Mrs Hulse's classes, I would complete my time there in the 'prefabs' in the charge of the guitar-strumming Mr Donovan. I enjoyed the classwork, regularly being incentivised by Dad to earn ten stars in a week, in order that I could be rewarded with a packet of Nice biscuits from the school tuck shop. I do not recall that I ever achieved it.

The highlight of the week was always Wednesday afternoons and hymn practice followed by football. I have never been a singer, but I did enjoy being part of the school choir and belting out such old rousing classics as 'Praise, My Soul, the King of Heaven', 'Faith of Our Fathers' and 'Onward, Christian Soldiers'. It provided great vocal training for the times ahead on terraces up and down the country.

Today, I cannot sing or hear the hymn 'Oh, the Love of My Lord is the Essence' without being immediately transported back to Mr Donovan's prefab and hymn practice, recalling the restless energy in anticipation of school football to follow.

I say football, when it was really more of a kick-about in the local Wythenshawe Park. Legendary City coach Malcolm Allison had trained his first-team squad in the park and if it was good enough for Colin Bell, Francis Lee, and Mike Summerbee, then it was certainly good enough for Dickie Denton. It was definitely the closest I had ever come to organised football. My only other opportunities to hone my beginner's technique was in the back garden at Winster Avenue – practice sessions which were usually cut short by Dad as he confiscated the ball as a result of a careless shot careering into his beloved dahlias. As I said, he was not a football man.

I so envied the boys in my class who had replica kits, even if they were all adorned in United red. All except for Paul Burns, that is, who was inexplicably the proud owner of an 'old gold' Wolves strip. Later in life I would take mischievous joy in reminding him of this aberration. The boys in kits, with proper football boots, looked like real footballers. They were smart and uniformed. With their iconic black socks, red and white trim on the overturned tops, they reminded me of the royal guardsmen that had captivated me during a recent family trip to London. Next to them, dressed in my yellow T-shirt, old shorts, and black plimsolls, I looked anything but the footballer. I so wanted a football kit, and I think that if any one of them had offered me theirs in exchange for my footballing allegiance I might just have sold my soul to the

Red Devil. They didn't, of course, and so, in the words of 'Oh, the Love of My Lord is the Essence', I did not 'turn from his presence' and 'walk other paths, other ways'.

It was another ordinary day when, one morning, Mum called a family meeting. Dad was at work and the six of us were summoned to the kitchen. That usually meant that one of us had done something wrong, and we were about to receive a lecture. After waiting until she had our undivided attention, she told us the news.

'We are going to move to a new house, in Leeds.'

'What?' 'Why?' 'When?' But most of all, 'Where?' or, as I really felt, 'Where the fuck is Leeds?'

Even though I had heard of Leeds, I did not have a clue where it was. I remembered hearing a report, a few weeks earlier, on the BBC about their football team's supporters rampaging round Paris's Parc de Princes stadium after the European Cup Final. These did not seem to be my kind of people.

I felt a little excitement, a sense of the adventure to come, but the overriding emotion was fear. The question I most dreaded asking was 'would I have to go to a new school' and of course the answer was 'yes'. As a painfully shy child, the prospect of a new school petrified me. My shyness extended to family. My cousins – who we did not see so often despite their proximity – put the fear of God into me and I would often be found hiding in the garden shed when they came to visit. There were so many of them; 18 between my mother's two siblings, mostly older and bigger than me. I just did not have a clue who each one was. A visit felt like a takeover of my home.

So that was it; by the end of the summer I would have a new home, new town, and new school. Somehow, I was going to have to make new friends. But if anybody was going to make me have a new football team, they would need to think again.

Only later did I come to understand the reasons behind the move. My father had started his career as a textile scientist at a research organisation in Didsbury. From there his skills had come to the attention of the industry and he was persuaded to join the splendidly named Macclesfield-based textile machinery firm of Ernest Scragg. I never knew exactly what Dad did at Scragg's but from time to time he went off on business trips, usually to the Far East. On his travels he could not help but notice the emergence of the textile industry in Asia with the increased investment in research and technology. This, together with the low wage base, meant the writing was on the wall for the north-west's declining industry. Lancashire's days as the world leader were no more. When Leeds University came calling in 1975 and offered the relative security of an academic life, the decision to move the family was one of pragmatism and prudence. His post at the university also allowed him to indulge his passion for education and research. As a reader in the Department for Textile Industries he became one of the world's leading authorities on synthetic polymers.

Although less than an hour away, and only just over the brow of the Pennine hills that I could see from my attic bedroom window, Leeds could have been a thousand miles away and the other side of the Alps for all I cared. Before I could get comfortable with the idea of leaving St Aidan's, my friends, and familiarity, the end of term was upon us. For the final time we stood outside the school gates and watched Mum drive the blue VW camper van up and along Rackhouse Road. Already feeling scared and uncertain, I awaited my new life in Yorkshire.

2

Different Colours

AS THE last sun of the school holidays faded, I counted down the days with increasing trepidation. I had reluctantly accepted the inevitability of what was about to happen, but nevertheless, I was determined that I would not leave my home town without attending to one important piece of business. I had sworn, to my best friend Paul, my unyielding allegiance to Manchester City but I could hardly call myself a proper supporter until I had seen them play.

Mum and Dad, ever mindful of their children's education, had decided that we would start the academic year at our new schools in Leeds, even though we remained some weeks away from moving to our new house. My father had been making the hour-long trans-Pennine commute for several weeks in preparation for the university term, establishing his presence in the faculty. It therefore made sense that he would take us back and forth with him each day.

My older sisters Elizabeth, Katherine and Rachel, and my brother Alban were at the city's two single-sex Catholic grammar schools, while David and I were seeing out our last years at primary school, so this entailed three different drop-off points. I would have quite happily eased the logistical complications and returned to my life at St Aidan's but my parents were having none of it. Whether it was my reward for enduring this daily ritual or sheer persistence I do not know, but I somehow managed to persuade Dad to forgo one of his hard-earned Saturdays and take me to Maine Road. I doubt that my negotiation skills were up to much, so I think that just spending so much time with him in the car slowly wore him down. The means and method were not important; at last, I would get to see City.

A week before finally leaving Manchester we made the short journey, on foot, to Maine Road. This time just Dad and I as my brothers' interest had somewhat waned. While they had been seduced by the offerings of Meccano, Hornby, and Airfix, I remained magnetised by football. I suspect my parents considered it a passing fad that would soon be forgotten. I am sure they would have preferred me to have adopted an interest that required less parental supervision but, for now, they were prepared to indulge my passion.

Dad's unfamiliarity with all things football was apparent as we walked around the four quite different Maine Road stands, wondering which gate to enter. Finally, we must have paid about £3 and to my delight, as we emerged from the dark concrete stairwell, I could see rows of blue wooden seats. I had assumed the luxury of sitting was only for the cinema or, in my case, the annual Christmas pantomime at Manchester's Library Theatre, but never for something quite so as prosaic as football. I would have been more than happy to be stood up, but on a seat high in the Main Stand I knew I would get to see far more of the actual match and come away with a nine-year-old's informed opinion of the tactics and finer nuances of the action playing out before me.

Once seated I knew beyond any doubt that I wanted to spend all my life watching football matches. When Joe Royle scored, and the stadium erupted in celebration, I knew I also wanted to spend all my life watching City. Dad did not quite share my enthusiasm, and that was a bit disappointing, but if he kept taking me to matches then I could live with his indifference. I did not appreciate it at the time but the team that day was a pretty good one that boasted the likes of Mike Doyle, Colin Bell, Rodney Marsh and Dennis Tueart. But it was the goalkeeper, Joe Corrigan, who really caught my eye. Tall and commanding with long dark hair, his bright green shirt contrasting with the Manchester murk, Corrigan was my first idol. I liked the fact that he wore a different shirt and played in a different position. He was his own man. I made my mind up that I too would be a goalkeeper and that being different was okay. That day, City beat Middlesbrough 4-0 and I came away convinced that not only had I chosen the right sport, but also a winning team. I had much to learn about life.

This short-lived exhilaration was a brief distraction from the reality that I would shortly leave it all behind. I had already said goodbye to my best mate Paul and my class-mates at St Aidan's and soon I would have to do the same to Winster Avenue and Manchester City. Moving day was quickly upon us and we made the final commute back from our Leeds schools for our last night at home. As we turned into the road, we could see the two orange Glaziers removal vans parked outside our house and the family's worldly goods being packed away. Suddenly it was alarmingly real. The angst of the move was briefly tempered by the sense of adventure and the rare treat of eating fish and chips out of newspaper as we sat in our empty front room surrounded by tea chests. The next morning, we set off through Manchester's southern suburbs, on to the M62, and over the Pennines. Later that evening we all returned to our new home, 282 Pudsey Road, Leeds.

My new school, Catholic and controlled by nuns in a way that only Catholic nuns can control, was Christ the King Primary in Bramley, a working-class suburb of west Leeds. The Irish headmistress, Sister Cecelia, was old-school, all 'hell, fire, and damnation'. She was about 5ft 2in tall and weighed no more than seven stone wet through, but she put the fear of God into pupils, teachers, and parents alike. My form teacher, Mr Foster, was from Newcastle, and he had an accent the sound of which I had never heard before. We did not watch *The Likely Lads* at home. To his pupils he was something of a minor celebrity as his older brother was none other than the famous athlete and BBC Sports Personality of the Year, Brendan Foster. At the end of my first year, when he told us that he was finishing term early so that he could go to Canada to watch his brother compete in the 1976 Montreal Olympics, we felt as if we were going there ourselves.

I recognised that while I held little influence over matters like choice of school, I remained adamant that there was one thing very much within my control. I maintained my resolve that changing football teams was out of the question, and I would not be supporting Leeds United. Admittedly, it would take me a little while to disclose that fact to my new class-mates. The new boy likes to fit in, especially when he is only nine.

For a confident and extrovert child I would expect that the process of adjusting to a new school in a new city is not an easy thing. As I happened to be neither of those it was always going to be a personal challenge. On many of those first few journeys along the M62, I sobbed silently as my stomach churned, dreading the day to come. I would be half asleep as we left Manchester shortly after 7am and started the slow climb along the motorway. The stone white rose that marks the county border at the top of the moors indicated the start of the descent into Yorkshire. The closer we got to Leeds, as the mileage signs indicated our growing proximity, I became more withdrawn. We passed signposts to Huddersfield, Halifax, Heckmondwike, Dewsbury, and then Leeds; signposts that even today remind me of that journey, each taking me closer to a fate I dreaded. I somehow kept my inner feelings hidden. Internalising anxiety was something that would be a big part of my life in the years to come; this was merely the rehearsal. By the end of the school day, when I saw Dad draw up in the camper van, I had largely overcome my turmoil but there was nonetheless immense relief.

Like most children, I did adjust and what I remember as being months of trauma was probably more like a week or two at the most. I did also have my brother David with me and that was a great support and comfort. As the two youngest in a large family, we had often been thrown together and in a school full of strangers we now depended upon each other. I was more dependent on him without a doubt. Only much later did I learn that one or two of my older siblings

also went through the same personal torment during that transition but, like me, kept it to themselves. I was not alone in my solitude.

The assimilation into my new school environment was gradual and unsurprisingly I found that Leeds kids were in many ways much the same as Manchester kids. They liked football, had fights, pinched money to spend on the penny tray in the newsagents and, given a half chance, would find any way to get out of schoolwork. They did have some funny words in Leeds that were completely new to me, like 'laiking' (playing), 'scran' (food), and 'ginnell' (alleyway). To my mind there was no question that they were tougher. Manchester kids were no shrinking violets and my playground fight with Noel Bayley at St Aidan's was the stuff of legend (in one of life's strange twists of irony, Noel later became editor of a fine 1990s City fanzine – *Bert Trautmann's Helmet*). I cannot precisely put my finger on exactly how the Leeds kids were tougher and more streetwise, but they seemed to talk harder, hit harder, and kick a ball harder.

Through the eyes of my new class-mates, I also became more aware and conscious of the colour of David's skin and his ethnicity. I do not think that Leeds nine-year-olds were any more or less racist than their Manchester counterparts, but before moving to Leeds this visual distinction had never been a part of my school life. David had been adopted before my birth, so I never regarded him as anything but my brother. Maybe because we had grown up with the same school cohort and maybe due to the colour-blindness of infant eyes, the shade of David's skin had never been a conversation, even less an issue in Manchester. In Leeds this was more than a conversation. It required explanation. Adoption was not the celebrated thing it is today, especially for families with five children, and a white boy having a brother with brown skin prompted a natural curiosity that could not be avoided.

'He is not your real brother is he? He's a different colour.'

'Why did they adopt him?'

'Why not adopt an English kid?'

'Is his mum a Paki?'

'Do your mum and dad treat him the same?'

And some of that was from the adults.

Fortunately, what I lacked in physical courage and bravado David made up for, and he happily took on all comers verbally and, occasionally, physically. Leeds felt to me like a hugely different place, but, in truth, my age of innocence was nearly over, and my senses were merely being opened to the real world.

Our address on Pudsey Road did little to help create a sense of identity in Yorkshire. Situated on the outskirts of Leeds and close to the neighbouring city of Bradford, it felt like it belonged to neither. The nearest town was Pudsey but Pudsey-ites would tell us we did not live in Pudsey. Nor was it in the next town, Bramley. The area in between the two had no name to speak of. We did have an address, and we got our mail, so the Post Office knew where we were, and the fact that none of these strange Yorkshire folks had a name for the neighbourhood did not stop it becoming our new home.

Mum and Dad again worked tirelessly using every free hour and spare penny to create our new family base. The emphasis on collective hard work and discipline was paramount and once homework and music practice were complete there were always extra jobs to be done. Dad was a passionate gardener and after years of hard sweat developing a beautiful garden at Winster Avenue, he set about his new cabbage patch in Leeds with similar gusto. He was also a hard taskmaster and thought nothing of conscripting his sons to spend the Saturday afternoons digging, sweeping, and generally making themselves useful. If we were lucky there was the prospect of a bonfire with baked potatoes at the end of an autumn day.

Whatever task was assigned to me – and they were many, various and, as the youngest and smallest, often the dirtiest – close by my side was my most treasured possession, a transistor radio. Its aerial was aimed in whatever direction would get me the best reception for BBC Radio Leeds, Radio 2 and, finally as the dusk drew in and the skies darkened, *Sports Report*, delivering all the day's football news with its iconic theme tune. Di dum, di dum, di dum, di dum, di diddily dum di de; you know how it goes.

During the weekends, in that garden at Pudsey Road, and later in my attic bedroom during midweek evenings, I came to fall in love with football on the radio. It provided my only access to live football. There was limited television coverage and my parents invariably switched channels when the start of *Match of the Day* was announced. This was of little consequence to me as it was past my bedtime. Radio was my umbilical cord to football. West Yorkshire was a big sporting conurbation, and the Radio Leeds coverage was widespread and knowledgeable. Despite the famed successes and failings of Don Revie's 'Dirty Leeds', the city's sporting interest was split between football and rugby league. Cricket, and more specifically 'Sir' Geoffrey Boycott, dominated the airwaves in the summer. Most of the live sport still took place on Saturday afternoon, so the entire coverage had to be condensed into a few action-packed hours. Sunday football and Sky Sports was not yet even a twinkle in young Rupert Murdoch's eye.

The rugby league from Headingley started at 2pm with legendary broadcaster Jack Wainwright. Leeds had a decent side, winning the Challenge Cup twice in the late 1970s and, as often as not, the battle was against one of their cross-Pennine rivals, Widnes, Wigan, or St Helens. On all things sporting I always sided with the Lancashire team, with one notable exception. As the rugby advanced into the second half, football matches kicked off across the county. Team news came from the grounds where the various West Yorkshire teams were playing. Leeds United were usually the big story and David Campbell or a young Harry Gration, now a veteran anchorman of *Look North*, would report from Elland Road or wherever Leeds were that afternoon. A collection of gravelly voiced, seasoned football journalists sat in press boxes and orated with equal doses of wisdom, cynicism, and very occasionally that rare Yorkshire indulgence, hope, on the exploits of Huddersfield Town, Bradford City and Halifax Town. Leeds Road, Valley Parade, The Shay, and other weird and romantically named lower-division grounds such as Sincil Bank, The Old Show Ground, and Gigg Lane entered my consciousness forever.

At half-time, Radio Leeds would join with BBC Radio Two for the nationwide commentary from the Football League. *'Would it be City this week? Please let it be City this week.'* If the Manchester derby was being contested then there was a good chance, but most of the time it seemed to be Liverpool on another unstoppable march to the title. I did not care. It mattered little as I would just absorb all things football. Had it been Rochdale against Torquay, I would have been just as interested. In my mind, I could have been at any and every ground in the country, kicking every ball, swaying with every person in the crowd.

Those images were so brilliantly and vividly described by the likes of Peter Jones – surely the greatest radio commentator of them all. There was also Jim Rosenthal, Des Lynam, and Alan Parry before they went on to their successful television careers. They were accompanied by the acerbic, incisive summaries of Denis Law and later by Jimmy Armfield. Through the magic of radio, I knew all about the surge of the Kop at Anfield and 'You'll Never Walk Alone'; the famed Clock End at Highbury, the notoriously muddy pitch at Derby's Baseball Ground and the intimidating proximity of the crowd at Upton Park. All pictures imagined by a young boy in wellington boots holding a yard brush taller than himself as the light faded and an autumnal Yorkshire sun started to set.

While the action in the commentary game held most of my attention, I would have one ear constantly alert, listening out for the scores from the other grounds, always with City's fortunes top of my mind. I would be back inside the house when the tune 'Out of the Blue' heralded the start of *Sports Report* and the announcement of the classified football results, always read by James Alexander Gordon. While other kids were watching *Play Away,* I absorbed the last detail of the afternoon's action, the interviews with disgruntled managers and delighted match-winners from around the country.

The holy grail was still to go to a live game. Very much regarded as an annual treat, Dad was clear which one it should be: Leeds United vs Manchester City at Elland Road. David had become something of a Leeds supporter so to my ever-practical parents it made sense to kill two birds with one stone. Six months after our move I prepared myself in eager readiness. Old Trafford, Maine Road, and now Elland Road, three of the north's greatest sporting venues in my first three games.

In 1975 the vogue was that young fans would sport scarves knitted by indulgent mothers, aunts, and grandmothers, rather than fork out for the official versions at the expensive souvenir shops. In keeping with the time-honoured tradition, I managed to persuade Mum to make me a City scarf. God knows how she found the time while settling us all into our new life and home. My older siblings had their own interests that required her attention too, be it art, music, woodwork, or destroying the house with chemistry sets. Remarkably, she managed to do it, and so resplendent with my blue-and-white knitted glory we set off to Elland Road: Dad, David, my eldest sister Elizabeth, and me.

Once more, the family's lack of familiarity with football stadia was evident as, ticketless, and directionless, we wandered around the perimeter of the ground and looked for a section that looked the least intimidating. Dad led us through the thronging crowds around the stadium and I constantly pestered him to go inside. I could hear the chanting from the terraces almost beckoning me in. My impatience was too much to contain. Finally, he made up his mind, selecting the stand that looked the most modern and, crucially, accepted cash at the turnstile. We made our way up the steps, oblivious to the strange looks we were receiving and eventually emerged into the light. In the distance, laid out in front of us like a snooker table baize, was the pitch, looking just as impressive as those I had seen before. This time we were behind the goal, a view that gave a new and different perspective. Of more immediate concern, especially for Dad, was the sight all around us. Not the rows of orderly seats he expected to see but a terrace full of Leeds United fans. We had inadvertently found ourselves standing in the middle of Elland Road's notorious Gelderd Road End, the 'Kop' as it was known to its regular inhabitants, and there I was, adorned in my finest City regalia.

In fairness to our fellow terrace dwellers, I do not recall any trouble at all. After all, my age was then nine, David ten and Elizabeth 14, with Dad looking as threatening as, well, a bespectacled university lecturer can look. I can only assume that we were given a pass on this occasion. David was probably the only 'Indian' in the ground that day so the whole collection of us must have looked more like figures of curiosity than hostility. Being small in size, I struggled to see the action, and Dad put me on his shoulders. From that vantage point, for the only time, I saw Colin Bell score in what was one of his rare comeback games following the horrific knee injury that would end his career. My innocent celebration was quickly muffled by Dad. Our safe return home was probably aided by the fact that two second-half goals from Leeds meant that, much to Dad's relief, the perilous prospect of a City win had been avoided. The natives all went to the pubs happy, no doubt telling their mates with amusement about the strange sight they had witnessed on their Kop that afternoon. Relieved at having escaped this close shave, Dad introduced a new family rule: for any future games, I would be required to queue and buy tickets for the seats in advance. He wanted to know exactly what he was letting himself in for when he next took his family to a football match.

Although totally engrossed in the action on the pitch, I was not so naive that I did not recognise the tribal rivalries and the menace of violence that were so manifest within football grounds. I felt some fear that day on the Kop, but also profound exhilaration and pride to have represented my team and my city among the rival supporters. It had touched me on another more human and base level. Football was no longer just about my team and the sporting contest but that afternoon on the Kop it unknowingly started to become a bigger cause, one of self-identity and belonging. Fuelled by this experience, and my increased personal stake in City vs Leeds games, I found Elland Road to be the most intimidating of away grounds, and for that reason I have always loved going there. Of course, I had naively expected to leave Elland Road with a glorious victory. My supreme confidence stemmed from the fact that City were going into the game as cup winners. Less than one month prior I had bagged my first trophy as a fan.

The League Cup had not been on my radar in 1976. I knew about the league championship – it seemed that Liverpool always won that– and I knew about the FA Cup. I could a vaguely recall Sunderland's famous 1973 surprise triumph over Leeds making the news. A couple of years later, a neighbour who was babysitting for us in Manchester had mentioned that the FA Cup Final was taking place the next afternoon. I had promptly watched West Ham beat Fulham. That was in 1975 and the neighbour was the same Mrs Levy of the donated Subbuteo set. A well-off Jewish widow, who lived on Winster Avenue, she frequently indulged her six young neighbours, leaving gifts of sweets and holiday souvenirs on our doorstep. She also correctly predicted L'Escargot's surprise victory over Red Rum in the 1975 Grand National. With hindsight I suspect that Mrs Levy's interest in football and the horses might possibly have extended beyond the sporting spectacle and down to the nearest William Hill betting shop along Barlow Moor Road.

As remains the case today, the early rounds of the League Cup were played during midweek so there was little chance for them to register in my consciousness. Bedtime radio was not permitted, though at that point I am not sure I was even aware that school-day football existed. When I did make that happy discovery, I had also become smart enough to acquire a set of earphones. City's progress therefore went largely unnoticed in the Denton household. While preparing for school one January morning I heard on Radio 4's *Today* programme that, the previous evening, Manchester City had won a place in the final of the League Cup. The mere fact that I had never heard of the League Cup did not matter. It was a cup final that was going to be played at Wembley, against Newcastle United, so it must be important. The chances of going to that final were zero; the thought never entered my head. Wembley cup finals were for other people. Paul Burns and his family were going. We had kept in touch since the move to Leeds via occasional letters. His were a lot better than mine, full of lots of exciting stuff he seemed to be doing every weekend while I swept the backyard. He had not held back in letting me know that he was a much bigger City fan than me, and that he had a ticket for the game. I envied him but was also happy and excited that I knew someone who would be there.

Cup final day arrived and just before 3pm I excitedly turned on the radio. I had made sure that any assigned weekend chores had been completed, thus ensuring uninterrupted listening. I also decided that for such an auspicious occasion the family's dining room radio should be commandeered rather than my small pocket transistor. I announced to the family during lunch that as this was the most important event of the day, if not the year, I should not be disturbed. That nobody else in the house was remotely interested was of minor significance. At least I had the room and radio to myself.

My eager anticipation soon turned to frustration and disgust when I discovered that the nation's broadcaster did not care much about the League Cup. The match took place concurrently with the rest of the league fixtures and the powers that be in the BBC's sports department had deemed that Derby County versus Liverpool was far more deserving of the nation's attention. Frantic retuning brought forth *The Goons*, Radio Luxembourg and Radio 4's afternoon play but nothing from Wembley. I therefore relied on the infrequent interruptions from Derby for news of the game. Young winger Peter Barnes had scored for City but Alan Gowling's equaliser had levelled the scores before half-time. Minutes into the second half, the radio coverage flipped to Wembley. City had taken the lead and Dennis Tueart had scored with a spectacular overhead bicycle kick. I did not know what an overhead bicycle kick was, never mind having seen one, but I did not care. It proved to be the winning goal in a cup final. Mike Doyle, a true City warrior, led his team up the Wembley steps to collect the trophy as I listened with excitement and dreamt of the many more trophies to come.

While the glow of victory was short-lived, its after-effects were much longer lasting and significant. The League Cup Final proved to be the catalyst for proclaiming my allegiance publicly. The time had come to step out of the closet and declare my support.

Like a politician, I had been somewhat economical with the actualité when it came to revealing my different colours in the playground. As the nervous new kid, my responses had been evasive when asked the question: 'Who do you support?' I do not think I ever said that I supported Leeds United, but neither was I unequivocal in my denial. Most Leeds kids were more concerned with a dislike of Manchester United so the first question this Manchester lad often got asked was, 'Do you support Man United?' That was an easy one and was answered with an emphatic truth, 'No, I can't stand them,' followed by an anxious wait for the inevitable next question. *Please do not ask me who I do support, please don't ask me if I am a Leeds fan.* Somehow, I managed to survive the interrogations.

The true cause of my 'coming out' was my Geordie form teacher Mr Foster. It only stood to reason that Mr Foster would support Newcastle United and, inevitably, considering he was planning to travel 3,000 miles to the Olympic Games, he had made the comparatively short journey from Leeds to Wembley. Had he known that there was a Manchester City fan in his midst he might not have been so forthcoming and generous with his sharing of the experience. At Monday's class assembly he told us about his trip to London and had his young audience enthralled as he held out the match programme, pictures of Wembley's twin towers, and the Newcastle and Manchester City squads across the front. A priest holding forth the holy grail could not have elicited more reverence from myself. Whoever could tell him something about the game would be allowed to read the programme during break-time. Discretion and inhibition went out of the window as quickly as my hand went up. I told him the score, the scorers, the referee, the City team rolling of my tongue, 'Corrigan, Keegan, Donachie, Doyle, Watson, Oakes, Barnes, Booth, Royle, Hartford, Tueart.' I told him everything except the programme-seller's inside-leg measurement (28 inches for the record). My subterfuge was exposed, but my pride was never greater. My own man, a lone Manchester City fan in a school full of Leeds fans. No longer living the lie, it felt wonderfully liberating. I pored over each page and fact in that programme during the break. Like many things in life, the fear was worse than the reality and my class-mates quickly got past the shock of having a City fan in their midst, thankful, at least, that it wasn't United.

Trips back to Manchester were infrequent but cherished. Usually they would be with Mum to visit my grandparents, but sadly never to see City. The one that had the most profound effect occurred shortly after the League Cup victory. I had been invited to spend a weekend with Paul Burns and his parents at their house in Northernden. Paul had brothers and sisters, all much older, who had left home and were earning good money, so invariably he had the best new toys. This was an opportunity not to be turned down. We spent the Saturday playing with Action Men and watching *Grandstand*, then kicking a ball around in the garden with old St Aidan's friends. On Sunday, after Mass, we headed off into town and in the direction of Maine Road. Much has been written about Peter Swales's tenure as chairman of Manchester City, most of it negative. However, in overseeing the foundation of the Junior Blues he created something of which he could be truly proud. When young supporters today are so much at the heart of every club, for community, corporate relations, and commercial reasons, it seems strange to think that in the 1970s this just was not the case.

Established in 1974, the Junior Blues was the country's first junior supporters' club. Open to all under the age of 16, members were presented with a membership certificate, a Junior Blues cloth badge, a team photo, an autograph album, and the promise of newsletters at various irregular intervals. Additionally, one Sunday morning each month, the Junior Blues met at the City Social Club behind the North Stand at Maine Road. Luckily for me, this was one such Sunday.

We entered the smoke-filled room, more of a home to working men's pipes, flat ale, and B-list cabaret acts than to throngs of excited boys and girls with their parents busily ordering lemonade and crisps. The meeting was hosted by ex-City chief scout 'Uncle' Harry Goodwin, who entertained his young audience before introducing some of the heroes from the League Cup-winning team. Mike Doyle, the skipper, was there on the stage saying how proud he was to have lifted the cup, then my idol Joe Corrigan followed by Asa Hartford, and then finally Dennis Tueart, the trophy in his hands. Afterwards there were photo opportunities and Paul's mum paid the £1 required. I still have the picture of Paul, his mum, and me holding the League Cup that February morning.

If I thought my day could not get any better, I was happily mistaken. As we were leaving the social club a suited administrator presented me with my Junior Blues certificate and badge. Paul's parents had enrolled me. I was now a Junior Blue and an official, registered City supporter. I glowed with pride as I tightly held on to my certificate, feeling like I had just signed for the club as a player.

Leeds life, with my new school and class-mates, settled into a familiar pattern. Thanks to the Junior Blues and the radio, City were never far from my thoughts. Slowly they were surpassing Leeds as a footballing force and finished runners-up in the league, missing out to Liverpool by just one point. There had been one big disappointment that season, when City were drawn against Leeds in the FA Cup fifth round at Elland Road. True to his word Dad agreed we could go if we obtained tickets prior to the game, and accordingly David and I queued in advance to ensure that this time we did not end up in the Kop. We sat in the relative calm of the West Stand and watched as Trevor Cherry scored a heartbreaking late winner for Leeds. I had been convinced it was City's turn to win the FA Cup. My bold declaration as a fan now had a price to pay on Monday mornings and I knew I would be relentlessly mocked at school. I had started to dislike Leeds United almost as much as their Manchester namesakes.

However, I simply loved the FA Cup and I always will. I consider that the FA's failure to protect the status of the competition and what it stands for against the relentless growth of the Premier League is one of the greatest examples of brand-owner neglect. Right up there alongside Gerald Ratner.

I had watched previous finals on television but the first one I truly embraced was that 1977 final, Liverpool versus Manchester United. David Gilpin was my first friend in Leeds, and we sat in his front room, decorated with homemade banners even though neither of us supported Liverpool or United. The day began at 9am with an *It's a Knockout! Cup Final Special*, on to *Cup Final Grandstand* and all the glorious, trivial build-up, climaxing with *Meet the Winners* once the match had concluded. We were glued to his television throughout, not moving from the sofa. His mum brought us baked beans on toast and orange squash at regular intervals. After the conclusion we then burnt off our pent-up energy by going out on to the adjoining Bramley Park to recreate the key moments with the other boys streaming out of their homes.

My time at Christ the King was always destined to be a short one as my primary education was coming to an end. Moving on to grammar school was subject to the minor obstacle of passing the 11-plus. My five older siblings had all passed the exam, so my parents' expectation was clear and expressed. I never held the mantle of star pupil but was consistently in the top five or six in my classes and if I were not so easily distracted I could probably have been placed higher. I was confident in my ability and enjoyed the challenge of tests but in the wake of my siblings' successes the task of upholding the family reputation did create a pressure that was new to me.

The day of the exam came and went, and I put it to the back of my mind and got on with life. A few weeks later the playground rumours circulated that the 11-plus results had arrived. As class was dismissed at the end of the day, we were handed letters 'strictly for our parents'. The letter was not in an envelope but was sealed with a small piece of Sellotape. Looking closely through the thin folded page, I could see the words 'St Michael's College' printed on the paper beneath. St Michael's was the Catholic grammar school that my older brothers now attended. I ran home desperate to have the news confirmed and breathlessly handed the letter to Mum. The smile and hug confirmed that my happy suspicions were true. Her joy, and that of Dad, was twofold. The alternative school, had I failed, had a poor reputation. I later found out that should I not have passed they were considering paying for a private education we could not afford.

It was the glorious summer of 1977, the year of the Queen's Silver Jubilee, of street parties, Virginia Wade winning Wimbledon, and England regaining the Ashes. The cricket was more celebrated than the royal jubilee in Yorkshire as Geoff Boycott famously recorded his 100th first-class century in the Headingley Test match. Nanna and Gangan also marked their 50th wedding anniversary and we celebrated with them as a family in Manchester. With the upheaval of the Leeds move a distant memory I awaited the next chapter of my life with confidence and optimism. I held lofty ambitions on two fronts. I would take on the challenges of grammar school, but more importantly City, with the addition of England's Mike Channon to their impressive ranks, would attempt to win the First Division title.

3

The Well-Rounded Person

THE PRAYER of St Michael the Archangel is not one to indulge the more tender virtues of compassionate faith. Instead, it embraces some of the more robust aspects of Catholicism:

Holy Michael, the Archangel, defend us in battle.
Be our safeguard against the wickedness and snares of the devil.
May God rebuke him, we humbly pray;
and do you, O Prince of the heavenly host,
by the power of God cast into hell Satan
and all the evil spirits
who wander through the world seeking the ruin of souls.

A jaunty little number isn't it? Maybe not a prayer for the faint-hearted and neither was my new school, St Michael's College.

Established in 1905 by Jesuit priests, the college's role was to enable the predominantly working-class Catholic community in the West Riding of Yorkshire to raise its social status and material wellbeing. The school's ethos was based on the fundamental principles of Jesuit education: 'Our ideal is the well-rounded person who is intellectually competent, open to growth, religious, loving, and committed to doing justice in generous service to the people of God.' That was the worthy aspiration.

The school was in the process of transitioning away from Jesuit governance into the mainstream education system. While its entrance and assembly hall were adorned with impressive statues, shields, and other relics of the Jesuit past, there were only one or two priests who remained in a teaching capacity and the headmaster, Mr Morris, was the first layman to be appointed to the school's top position. Located in the centre of Leeds and one of the city's leading Catholic boys' grammar schools, its catchment area was wide and encompassed all socio-economic classes, extending out from the inner-city council estates to the more salubrious and countrified suburbs of Roundhay and Alwoodley, and as far as Selby, Wetherby, and York. Also among its intake were Leeds' large immigrant communities from Ireland and Poland, with their strong Catholic heritage.

Aged 11, I presented myself at the doors of the imposing, red-brick gothic building for my first day, proudly wearing my oversized blazer that had been bought with plenty of growing room. I arrived full of positive intent. In theory adjusting to this change of school should have been a lot easier than my previous one as every boy in the class would be new. I also had my two older brothers at the school, and additionally the familiar company of the ten or so other boys from Christ the King who had passed the 11-plus. The uniform made a bold statement: a royal blue blazer with the badge of St Michael, depicting a flaming sword. The matching tie ensured that a St Michael's boy did not go unnoticed in public and was easily identifiable if caught getting up to any sort of mischief in the city centre on their way home or, worse, during school hours. The strict uniform code was constantly in conflict with the rebelliousness of youth, and imaginative ways were found to reflect the prevailing fashion trends through ingenious methods of customisation, be it mod, rocker, or new wave. The irony of swapping one uniform for another.

My first-form teacher went by the name of Finbar Laverty. He was Irish and happened to be an avid Manchester United supporter. He was the finest teacher that I encountered throughout my education, a 'Mr O'Chips' with an innate ability to move with the times. He was able to contextualise and relate to what was going on in the world his charges were growing up into, while retaining his authenticity and authority. I settled into my new surroundings with relative ease, my introverted nature keeping me in the company of those I knew, and within my comfort zone of acquaintances. I certainly was not yet ready to be the centre of attention. That would all come later.

I had, by now, become accustomed to the range of questions that stemmed from curiosity regarding the colour of David's skin. Answering the same questions was initially an inconvenience rather than a problem, something that would settle once the novelty had worn off. Across a school headcount of over 800 there were possibly 15 who were 'non-white', so David's distinctive presence and our unique family dynamic was always going to be conspicuous. I never discussed these conversations about race at home, mistakenly believing that it would all go away. In my silence, I was creating a future problem for myself by internalising my discomfort. Without realising it, I had slowly started to build walls from which I would later struggle to escape.

Keen to make a good first impression and, knowing my parents would be closely monitoring my scholarly progress, performance was solidly average. At primary school I could sit comfortably in the top 20 per cent without a great deal of effort. However, this was now a different league. With the larger catchment at St Michael's comprising a more academically able demographic, each one an 11-plus graduate, I now languished in mid-table mediocrity. The new reality was that if I was not on my A-game then I would be in danger of heading towards the relegation zone.

Back across the Pennines, my football team were facing a similar challenge in fighting off keen new competition. The glorious capture of the league title that I confidently predicted had not gone to plan. Surprisingly, and to my mind unreasonably, it was not Liverpool who were proving to be the obstacle, but Brian Clough's newly promoted Nottingham Forest. Too young to be able to appreciate the genius and individuality that Clough represented, I just saw an arrogant egomaniac (whom I thought looked, talked, and dressed more like my father than a football manager) stealing the league title that, for no rational reason, I felt City were entitled to.

A series of disappointing results in autumn saw City languishing in mid-table. The January FA Cup third round draw once again paired City with Leeds at Elland Road and with it another rare but welcome chance to see my team play.

The prospect of ridicule on a grammar school scale should we lose was no deterrent. David and I queued for the tickets again and this time, with both Mum and Dad accompanying us, we took our seats in the Lowfields Road Stand. I once again wore my blue and white. Football 'hooliganism' – as a multitude of sins was commonly referred to – was probably nearing its shameful peak. From the outset the atmosphere inside Elland Road had been intense and confrontational, the cross-Pennine rivals exchanging dubious new year pleasantries across the terraces.

A goalless and bad-tempered first half did little to becalm the simmering mood and then City ripped up the local script, scoring two goals in quick succession. The home crowd was silenced and the game seemed to be heading to its conclusion, when all eyes turned to the City penalty area. There stood Joe Corrigan, defiantly fighting off the two Leeds fans who had climbed over the Kop wall and wished to engage him on any range of matters. To see my idol assaulted felt like a personal affront. Two assailants soon became ten and the ten quickly became hundreds. Presumably, sensing a chance to get the game stopped, a multitude of youths adorned in white-and-yellow scarves piled through the hoardings and on to the pitch. The referee, Colin Seel, led the players to the safety of the changing rooms and took control, making his famous 'this game will not be abandoned' speech via the intercom. The large gates in the corner of the stadium were swung open and in rode the cavalry of the West Yorkshire Constabulary Mounted Division. As the pitch was cleared and order was restored, Dad, no doubt counting his blessings that we were not stood on the Kop that afternoon, leaned across to me and muttered, 'Give me your scarf, you are not wearing that outside here.' For once, I did not argue. Play did eventually resume, and Leeds scored a consolation goal, but City held on for the victory. We made it home late but safe.

My first exposure to crowd violence had done nothing to lessen my appetite for football. Steadfastly in love with the game, I took in every little detail on the television news. Of course, winning meant that I would have the Monday morning school ritual to deal with. Being so proudly City in a Leeds school was a lose-lose situation. If we lost, ridicule and humiliation. If we won, then invariably the threat (but rarely the reality) of a congratulatory kicking from the disgruntled Leeds fans, courtesy of 'Dr Marten'. But I really did not care as long as we won. In the fourth round City drew Nottingham Forest and lost 2-1. Brian Clough was really starting to annoy me.

Domestic life for the Dentons had its own routine. My three sisters were at the Notre Dame Grammar School and the three younger boys at St Michael's. Both were within a mile of Dad's university post so the mechanics of getting us to school were quite straightforward. Dad would take us in at 8am and we would all make our own way home on public transport. We even had a rota determining whether we would be dropped off closer to Notre Dame or St Michael's depending upon the quantity and size of any musical instruments needing to be carried. These ranged from flute and recorder to euphonium and double bass with bassoon and French horn in between.

Dinner would be prepared by Mum while listening to Radio 4's current affairs programmes and promptly served against the backdrop of the 6pm news. It was a family affair, starting with the saying of grace. There were no TV trays. Portions were put aside for latecomers, to be heated up in the microwave oven once back from whichever approved extra-curricular activity had detained them, usually music lessons or band practice.

Independent travel was briefly interrupted in the early 1980s as the activities of the Yorkshire Ripper became more frequent and local. This was particularly felt following the murder of a Leeds University student, Peter Sutcliffe's final victim. Following this, Dad opted to drive my sisters around to their various engagements or send out the boys to meet them at the bus stop, ensuring that they did not have to take the short walk home alone in the dark. Once dinner and the associated washing up-related chores were done, there was homework. There would be no television until it was complete.

While I loved television, especially the comedies, and more so due to the strict rationing, it proved to be no competition for football should there be a live midweek commentary on Radio 2. The launch of Radio 5 Live with its wall-to-wall sports coverage was years away and football had to battle with light entertainment for airtime. Coverage began at 8pm, capturing the final 15 minutes of the first half. The first 30 minutes had been pre-recorded and the formula was simple, with any goal highlights being replayed as part of the build-up to the live commentary. There was no teletext and definitely no social media. It is hard to imagine it now but, apart from being at the game, there was no other way of knowing the live score. My midweek memories are invariably of Liverpool and the great European nights. England internationals were a novel treat, especially a 5-0 win against Luxembourg on my 11th birthday, and mammoth FA Cup replays, usually involving Arsenal had me thoroughly engrossed. The constant throughout this was the voice of my broadcasting god, Peter Jones, his combination of Welsh and Cambrian tones exuding gravitas, passion, and a sense of occasion.

Radio sports coverage was not confined to football, and I remember some epic boxing nights from Wembley, Golders Green and especially the Kelvin Hall in Glasgow as Jim Watt defended his world lightweight title on multiple occasions. In the summer there were athletics meetings and the epic Coe vs Ovett middle-distance races around the running tracks of Europe. If there was any sport on the radio, but especially football, I did not need to be told to go to bed. I never felt happier than when lying under the duvet, earphones in place, not missing any precious moment of the action. In the shared bedroom, not only did the earphones conceal my secretive, clandestine listening, they also made for a more intimate experience. The programme would finish at 10pm with the quintessential BBC sign-off, 'That was a BBC outside broadcast unit production.' Then back to *Humphrey Lyttleton's Band Night* or *Music from the Movies* and it was time for me to switch off the radio and drift off to sleep, reliving the sporting action in my head.

From the perspective of time passed I can now see the wonderful coexistence between the academic and the football calendar. Both run pretty much in parallel, starting in the late summer and concluding in the following late spring. The new 'campaign' for both is awaited with nervous excitement, lofty ambition, and a little dread. For both City and me the first part of the 1977/78 campaign was 'satisfactory but could do better with more application' while the second half was a story of declining form and unrest. City did finish a disappointing fourth in the league and qualify for Europe, but some distance off the champions, Nottingham Forest. There were also rumblings of discontent at Maine Road, and while the physical toll of long service was calling time on some members of the squad there was also talk of a few at the peak of their careers – Watson, Tueart, and Barnes – feeling unsettled. I regarded it as a minor blip and nothing to worry about. We would be back stronger. The same unrest applied to my academic life.

The initial impetus that joining a new school had given me lost its momentum as the term progressed into the winter months. There is no doubt that David's conspicuous ethnicity and my brazen support of Manchester City meant that I stood out as a figure of curiosity and difference. I remained a rather shy boy, but I had also become stubborn and proud of my unique footballing and family identity. At the same time, I also wanted to fit in, even if it was at the expense of my studies. My distraction was increasingly reflected in the quality of my work and did not go unnoticed by the teachers. I had briefly reversed the poor mid-season form following a post-parents evening bollocking and a heart-to-heart with the inspiring Mr Laverty, but was unable to maintain any consistency. Like City, my end-of-season form was giving cause for concern. The reminders that I was approaching a critical juncture were constant. At the end of the second year there would be a new intake of pupils under the 'comprehensive education' system introduced by the Labour government. The whole of the year group would be split into 'streams' based on academic performance. There would be an upper stream for the higher performers, and a lower stream for the rest that would be integrated with the new intake who had failed the 11-plus two years previously. I did not want the stigma of the lower stream. It was the glamour of the First Division vs the stigma of the Second Division.

By now, my parents, becoming increasingly conscious of football becoming the dominant influence in my life, were concerned that something which, at first, they might have thought to be a transient interest was now becoming my obsession. They were quite correct in that respect. I suspect the tipping point that summer might have been my confirmation, the Catholic sacrament of mature initiation into the church. As part of the gig, celebrants get to choose a 'confirmation' name. After due consideration I opted for 'Joseph' and, quite understandably, the assumption was that I had chosen the name in recognition of our local parish and church, where I was an altar boy. When I disclosed that it was in honour of Joe Corrigan, the realisation dawned that perhaps the battle for my soul was a losing cause.

When the respective new campaigns began in August the best thing for both City and me would have been to stick with the existing leadership. Despite my erratic own performance, I had, in Mr Laverty, a teacher who could inspire and motivate. It was a healthy relationship, the friendship secondary to the authority. In Tony Book, City had a manager who represented substance over style, and one who had the respect of the senior players. Both were to change before long.

Most of class 2 Alpha were excited when we found out that Mr Vaughan was our new form master. Not long out of university, Mr Vaughan was the epitome of a trendy 1970s teacher, the Kevin Keegan of the teaching world. More relatable than the older staff members, he had long hair, wore fashionable flared trousers, and he even went to watch football on Saturdays. He also cut me a bit of slack, possibly more than was good for me, as slowly other distractions were affecting my studies. Some were of my own making, others were not.

It is a harsh but accurate reflection of the times that the presence of bullying in a solely male environment was seen as a part of growing up. That which does not kill you makes you stronger, etc. Much of it started off as a bit of a joke so the thought never really occurred to me to call it 'bullying' and the idea of discussing it with a member of staff did not even cross my mind. That was not the way it worked, especially as it was nearly all verbal rather than physical. At first, I tried to laugh it off; after all, it was only words. I conditioned myself to believe that I possessed the resilience and maturity to cope. The football jibes I could take – that was self-inflicted. It was my choice to support City and I did not shy away from making my allegiance known. I could accept that. The racist jokes were a different matter. It was not physical or violent. I do not suppose that it was especially hateful in its intent. To begin with it was not particularly overt and obvious, but it was frequent and exhausting.

In my presence, David was referred to as 'Paki Denton' by pupils and, troublingly, some teachers. David was in fact of Indian descent, but I hark back to a time and a place when any sub-continental Asian was known as a 'Paki', any oriental Asian a 'Chink', and any Afro-Caribbean a 'Wog' regardless of actual origin. 'Just because your mum slept with the Paki milkman' was a favourite playground taunt and 'Paki lover' appeared in words, song, and graffiti, scrawled across the cover of my exercise books and my school bag. In the absence of smartphones, it was the social media of its time. I felt resentment and humiliation and because of this I also felt guilt. I loved my brother whether he was a 'Paki' an Indian, or an Englishman so what right did I have to be upset about being called a 'Paki lover'? Should I not be proud of it rather than ashamed? By laughing it off, was I also enabling it with tacit acceptance?

As it slowly became pronounced, I did briefly consider talking to my parents, but it was not physically aggressive and after all what real harm could words do? I liked to think I could withstand it and, perversely, I still craved popularity from the boys who were saying these things. In my confused mind I feared that I would be told to 'rise above the words' in an upstanding Christian way. I did not need that either. I was also too embarrassed to talk about the comments aimed at my mother. With all this going on, qualifying for the upper stream was not foremost in my mind. Getting through the week with my mental wellbeing intact was a bigger priority. What I wrongly perceived as my strength, my ability to contain my troubles within my own world, was becoming my greatest weakness.

If I believed that I would find solace and strength in City's form, then my judgement was sadly misplaced. The winter of discontent had descended upon the nation as bins went unemptied and bodies unburied. The same discontent was moving towards Maine Road. Shortly into the new season and with a serious challenge for the title looking increasingly unlikely, Peter Swales had made changes. Driven by insatiable ambition, for both City and himself, he had turned back the clock. The respected and loyal Tony Book had been demoted, and Malcolm Allison had been brought in as chief coach. Whatever way it was packaged, it represented a humiliation for Book. Allison was revered by a generation as the swashbuckling, maverick coach of the 1960s who brought style and flair to Joe Mercer's industrious team. For a brief time they matched Matt Busby's United of Law, Charlton, and Best. Between them, and with Book as their captain, they had won the First Division, the FA Cup, the League Cup, and the European Cup Winners' Cup. Nevertheless, the change of leadership was not popular with the playing staff. As the team dropped below mid-table there was an inevitability that Swales would soon have to back either Allison or his senior players.

Life at St Michael's had its challenges and was often not a happy place, but it also had some pleasurable advantages. As one of the city's leading schools, the PE department was allotted some free tickets for Leeds United's home games. They were located in the Boys' Pen – Leeds' concession to supporter development being a triangle of terrace between the Kop and the Lowfields Road stands set aside for under-16s. The Boys' Pen developed many things but probably not upstanding junior supporters and my memories of it are as a hugely hostile environment where I spent most of my time scared out of my wits. Nevertheless, motivated by the prospect of free football I managed to ingratiate myself with the gym masters responsible for the allocation of tickets.

I now needed to convince Mum and Dad to agree. Their most recent and abiding memory of Elland Road had been of the attack on Joe Corrigan and the subsequent pitch invasion, so I knew it would be a formidable task. I painted a picture of the Boys' Pen being an oasis of calm and serenity among the surrounding chaos. I assured them that the area was supervised by responsible adults and any swearing was forbidden. I also left them with the impression that I would be accompanied by one of my friends' parents. A bit like a boy scouts meeting held in a football stadium. I am not sure that they completely bought into the embellishment but to my surprise they allowed me to attend my first unaccompanied matches.

Aged 12, it was a daunting but wildly exciting adventure to make my way to the ground on my own. From the moment I left home on foot I felt an irresistible force pulling me towards the ground and ended up running most of the three miles. As it happened, I did meet some school friends, albeit minus their parents. The Boys' Pen was pretty much unmanned by any stewards, and we could have our pick of the less crowded and less intimidating Lowfields Road terrace. Elland Road produced a passionate and tribal atmosphere and I enjoyed going to those games. Occasionally my school-mates would think it entertaining to announce to the crowd around us that I supported Manchester City, but no harm came of it. I liked being able to go into school on Monday morning and talk about the game with first-hand knowledge. Becoming an authority on what had happened at Elland Road on Saturday made me feel more accepted.

There was never any notion of supporting Leeds. They were now a bigger nemesis for me than United. At the games I would outwardly be making all the right noises, especially when Leeds went close or scored but, inwardly, I was passionately hoping they would get beat. My shouts of 'shit, shit' when the opposition scored were massively hammed up as I tried to conceal my delight. This was never more so that when City played at a snow-covered Elland Road in January 1978. For most of the match, disguising my allegiance had not been too much of a problem, as well into the final minutes we were trailing 1-0. That was until Brian Kidd picked up the orange ball, took a few strides forward towards the Kop end and fired a 25-yard bullet into the top corner. As the 30,000 around me cursed and groaned I struggled to contain the little somersaults of joy that were going on inside me. It was the best feeling.

When not at Elland Road, I would take myself off to watch my local rugby union club, Headingley. In the shadow of the more celebrated Yorkshire cricket and Leeds rugby league clubs, Headingley were a top-tier side and had the likes of Ian McGeechan and Peter Winterbottom in their ranks, both of whom played many internationals for their respective countries. In truth, if there was live sport then I wanted to watch it. Football first, but if not football, then anything else would do. Each Saturday afternoon, whether I went to Elland Road or Headingley, my mind was always with City and their fortunes. I carried my pocket radio with me so could listen to *Sports Report* as I walked the good hour it took me to get home. On more than one occasion I took my life into my own hands as I would step across roads, more concerned with the voices in my earphones than the cars around me. I obsessed with every result, analysing the *Sunday Times* reports after we had been to church and then eagerly looking out for whom City would play the next week. The Junior Blues had affirmed my belief that I was part of a meaningful relationship with the club, and I even penned a poem, published in the monthly magazine:

A is for Asa, Hartford is his name,
B is for Book, best manager in the game,
C is for Corrigan, brave and strong,
D is for Dave Watson; he'll never go wrong ...

And so, it continued. More William McGonagall than William Shakespeare, but you get the drift. I can't recall what I put for X or Z, especially as Pablo Zabaleta had not yet been born.

The Junior Blues was a fine organisation, pioneering in its inception and wide-reaching beyond Manchester's metropolitan boundaries, but they did not get it right all the time. It might have been because I lived in Leeds rather than Manchester that announcements about club meetings invariably arrived after the gathering had already taken place. My membership certificate usually landed on my doorstep creased and battered. I was inclined to largely overlook these shortcomings in return for feeling part of something so much bigger and more important. It felt petty and, even worse, disloyal to complain about such minor indiscretions. From the bay-windowed front room I could probably see half a mile up Pudsey Road so had advance warning of the postman's arrival. When I knew that something from Manchester was due, I would look from the living room, spotting him emerge from the front gardens at the top of the inclined road and watch him deliver to the other houses before finally coming up the driveway of 282 and depositing our mail. Usually, it would be bills or academic correspondence for Dad, and I would go back to wait another 24 hours' hoping that tomorrow would be the day.

On a rainy Saturday morning in January 1979 a damp, torn team poster and membership card belatedly and limply fell through the letterbox. My disappointment and frustration ran deep. This was compounded in the afternoon when City were dumped out of the FA Cup. I had once again been convinced that there was only one name on the trophy, but Shrewsbury Town of the Third Division inflicted the cruel humiliation. Enough was enough. I reached once more for the Woolworths pad, wrote what I considered to be my finest strongly worded letter, had it endorsed and countersigned by Dad and posted it. Being treated like shit at school was bad enough, but I was buggered if my football club, the football club I bravely stood up for every day in the playground, was going to treat me with the same disrespect. I did not articulate it quite that way in the letter.

For once, the reply was surprisingly prompt, but the envelope was disappointingly thin. Where was the complimentary scarf, hat, mug, and shirt by way of an apology? I tore into it with more hope than expectation – but my lack of faith was misplaced as the envelope contained more than I could ever have imagined. The correspondence was not from the secretary of the Junior Blues, nor from an office administrator. It came from the Junior Blues president, Joe Corrigan himself, personally signed. He said how sorry he was to receive my letter, that a replacement team photograph was on its way to me, and should I ever wish to go to a game at Maine Road then he would be happy to send me some complimentary tickets. A letter from Joe Corrigan, my first football hero! True to his word the team photograph arrived, this time sent by courier and in pristine condition. Additionally, it had been autographed by each one of the first team including the new headline signing from Poland, the enigmatic Kazimierz Deyna (the concept of a foreign import was a new and exciting innovation in 1979). The poster went straight up on my bedroom wall, the letter was immediately taken into school to be shown to my class-mates.

I perused the remaining fixtures of the dwindling season to find the stand-out match. All the big teams had already come and gone, most of them with victories, so I chose a game against Queens Park Rangers. I promptly wrote back to Joe – I considered that we were now on first-name terms – and requested that, as I would be bringing my big sister, we should be afforded tickets for the seats. My eldest sister Elizabeth and I took the early morning National Express coach, visiting my grandparents for lunch before heading to Maine Road. I secretly hoped that at some time during the game a club official might locate us and invite us into the inner sanctum of the dressing room to meet the players. That did not happen, but I was not too disappointed; I would not have known what to say anyway. City stumbled their way to an unconvincing 3-1 win and that was the most important thing.

I am a notoriously bad traveller and get car sick very easily. I get seasick sat in the bath. Consequently, I rarely, if ever, read when travelling. But somewhere on the journey back to Leeds, over that well-travelled route, I must have read the matchday programme because by the time I arrived home and opened the big green front door to our house on Pudsey Road my plan was formed. I now just had to do another big sell on Mum and Dad. A few pages in from the back of the programme, I'd seen a notice about the sale of the following year's season tickets. There were special discounts for those committing to and paying in full before the end of April. The prices were listed in descending order, from the best seats in the Main Stand through to standing on the Kippax Road terrace. The last line had caught my attention:

'Junior Blues Special – Platt Lane Stand Seats £5 (£4.00 before 30 April).'

'Surely there must have been a typing error.'

'Was that price per game? No, it couldn't be, that would be ridiculously expensive.'

To my mind, season tickets were only for the rich and fanatical and, while every bit as fanatical as the next man or boy, I certainly could not be described as rich. But £4? I could afford £4. On the way home I did the math. On top of the ticket, I needed my coach fare multiplied by 21 times, assuming I went to every game. I certainly intended to be at every minute of every game. I also needed six bus fares per trip, to and from the coach station in Leeds, to my grandparents' house in Manchester and from Maine Road to the coach station in Manchester. I could walk the couple of miles from my grandparents' to the ground and that would save a pound or so across the season. I knew roughly what was in my Halifax Building Society account and I worked out that I could afford it for one season only – but what a season that would be.

The initial parental reaction was, like my own, sceptical. There must be some sort of typing error; the pricing could not be right. But there it was in black and white, 'Binding!' as Dad proclaimed. Ever the opportunist, I also ruthlessly leveraged other factors to my advantage. My parents loved a bargain, especially my mother, so I immediately had her attention and the fact that my grandparents, her parents, were in Manchester meant that I could call on them beforehand and get fed and looked after. Nanna and Gangan rarely travelled beyond Manchester's boundaries and profoundly missed their Yorkshire-based grandchildren. Also, to my advantage, the parental 'we'll think about it' in the hope that whatever 'it' was would go away over time could not be deployed, as the offer would expire in nine days. The imminence of the deadline eliminated the possibility of that other time-honoured parental caveat: a positive response being contingent on school results. The odds were stacking in my favour. Ultimately the hard sell that I had envisaged was not needed. I think my parents appreciated that my interest in football was genuine, and they were keen to encourage their children to 'stick at things'. They had by now accepted that this was more than the passing fad they had anticipated. I paid Dad the £4 and he wrote the cheque. I ran across the road, deposited the envelope in the red post box and now just had to wait the four long months until August.

Before the new season would start the old school term had to finish. I do not think that, had my parents been able to incentivise my season ticket against school results, it would have made much difference. The damage had long since been done. My inattentiveness coupled with the personal challenges I faced on an almost daily basis meant I struggled to focus academically or motivate myself sufficiently to push into the top half of the class. At times I could be massively motivated but rarely around my studies. Mr Vaughan was an enthusiastic and energetic form teacher who inspired the class to raise record amounts of money for chosen charity causes and I threw myself into these activities with passion and commitment. I became a keen, dedicated member of the athletics team and what I lacked in technical ability at ball sports, I made up for in doggedness and stamina when it came to long-distance running. I represented the school at both cross-country in the winter and the 1500m in the summer. This was the longest my age group was permitted to run, which was a regret to me. I found peace in the 'loneliness of the long-distance runner' losing myself in the solitude of the activity and for a short while forgetting about everything else around me.

I also became an accomplished swimmer, achieving all my life-saving awards and several long-distance swimming certificates. My parents had a love of music and encouraged us all to embrace this pursuit, more so than sport. I never rose to my sisters' heights of accomplishment on the flute, double bass, and bassoon but I did enjoy playing the euphonium, especially as a member of the Leeds Schools Brass Bands. I could lose myself as a small part of the collective group, each contributing to bigger, bolder outcome as we performed our repertoire around the city.

Academically, however, the final whistle had long since sounded, and the increasingly inevitable outcome was decided on the last day of term. I would be in the lower stream going into my third year at St Michael's and there was nothing I could do about it. The second division awaited me. I had failed to show enough dedication or academic ability to convince the teachers that I could cope in the upper tier. My pride and confidence were massively hurt. On paper it meant a new group of class-mates, including the new comprehensive intake, and a supposedly less challenging syllabus that would determine the public examinations to be taken at 16. In reality, it meant much more.

4

Against the World

DURING THE summer I came to terms with my reduced academic standing and convinced myself to adopt a positive attitude to it all; I saw the possibility of a new start and the chance to be one of the stronger class performers. I could rebuild my damaged self-esteem and wounded pride. I resolved that with more focus and dedication I would give it my best shot.

In Manchester there had been changes too. The changing room unrest that had been growing since the arrival of Malcolm Allison had forced Peter Swales to make a choice. He had backed his coach over his players. The summer had resembled a car boot sale with many of the established players departing. Gary Owen, the local lad and bright new hope for the club, was heartbroken to leave. His father famously described the journey to sign for West Brom as being 'like taking your dog to the vet to be put down'. It brought to mind some of my own feelings on those first journeys from Manchester to Leeds. Allison's ambitious vision would be built around the remaining long-serving personnel and a handful of promising but unproven youth team graduates. There were new signings, all bought in at fees disproportionate to anything their previous achievements had merited. Three games into the new season Allison smashed the British transfer record to sign Steve Daley from Wolves for over £1m. It was a bold, brave, and ultimately misplaced gamble, but Allison was never one to doubt his own ability, especially when indulged by a chairman with an equally large ego.

In June my season ticket arrived. Maroon and blue, each page with an individual match number. During the long summer weeks, I leafed through the magnificently meaningless pages countless times, each one betokening the glorious victories to come. The fixtures for the new season were due to be published the following month. I desperately hoped that City would be at home on the opening day as I did not want to wait an extra week for my season to begin. My wish was duly granted. Newly promoted Crystal Palace would be visiting Maine Road; Malcolm Allison versus his protégé, the young and innovative Terry Venables.

At long last the day arrived. Proudly sporting my new pair of green denims, bought especially for the season, I confidently left home looking quite the part. It would be the first of many such trips. From Pudsey Road the number 5 or 11 bus would take me to the National Express Coach Station on Wellington Street where I would buy my junior return ticket. Four years previously, crossing the Pennines in the opposite direction, I was scared and anxious. Now there was only a light-headedness. After the coach dropped me off at Manchester's Chorlton Street Station, I'd hop on the bus from Piccadilly Gardens and then quickly find myself outside my grandparents' house, 4 Brixton Avenue, Withington. The small pre-war terrace they inhabited for the last 40 years of their married life was full of nostalgic paraphernalia. Faded volumes of books adorned the walls, along with sepia photographs of old unrecognisable relatives, mixed with the bright colour of a newly born grandchild or first communion celebrant. Weird mechanical toys from their own childhood days, once occasionally taken down to amuse grandchildren, gathered dust. The walls and ceilings were yellow with Gangan's pipe smoke and the smell of tobacco lingered on the upholstery and in the air – Balkan Sobranie tobacco, always Balkan Sobranie. That small, unconditionally welcoming house became a second home for me; and a refuge from my teenage demons.

I arrived before lunch and helped Nanna with some chores before being dispatched into Withington village with a shopping list of varied groceries. Pork sausages from Norton's the butchers and a white unsliced loaf from the bakery. Inside the cosy tobacconist's with standing room for no more than half a dozen people, I was hemmed in by all manner of tobaccos and smoking accessories. I asked for two ounces of Balkan Sobranie for Mr Clift. The obliging proprietor benignly turned a blind eye to my young age in full knowledge and respect for whom Mr Clift was.

There was no central heating in the house, but there was a wonderful, coal-powered Aga stove. I brought in the coal from the outside bunker and made myself useful however I could. Gangan was a keen photographer and obsessed by growing tomatoes in his lean-to greenhouse in the tiny back garden. We went out and made admiring noises at the plants and I posed for photographs on his old wooden chair as he puffed on his freshly reloaded pipe. There was a reassuring comfort about the scent that wafted up into the Manchester air. Under his watchful supervision, I put the compost into the new tomato pots ready for his next attempt.

Lunch, homemade by Nanna, was traditional Lancashire fayre; usually a meat and potato pie that was hearty enough to see me through until I got back home late in the evening. As lunchtime became early afternoon I glanced at the clock, not wanting to miss the BBC's *Football Focus*, presented by Bob Wilson. Would City get a mention during the preview of this afternoon's games? Finally, at about 2pm I would say my goodbyes and leave. Nanna handed me a brown paper bag with an apple and a piece of cake for half-time, although rarely was either eaten. It would become a fondly familiar routine for the next few years.

The feelings of warmth and security of 4 Brixton Avenue was replaced by an impatient energy as I set off. At the end of Burton Road, I passed the Victorian nursery school building which I once briefly attended while living at Winster Avenue. I turned left on to Yew Tree Road as more supporters, scarves draped around their shoulders, emerged from homes and pubs. Yew Tree Road was a long, straight thoroughfare leading almost to the stadium. It took me past the back of Platt Fields Park where the Dentons had attended the Manchester Flower Show as an annual pilgrimage. As I crossed Platt Lane the numbers would swell, and I became part of an expectant throng. It was as if my shyness miraculously disappeared as, in my excitement, I felt the urge to talk to any one of these strangers about the afternoon's game. My season ticket was in the Platt Lane Stand so I must be near now. Peering through the tight alleys nestled between the rows of the red-brick terraces of Moss Side, I could see the back of the Kippax Stand rising above the houses. The narrow street opened on to the pot-holed car park and in front of me was the full impressive splendour of the Kippax. I had finally arrived.

Still much too early for the kick-off, I nevertheless rushed around the ground, past the length of the old terrace and around the outside of the new North Stand. It was just metres from the adjoining residential backyards and the enterprising occupants were offering to look after bicycles for 50p. I peered through the dirty window of the small, cluttered souvenir shop that preceded the days of City Superstores and looked on with envy at the people who were buying the associated tat that lay within. Maybe a scarf or an autograph book or perhaps a metal pin badge just like those Paul Burns had worn on his denim jacket. The souvenir shop adjoined the social club, where I proudly held the League Cup and Paul's parents had enrolled me as a Junior Blue. I walked past the outside of the Main Stand. High up in those seats, Dad and I had sat and watched my first City game. I could tell if today's game was going to be on either *Match of the Day* or *The Big Match* by the presence of big TV vans parked on the concourse, miles of cables leading up to gantries and cameras. At the main entrance I stopped to celebrity spot. Could I see any players arriving or anybody else from television that I might recognise?

As I came to the Platt Lane Stand and retrieved my season ticket from my coat, I noticed my hand was trembling. I feared losing it or having it stolen. I tore out the page with corresponding match number before quickly putting it back in my pocket and zipping it up. I handed the small piece of paper to the turnstile operator, still half-expecting to be told to go away, that this was not a ticket but a dream. He took it from me and nodded, the rusty iron turnstile gave a heavy click as I gave it a push and slowly it turned, and then I was in the ground. I found my seat in the right-hand corner of the stand – not just any seat but *my* seat for the season. I did not care that it was really a section of maroon wooden bench with a number on it. Block E, Row 12, Seat Number 7. Just 12 rows back from the goal.

In his wonderfully moving and amusing book, *I'm Not Really Here*, the ex-City player Paul Lake recounts his own journey to Maine Road as a young supporter. We are 18 months apart in age so it would have been a similar time. Maybe on one of those Saturdays we passed each other, filled with the same boyish excitement. I like to think so.

That first game against Crystal Palace was a 0-0 draw, but the day was by no means an anticlimax. The sheer exhilaration I felt ensured that. After the final whistle I walked through the Manchester dusk to the bus stop, my faithful radio always in hand, catching up on the other scores. The coach headed back out through the industrial landscape of Manchester, up on to the now darkening Pennine moors and back down into Yorkshire. Mum and Dad were relieved to see me back safe, and I think a little proud of my independence and dedication. Any sense of pride would not mitigate having to make up for my Saturday excursion by completing my share of household chores and weekend homework assignments the next day. I called Nanna and Gangan to let them know of my safe arrival home and my day was done. I ate my tea, reheated in the microwave, and relived the action as I read through *The Pink*, the *Manchester Evening News* sports paper that I had acquired at the bus station.

A week later I saw my first City goal as a season ticket holder, scored by Paul Power running through the Brighton defence. After what seemed like years of having to bottle up my true feelings at Leeds games, I could finally cheer a City goal and was ready to make up for lost time. I forced myself to hold back tears, too emotionally immature to understand why a simple goal could make me feel this way. It meant so much more than a goal. For that brief moment, nothing else in the world mattered.

My resolve going into the new academic term had resulted in a solid if unspectacular start. Despite the turmoil of seeing the class I yearned to belong to being led off in one direction, and my new form of strangers and to my mind failures, being led off in another, I was determined to overcome my disappointment through achievement. My early results were encouraging; however, like my football team, confidence was brittle and resilience to setback was weak. I had hoped to be appointed as 'class captain', a position of no great importance but one that would have given me a much-needed boost, although that did not happen. Soon my focus gave way to a desire to fit in with my new class-mates.

The racial jibes continued. As in the past, it had started with amused curiosity as a new intake discovered I had a 'Paki' brother. The questions were the same, this time with a different, older, and more streetwise audience. I increasingly defaulted to classroom antics as a futile attempt to divert conversation away from race and pretend that none of this was really happening.

The verbal assaults were by no means from all the class. In form 3F there were also caring boys who wanted no part of it and, with more insight and maturity than I could muster, were able to see what was happening and its effect on me. I will never forget the kindness of Patrick Buggle, a boy who was going through his own academic struggles but often took time out to just talk to me. He never mentioned what was going on around me but somehow we both knew the unspoken conversation that was taking place.

The 'jokes' usually centred on colour and family, curry, and anything else Asian. On one level it might have been considered as harmless fun, especially if the nation's family entertainment was any barometer. Much as I enjoyed television sitcoms such as *Mind Your Language*, *It Ain't Half Hot Mum* and *Love Thy Neighbour*, their characterisations, and parodies of Asians, did not help. At school, the racist incidents were becoming more organised, more of a group activity. The tribalism that had drawn me to football was now coming back to haunt me in a different way. As a peer group we were all getting older and more socio-politically aware of movements like the National Front and the BNP. I had, occasionally, heard their anthems sung at Leeds home games and quickly they migrated to the classroom. I would be at my desk, waiting for the teacher to enter, when the soft whispered incantation from a few boys around me would start up:

There ain't no black in the Union Jack, send the Pakis back.
There ain't no black in the Union Jack, send the Pakis back.

If I had any doubt as to whether the sentiment was aimed at me, my suspicions were soon confirmed, as the lyrics were not so subtly twisted:

There ain't no black in the Union Jack, send the Dentons back.
There ain't no black in the Union Jack, send the Dentons back.

The hushed tones, accompanied by rhythmic drumming of fingers on desktops, increased the sense of menace. Sinister as it was, it was barely audible to the approaching member of staff and stopped immediately when the master entered the classroom.

I remain convinced to this day that there were teachers at St Michael's College who were aware that this was going on, and not just to me but others too, and chose to turn a blind eye. I can only surmise that their reasons might have been apathy and lack of understanding of the impact it had. I prefer to think that it did not betray sympathy with the wider sentiment. Evidence of this complicity was provided one lunchtime. Some boys were jostling me to the back of the school dinner queue for 'having a Paki brother'.

'Fuck off Denton, Pakis at the back.'

Not five metres away there was a teacher supervising. I looked at him and he looked at me and raised his eyebrows as he looked towards the back of the queue. I do not know whether he was indicating that he agreed or whether he considered my best and easiest course of action was to go to the back. Regardless, I did not intend to humiliate myself any further. Barely holding back the tears, I walked to the back of the queue and then kept going on and out of the school gates.

I would go hungry before I cowed before these racist bullies. Observed leaving the school by a prefect, I was punished with a half-hour detention for being off school premises without permission. Things were not going to plan in Leeds, and nor were they in Manchester.

City's young team had also been having a difficult autumn term. The inexperience had been evident as they suffered big defeats against Liverpool, West Brom, and Ipswich, but I was also there to witness victories against European champions Nottingham Forest and in the 100th Manchester derby, goals from Tony Henry and Michael Robinson put United to the sword on a never-to-be-forgotten November afternoon. Matches against Leeds were never tame affairs, and I once again feared for my safety in Elland Road's Boys' Pen as City won 2-1 in a bloodbath of an encounter. I remained besotted with everything about my football.

Out of the blue I presented my parents with a small glimmer of hope that I might have a career ahead of me. The November Junior Blues newsletter competition was to write a report on a City match. English was one of my stronger subjects and I quickly penned my account of the derby victory. To everyone's surprise, a few weeks later a package arrived in the post with a note telling me that I was the winner and with it came my prize – Kevin Keegan's book, *Against the World*. It felt like a title that summed up my life. Encouraged by this rare scholastic achievement my father wasted no time in suggesting the possibilities of a journalistic career and insisted I write to the competition adjudicator, journalist Ron Crowther of the *Daily Mail*, for his advice. He kindly took the trouble to write back to me with words of encouragement.

Soon my involvement with City would hit heights greater than even I could imagine, but that was not before a new low. On Boxing Day I ventured overseas for the first time. My sister Kathy had been part of a school exchange trip to France and stayed with a Normandy-based family, the Huets. They were Catholic, of course, and their seven children's ages roughly corresponded with the Dentons. It made good sense that we kept the exchange relationship going through the family. Other siblings had also exchanged visits with their Huet counterparts. Kathy had a talent for languages and was studying French at A-level so it would be good preparation for her forthcoming exams to visit the Huets again and brush up on her verbal skills. Out of nothing more than opportunist curiosity, I requested if I could go too and when the unexpected answer was 'yes' I immediately regretted my ill-considered eagerness. I did not really want to go to France, I did not want to meet people I did not know and could not talk to anyway. I certainly did not want to miss any of the Christmas football fixtures. I had, however, dug myself into a hole and there was no getting out of it. We set off from Newhaven to Dieppe in the midst of a gale force storm and were both spectacularly seasick as the ferry got tossed from wave to wave on the cold, grey English Channel.

For the next ten days the seasickness was replaced by profound homesickness. I missed everything about the UK – well, maybe not school so much. All of this was in no way down to the Huets, who were the most generous and welcoming hosts. Conscious that Kathy had also suffered from homesickness in the past, I tried to hide my feelings as I counted the days until we went home. Having become something of a master of concealment, it was not such a difficult task. The days slowly went by and we returned home on the first Sunday in January.

While happy to be back home among family, my real priority was to catch up on City. How had they fared while I'd been away? I had not seen any of the results from England. The third round of the FA Cup, one of my favourite events in the football calendar, had taken place the day before, and I had to know that we had progressed. After exchanging the obligatory 'hello, pleased to see you' as Dad met us at Leeds station, I asked him about the football. 'They lost to Halifax Town,' he told me in his matter-of-fact style. He was not one to sugar-coat bad news. My heart sank. Halifax were bottom of the Fourth Division; it was one of the FA Cup's biggest ever shocks. For the last week I had looked forward to returning home to hear about City winning but they had let me down. More than that, they had humiliated me and I knew the teasing would be merciless when the new term started the following day. If I had been given the choice between school the next morning or returning to France it would have been a close call.

Ultimately relieved to be repatriated, I settled into my familiar regime, managing my academic and emotional challenges. The next trip to Manchester was always front of mind and football gave me something to look forward to. Unexpectedly, I once again found salvation within the pages of the matchday programme:

'Would you like to be a ball boy at City home games? If you would and you are a Junior Blue, then please write to us and tell us why you should be a ball boy.'

Five years had passed since I had sent my unsolicited letter to United. They had not even bothered to reply. I was determined that this was going to be different. Once more the Woolworth's pad came out and the letter scribed and mailed. I have no recollection of what I wrote; I expect I referenced the fact that my loyalty and dedication could not be questioned as I travelled over from Leeds for every home game. It must have sufficiently impressed those in power as I soon received a reply inviting me to attend a meeting at Maine Road to 'discuss the expected duties of a ball boy'. The 'interview' was on a school day and my form teacher, suitably amused by this auspicious summons, granted me the afternoon off. It felt strange to be at Maine Road with no crowds; the concourses around the stadium, usually so busy and energetic with pre-match activity, were eerily empty and quiet. A few solitary figures were visiting the ticket office and buying gifts from the souvenir shop. I duly presented my letter of invitation at reception. My fellow competition winners and I were escorted down a sky blue-carpeted corridor past the perennially empty trophy cabinet and through to the Chairman's Lounge. The 'expected duties of a ball boy' were not a great surprise: give the ball back to the players and don't run on the pitch.

What was not foreseen was that the duties extended to reserve-team fixtures, and I would be required to attend every Saturday and not just the alternate first-team games. Although concerned that my detailed budgetary planning had not accounted for these extra trips, I nonetheless did not have the nerve to enquire about expenses. From the newspapers I was aware of the club's increasingly precarious financial position and did not want to add to the cash-flow pressure that the cost of my junior return ticket from Leeds would have entailed. I eagerly accepted the invitation to serve until the end of the current season when the position would be reviewed. Schedules needed to be adjusted for my new and important role at the heart of the club, with my duties requiring me to be at the ground by 1pm for reserve-team games. Nanna and Gangan happily obliged, rearranging lunchtimes, accommodating me every weekend, proudly sharing the news with their neighbours and old friends. Between them and my parents they even paid for my extra travel expenses.

Ten days after my interview, I reported for first-team duty. I tentatively showed my letter to the uniformed commissionaire in charge of the cordon outside the busy entrance to Maine Road. This time the throngs of matchday crowds had already gathered, waiting to catch a glimpse of the players arriving. I expected to be turned away, but he pointed me to the players' entrance. As I walked to the narrow wooden door, my Adidas bag containing trainers and T-shirt in hand, I could hear voices behind me wondering who this young lad heading into the players area was.

'Do you recognise him?' 'He might be from the youth team.' 'Maybe he's a reserve.' 'Bit young, isn't he?'

It had been barely a year since I had sent that strongly worded letter expressing my disappointment with the Junior Blues and I was now entering Maine Road through the same door as the first team. I had come a long way in a short time.

The entrance led to a short, sky blue passageway and immediately the smell of football dressing rooms, liniment, Deep Heat, and hot, strong tea hit me hard. I came to the end of the passage and there on the right was the wood-panelled home team changing room, and on the left, the visitors. There was an urgent but controlled energy about the place as club officials wandered about performing their various matchday duties. Next to the visitors' changing room was the ball boys' room. I say ball boys' room as that was its purpose for a few hours each week. The rest of the time it served as a store for corner flags, nets, training bibs, and other assorted accessories. Luxury it was not, but we did not care.

Occasionally, comedian and long-time City fan Eddie Large would come in and joke with us, trying out his material on a not-so-critical audience. My enthusiasm was bettered by my fellow ball boys, as I was the last to arrive. There were ten of us and just eight places. The two reserves would sit in the stand just in case anyone should pick up an injury, rendering them incapable to carry on (seriously). The fairest way to decide was deemed to be based on who had arrived first, so I duly took my place on the bench for the game. I decided that I would learn from the others, see where they screwed up, and make a stunning 'debut' in due course. My delayed appearance did not dilute my excitement and I still felt massively involved. The game was against Norwich. Dennis Tueart had re-signed for City and was making the first appearance of his 'second coming' so there was a sense of optimism and anticipation. Premier League anthems and orchestrated processions on to the pitch were still a thing of the far-off future so we had to be alert and look out for the players to emerge. The home team changing room door opened and the captain, Paul Power, moustachioed and ball in hand, stepped out, the tall Joe Corrigan towering behind him. The ball boys, in purple tracksuits with the sponsor's logo (Associated Tyre Services) on the back, sprang into action and ran out through the tunnel and out to take their positions.

I made my debut two weeks later against Arsenal, by which time the pre-kick-off ritual had been tweaked to my advantage. Instead of the ball boys coming out and immediately taking their positions, we were to run on to the pitch just before the players and stop in the centre circle, where we would wave to our adoring public and disperse. Having missed out two weeks earlier, I was chosen to lead out the group. At five to three I could hear the clatter of metal studs against the tiled floor of the adjacent Arsenal changing room as the players went through their last-minute preparations. Just the other side of the wall were the likes of Pat Jennings, David O'Leary, and Liam Brady, all household names I had seen on television so many times. I led my team out of our pokey little cupboard. I could hear the crowd singing in the stands above me, and through the dimly lit tunnel the bright spring afternoon was illuminating the pitch. Beyond the green of the grass, I could just make out the massed ranks of the Kippax. I broke into a jog and moved forwards. Photographers, ground staff, and various matchday officials were congregated at the end of the tunnel. For a moment, I knew what it felt like to be Tony Book, Mike Doyle, Paul Power, and all those other City captains who had led their teams out on to that Maine Road pitch. The players had emerged just behind us and, as we got to the centre circle, the tumultuous cheer from nearly 50,000 supporters went up. That the cheer was not meant for me did not matter one jot.

I milked every last second of it before running up to take my position behind the North Stand goal from where I then had the best view of City getting beaten 3-0.

Pitchside positions were keenly fought over in that crowded ball-boys' room. Prime location was the Kippax. The atmosphere was the best in front of the massive terrace, and with the camera gantries being high up in the opposite Main Stand it provided the best chance of a TV appearance on *Match of the Day*. After that was behind the goals, less running to do and a sense of proximity to the action, plus also the chance of some TV exposure whenever there was goalmouth action. Whoever was on duty at the North Stand also had the additional task of taking a sprig of lucky heather from Helen 'The Bell' Turner and placing it in Joe Corrigan's glove bag. From the 1970s through to the 1990s, Helen, with her distinctive bun of blonde hair, could be seen and heard ringing her big brass bell from the front row of the North Stand. For the Central League reserve games where the attendance was generally below 1,000, the two reserve ball boys were positioned on the empty Kippax terraces, returning the ball should it be kicked into row Z. I liked being there as it meant I could listen to my radio at the same time, keeping tabs on the fortunes of the first team, wherever they happened to be playing.

Following on from my magnificent debut, we sufficiently impressed in our duties to be told that we would be staying on into the next season and, equally importantly, City performed sufficiently well to retain their place in the top division. We celebrated the final game with victory over high-flying Ipswich. Relieved of ball boy duties for that last game and given the choice of watching from anywhere in the ground, I made the brave decision to stand on the Kippax among the older, bigger, seasoned veterans of Maine Road. I joined in all the songs when I knew the words, with my falsetto voice, and listened to the gnarled wisdom and wit around me. In no time the shy kid from Leeds, surrounded by a thousand strangers, felt among friends.

The big football story of the summer of 1980 was Kevin Keegan's return from the Bundesliga and Hamburg to sign for Southampton. The opening day fixtures duly scheduled City to start their campaign away on the south coast, and the Keegan-inspired Saints won 2-0. In contrast City had been uncharacteristically quiet in the transfer market, Allison believing he could build on the squad he had assembled. However, it soon became apparent that what he had was not good enough. The season started off poorly and continued in the same vein. October came and City languished without a win, sitting second from bottom. The various graphs I had optimistically prepared and stuck on my bedroom wall to record the anticipated spectacular progress all had an ominous downwards trajectory. At least they would have if I could have been bothered updating them after the first few weeks. I preferred to avoid the sight of the depressing data being displayed for all to see. Hiding from bad news was becoming a common theme in my life.

I resumed my ball boy duties, watching the first-team struggles at close quarters and failing to spot any bright new talent in the reserves that might give a glimmer of hope. My hero Joe Corrigan, although coming to the latter days of his career, was frequently and heroically keeping City in games they should have long lost. When he incurred a rare injury in a League Cup tie at Stoke the signs were bad. Joe's misfortune, however, became my good luck as it meant that I would at last meet my hero. At the following reserve game, I took up my position behind the North Stand goal. With Keith McRae deputising for Joe it meant that youth-team keeper Alex Williams was promoted to the reserves. Midway through the first half, a ripple of applause from the paltry crowd in the Main Stand drew my attention. Joe, leg bandaged and on crutches, was hobbling around the perimeter of the pitch. He wanted to be there to support and coach Alex, and as a goalkeeper the best and only place was from behind the net.

He stopped at the goal and beckoned me over: 'Bring me a chair please, will you?'

I ran off and found one of the white plastic chairs that were used by stewards on matchdays. As I placed it for him, I wondered if I should tell him about the letter he had written to me so many lifetimes ago and how it had indirectly led to me being a ball boy here today. I decided that he had more important things to concentrate on right now so wisely decided not to. Inside, I also feared that he would have no recollection of his letter or that a secretary might have signed all his letters, and that would have hurt me badly. In the end we did exchange a few words over those 20 minutes or so. I said that I wanted to be a goalkeeper and he said, kindly, that I looked a bit small. I told him that I travelled to the games all the way from Leeds. He seemed suitably impressed by my dedication. That was enough for me.

Through my position I was privileged to have occasional access to my heroes like Joe, but then in 1980 football was hugely different to today's game. That City squad was all-British with a big proportion from Manchester. The players and their salaries, while being way beyond the working man's, were much more 'of the real world' and the players were accessible in way they simply are not today. I distinctly remember being on the number 48 bus heading to Maine Road for a reserve game, when at the bottom of Yew Tree Road, a young first teamer boarded the same bus. Steve McKenzie, at one time the country's most expensive teenager, paid his eight pence fare like me, and got off at the same Platt Lane stop. We walked to the ground and entered the same players' entrance, and there we went our separate ways. Not quite the comic-book image of 'cycling to the game with boots tied around the neck before scoring a hat-trick in front of 50,000 people' but a long, long way from arriving in a pimped-up Bentley convertible. Less than nine months later my fellow traveller scored one of the greatest ever FA Cup Final goals in front of 100,000 people at Wembley. He's probably never been on a Manchester bus since.

Relegation was again looking more like a probability than a possibility when Swales finally lost his nerve and fired both Allison and Tony Book. He then acted with uncharacteristic good judgment in appointing the Norwich manager John Bond. Ironically, Bond was a graduate of the same West Ham academy that had nurtured Allison under the tutelage of Ron Greenwood. He had kept Norwich in the First Division, playing good football and achieving consistent results on a limited budget, and had been astute with his signings and his man-management. Unlike Allison he was a pragmatist and was willing to make the necessary compromises to style to get the required results. He quickly spotted the issues: a lack of maturity in key positions, a shortage of confidence, and overly complex tactics.

Bond made three swift signings and the change was instantaneous and dramatic. After losing his first game at home, results under his leadership went from good to better, with impressive wins before Christmas over Leeds, Coventry, Tottenham, and others. The opening-day defeat at Southampton was avenged with a stylish 3-0 win at home, a match that gave me an opportunity to ask Kevin Keegan to sign his book won in the Junior Blues competition. He duly did so, and it remains on my shelves today. Progress in the League Cup was just as impressive as the new-found confidence flowed through the team. Dennis Tueart scored four in a demolition of Notts County, and by Christmas, City were in the semi-finals, one round from Wembley. The team were now playing with purpose, discipline, and authority, and those players who had looked lost and confused only months earlier were now enjoying their work and delivering results consistently. If only I could say the same for myself.

While my footballing fortunes had turned a corner, how I needed a John Bond in my school life. Having failed to avoid relegation to the second division, I now trod water in mid-table. A new academic year had not resulted in a dramatic upturn to match City's and the bullying continued to sap my energy and attention. My results were never so bad that they would raise massive alarm bells at home or school, but term by term they were slowly and irrevocably deteriorating. I knew that I could do much better even if consistently failing to show my teachers any evidence of that. My position was becoming increasingly unsustainable. A pressure cooker kept in check by my stubborn internalisation. That it would, one day, all come to a head was becoming more and more inevitable. I was sure that David must have suffered incidents of bullying like my own. I had occasionally witnessed it at a distance, but I did not need first-hand evidence. It stood to reason that was the case, but he had made it to the upper stream and I think with a more academically able and focussed class he was better able to prevent it affecting his schoolwork. He was also smart.

Just before the end of the autumn term we were talking at home. He told me that he had been having trouble from one particular teacher. The member of staff in question also happened to be my own form teacher. I do not remember it as a long conversation; we did not talk a lot about any troubles we might be having at school. I gave it little subsequent thought, but I did interpret his 'having trouble' as him feeling victimised over his colour.

The following day was the final one before the Christmas holidays. Like every other boy I was in an excitable mood as we assembled for afternoon registration. City were doing well, and I felt optimistic and confident about the forthcoming holiday fixtures. Christmas was coming and with it a break from school. We were to be dismissed early, as was customary on the last day of term. My form teacher walked in and sat down, placing the black class register on his desk. He was a tough-talking, ginger-bearded figure, suited but at the same time a bit scruffy, chalk dust on his cheap grey jacket cuffs and his fingertips yellow with nicotine stains. He opened the register and addressed the class in a manner I had not heard before (upon adult reflection, I suspect he might just have spent that lunchtime having a Christmas drink with a few of his colleagues).

'In a minute, a silly boy who is not one of us is going to walk into this classroom,' he said. 'When he comes in, I want you all to laugh at him.'

That was all he said; on the face of it, something that could be considered a harmless end-of-term joke. But something inside me told me that it might not be all that harmless, that there was more to it. There was mild confusion and intrigue in the class. We were all a bit old for a visit from Santa Claus. 'Who is it going to be?'

I instinctively joined the dots between David's conversation of the previous evening and the master's instruction and immediately I feared the worst. I had learnt to recognise the language of insidious racism and I knew enough to know what the 'not one of us' meant. It was going to be David, and I could not let him come into the classroom. Motivated by self-protection and concerned for my own pride as much as his, I knew I simply had to stop him. I got up from my desk and moved towards the door, but I was too late. David was already stood there, and about to enter. I could see that he was oblivious to what was about to happen. I slumped back into my seat and feared the worst.

He walked in and the laughing started. Not natural warm laughter borne out of something genuinely funny but a false, phoney, ridiculing laughter. Laughter and pointing. David was confused and understandably humiliated. I sat at my desk, broken and by now on the brink of tears. Some of my class-mates had made the family connection that my form teacher had so ignorantly failed to do. Embarrassed and sensitive to my feelings, they stopped laughing. After probably no more than a minute, it abated, starved of the oxygen of any reaction. The master was oblivious to my emotional state. I am not sure if he even realised that David was my brother.

He was told to stand at the front of the class while the register was taken.

'Adams?' 'Present.'

'Allenby?' 'Present.'

Soon it would be 'Denton'. How would I react? I did not know.

'Brearley?' 'Present.'

'Brokowski?' 'Present?'

'Cullen?' 'Present.'

If I just confirmed my presence, I would be tacitly saying that what was happening was okay. I would be saying that it did not matter. I would feel complicit. It had to be now or never.

'Davidson?' 'Present.'

'Denton?' Silence. What should I do? I had to do something, I had to say something. 'Denton?' He looked up at my desk. 'Denton?' The impatience grew in his voice. And finally I snapped.

'Fuck off. Just fuck off!'

It did not constitute the most subtle or erudite of responses, but it felt like the right one. It certainly got the room's attention. You simply did not tell a St Michael's teacher to fuck off.

'What's up with Denton?' asked one of the boys at the front of the class.

'I don't know,' sighed my form teacher. His air was one of irritation and boredom, as if itching to get back to his end-of-term revelries. His calm and disinterested response added insult to injury. I wanted a reaction. I needed a reaction. I needed to know that he had felt my anger and pain.

'Well, if you do not know I am going to tell you,' I thought, and through the tears it all came out. 'You are always picking on kids like him. Just because we are different. What did you have to do that for? Just because he's coloured.' I shouted through the tears, determined that the entire class should hear my voice.

I said the unsayable and accused a teacher of racism in front of the whole class. I needed to be put back in my place. However, my teacher was by now also aware that he had put himself in a difficult position and he acted swiftly: 'I don't want to hear another word, Denton, and we will talk about this later.'

He quickly reasserted his authority and dismissed the class except for me. David, who was also now in tears, was also dismissed, and I never did find out why he was summoned in the first place. My class-mates left quickly, to spread the big news around the demob-happy school that 'Dickie Denton had told Mr X to fuck off', and we were left alone.

The teacher apologised and admitted he had made a misjudgment, although I suspected that he was sorrier about my response than his own actions. Three and a half years of my pain and frustration had been offloaded on to him in a few seconds and it felt cathartic. We agreed to move on in the new term. I had no appetite to take it further and bottled out of the inevitable teacher and parent interviews that would ensue if I did. I also now knew that I could stand up to the bullies. I felt strangely empowered.

I have thought about what happened that afternoon every day of my life since. I thought about it in the hours after Sergio Agüero scored *that* goal.

5

Final Score

MY EXPLETIVE-LADEN outburst had given me a certain elevated status when I returned to school after the Christmas break. A new level of respect was briefly bestowed upon me as I now represented something of an anti-authority figure. Despite the macho, hormonal-driven posturing in an all-boys school, not too many had the balls to tell a staff member to 'fuck off'. I also believe that, for some people, my reaction had held an uncomfortable mirror up to their own behaviour. For the hardcore few the 'fun' continued but I had by now learnt to live with that. There was no dramatic upturn in results, but at least the slide in both my mental state and academic performance had been temporarily arrested.

Happily, the dramatic upturn in results was still manifest in Manchester. City continued to climb the table and after an impressive Christmas they were unfortunate to exit the League Cup in the semi-final, but by then attention had already turned to my beloved FA Cup. I had secured the prime ball boy location in front of the Kippax when Malcolm

Allison, now back in charge at Crystal Palace, ran out on to the pitch to greet the home fans, who still regarded him with great fondness. By a quirk of fate, City and Palace had been drawn together in the third round. The greeting was loud and genuinely affectionate for Allison and the Cockney-cum-Mancunian was no doubt hoping that such a public spectacle of adoration would unsettle his former players. Ferguson-esque mind games pre-Alex Ferguson. However, this was a wiser and mentally stronger side than the one that Allison had left behind and, after a goalless first half, City went through the gears to record a 4-0 win. A tricky tie negotiated with some style.

The fourth round matched John Bond's new club with his former club. Norwich had struggled since their manager had left and were now facing likely relegation. A rampant City wasted no time in putting them to the sword, with all six goals coming from different scorers. Two rounds negotiated, ten goals scored, and none conceded; City progressing with indecent efficiency. Given the failures of the previous two seasons the fifth-round draw was one to put fear into the heart of all supporters. 'Peterborough United will play Manchester City' was the Monday lunchtime radio announcement as the numbered balls were drawn out of the FA's famed velvet bag. After suffering at the hands of Shrewsbury Town and Halifax surely Peterborough wouldn't be next on the list. Happily, long-serving centre-half Tommy Booth, match-winning scorer in the 1969 semi-final, poached another vital goal to earn a 1-0 victory and avert a potential third humiliation. The quarter-final awaited and dreams of Wembley in May started to become a little more real.

The draw took us to Everton, a north-west derby and about as tough as it could get. Everton had knocked out Liverpool and Southampton in the previous rounds and were therefore feeling the same degree of belief that this could yet be their year. Their fans had been equally starved of success and were bound to make Goodison Park as hostile and unwelcoming as they could.

When Trevor Ross scored a penalty to put Everton 2-1 up midway through the second half, I told myself that City's race was run. With just minutes left I went into the living room and switched on *Final Score* just in time to see the goal flash. Paul Power had equalised, and City had unexpectedly rescued the tie.

The bigger surprise was yet to come. Times were changing in mysterious ways in the Denton household. I headed into the kitchen to share the good news with Mum and was shocked when she asked me if I wanted to go to the replay. Going all the way to Manchester on a school night to watch a football match, it was unheard of. I also needed to get a ticket, so my hopes were not high. While it would be an exaggeration to say that my parents had, by now, embraced my obsession, they had at least become far more accepting of it, while still harbouring concerns that it was at the expense of my academic progress. Their support had even gone to the extent of encouraging my brothers to accompany me to games and take advantage of the season ticket that temporarily laid unused. Mum liked to extract full value for money and hated to see a 'paid-for' asset sit idle. She would often drive us to Manchester, enabling her to spend time with her beloved and ageing parents.

By this time my tenure as a ball boy had come to an end and I had returned to the ranks of the regular match-goers. I felt good going back to my old seat in the stands. I loved my time as a ball boy and the access and insight it had given me, but by now I was becoming drawn to the banter of the stands, the songs, and the sense of adult camaraderie that it all entailed. Much to my delight, Mum had a quarter-final plan. She would visit my grandparents the following day, Sunday morning, thereby enabling me to collect my ticket. The next Wednesday, after school, my father would take me to the game and visit his in-laws while I was at the stadium. I think that my parents might actually have been a little caught up in my cup fever and wanted to be a small part of it.

The atmosphere that Wednesday night was the best I ever witnessed in the wonderful old Maine Road. The stands reverberated to all the old songs as two traditional, proper football teams contested a hard-fought game. The half-time stalemate was broken by an unlikely hero. Just as Everton were gaining the ascendancy, Bobby McDonald popped up from left-back with two goals in as many minutes. The ground erupted. Paul Power added a third and the drive back across the Pennines was never sweeter. We were in the semi-final; one game from Wembley and the FA Cup Final. Standing in the way of our big May day were Ipswich Town. Bobby Robson's exciting team was at its impressive peak. They were rightfully favourites, but City had one thing in their favour as Ipswich were fighting battles on three fronts: the First Division championship, the FA Cup and the UEFA Cup. City only had the FA Cup to go for. Ipswich's supremely talented but small squad was running out of steam whereas City had the momentum and singular focus.

The benign and generous attitude that my parents had displayed towards the quarter-final did not extend to the unfamiliar territory of Villa Park, Birmingham. I therefore relied on my loyal and trusted companion, Peter Jones, and BBC Radio 2. Concerned about showing my distress if things did not go to plan, I shut myself away in my bedroom shortly prior to kick-off. I lay on the bed, then got up and paced around, staring out of my window into the neighbours' gardens and repeating the sequence time and time again throughout the long afternoon. Shortly after 5pm, I emerged from my self-imposed confinement exhausted and ecstatic. In the tenth minute of extra time Paul Power had curled a free kick beyond the Ipswich wall and into the net. There was no way back for tired Ipswich and Peter Jones had never sounded better as he eloquently described the final minutes of play.

I wandered downstairs in a happy daze. My parents, ever keen to manage expectation, shared my joy, but were clear that I could only go to Wembley if I got two tickets, for the seats of course. It was my turn to provide the shock when I told them that I preferred to watch it at home. The FA Cup Final was one of my favourite days. For years I had watched *Cup Final Swap Shop*, *It's a Knockout!*, *Cup Final Grandstand* and *The Road to Wembley*, relishing the saturated television coverage, the trivia, the goals from the past and present, and player profiles. I was so jealous of the other clubs and their supporters that had won their way through to the final. Now I wanted to soak in every minute of it. City, my team, would at last feature. I loved each minute detail, and I did not want to miss one moment, even if it meant forgoing a trip to the game itself.

Spurs were the Wembley opponents. The two teams were well matched, with City's organisation and work ethic being countered by the flair and artistry of Spurs. Northern soul against southern style. Spurs also had the edge in the nation's affection with Ossie Ardiles's 'Wembley Dream' (a song featuring the seminal lyrics, 'Ossie's going to Wembley, His knees have gone all trembley') pulling at the heartstrings on *Top of the Pops*. The wait until 9 May and the 100th FA Cup Final was an interminably long one. The league campaign had to be completed, and with the safety of mid-table obscurity now assured, form understandably tailed off, as inevitably did my schoolwork. My mind was full of only one thing and that one thing wasn't the fall of the Holy Roman Empire or differential calculus. I read and listened to every preview I could find and my school exercise book covers were quickly adorned with potential tactical formations. On the preceding Friday afternoon, some class-mates, and teachers, sensing how much it meant to me, had even wished me good luck. I was as ready as I could be for what was to come, or at least I thought I was. I prepared myself for either victory or defeat. Almost as if a player, about to be interviewed by Jimmy Hill, I had an idea of roughly how I might feel and react and what I might say. However, I had not prepared for the game to be a draw. None of the cup finals that I had ever seen had ended level.

The big day arrived. Dressed in my newly acquired City shirt and with my scarf tied around my wrist, I parked up in front of the TV at 10am and remained there for the next eight hours. Tommy Hutchison's flying first-half header gave

City a lead that was comfortably intact as the clock moved into the last ten minutes. Then, in typical fashion, City were instrumental in their own downfall as a free kick deflected off Hutchison's shoulder, wrong-footed Joe Corrigan and flew into the net. Extra time was a slog on the wide, heavy pitch, like two heavyweight boxers out on their feet, trading tired blows but unable to deliver the knockout. It yielded nothing and the teams would have to come back again on Thursday evening. Much as I would have loved to have seen City hang on for victory, there was a positive side to the rematch. We would be in the papers for a few more days and for those few days I would not have to return to my real world beyond the FA Cup Final bubble. I would get to see my City on TV again.

The popular media view was that City had done well in the first game whereas Spurs had underperformed. From the start, it was obvious that Spurs were not going to waste this second chance and came flying out of the blocks, scoring after just four minutes. The goalscorer was the biggest underperformer of the previous weekend, Ricky Villa. City were not done for quite yet, and my erstwhile number 48 bus companion, Steve McKenzie, replied a few minutes later with a brilliant, but so often overlooked, 25-yard volley. Half-time came and went. Whoever scored the next goal would surely win. Other than getting up from the sofa to celebrate and take a half-time bathroom break, I remained fixed in my seat and glued to the television. Dave Bennett burst between two Spurs defenders in the penalty area and was fouled. Penalty! Kevin Reeves converted the spot kick with cool assurance; 2-1 City. Surely, with just 20 minutes to go we would hang on?

By now Dad and one or two of my older siblings who, to my incredulity, had been to Leeds Cathedral choir practice during an FA Cup Final, had arrived home. This now officially constituted a family event, but not one with a happy ending. I watched in increasing agony as Garth Crooks stabbed home the equaliser, before Villa's mazy, crazy slalom through the City defence extinguished any remaining hope. Spurs had won one of the great cup finals, 3-2. City were rightfully lauded for their part in it, but that was no consolation as Steve Perryman lifted the famous cup and proudly showed it off to the Spurs fans. The cup that I so desperately wanted. Manfully, I watched through to the end, eyes pointed to the TV so no one could see the tears starting to well up. I watched the interviews, the analysis, and the replays, my family feeling my pain in silence. Then I got up, went to my room, put my head in my pillow and cried.

I had just been studying the book *A Kestrel for a Knave* at school (later made into the film *Kes*). Downtrodden Billy Casper was about my age. He used his love of falconry as an escape from his otherwise desperate existence. The freedom of his kestrel, soaring above the South Yorkshire coalfields, is the antithesis to his life, trapped by economic and cultural deprivation. The traumatic end of the story is the cruel slaying of Kes and the destruction of the one good thing in Billy's life. The FA Cup dream had been my Kes, or so it felt at that moment.

The summer of 1981 was dominated by three contrasting news stories. While the royal wedding of Charles and Diana gripped the nation, my attention was held by the exploits of Ian Botham and the England cricket team's amazing Ashes triumph. It had all started just a mile or two from Pudsey Road at Headingley. On the last morning of the Test match Dad had jokingly offered to pay the 50p discounted entrance fee for any of us who wanted to go and watch England's inevitable defeat. We all declined, as we expected that, despite Botham's heroic century the previous day, Australia would comfortably knock off the 130 runs required. David and I were so sure of England's defeat that we were out playing knockabout cricket in the garden when *Test Match Special* reported that the Australian wickets were starting to fall. Sensing something special was about to take place, we went inside and then sat cheering, spellbound, as Bob Willis charged down the hill at the Kirkstall Road End to take his 8-43.

While Botham, Willis, and team-mates then took the roadshow off to Birmingham, Manchester, and London, the third significant happening of the summer was also making its way around the nation's cities. Race riots engaged the youth population in a totally different way, and few cities in England escaped some sort of unrest during the summer of 1981. Years of perceived injustice, underfunding and distrust of police and authorities in Afro-Caribbean communities came to a head. While the violence itself was localised and short-lived, the TV pictures hung around for weeks, and the impact went beyond the small communities that had been the focal points. Leeds was no exception, and the Chapeltown riots were talked about in the playground every bit as much as Botham's heroics as the new school term commenced. Most boys had no views on the rights or the wrongs of the riots, their causes, or the catalysts, but were entertained and amused by the anti-establishment uprising regardless of the ethnicity of the protagonists.

In theory the 1981/82 academic term could have been my last at St Michael's. Now 15, I would take O-levels at the end of the year and be free to leave mainstream education. In reality, that was never going to happen. Even if I had been ready for the outside world, and that was far from the case, my parents were adamant that I would be going on to sixth form and to study for A-levels. I knew that come the summer a good proportion of my age group would be opting out of sixth-form schooling. I told myself that if I could get through the next nine months, I should be fine from thereon in.

Despite contrasting experiences in two northern cities, my existence was far from a simplified and binary *Animal Farm* world. Manchester: good; Leeds: bad. That was far from the case. Two elements that represented the best and the worst of my life, football, and school, were by happenchance activities that took place in two different cities. The disappointment of countless football defeats was by no means the only misfortune I encountered while visiting Manchester. On one occasion, waiting to cross a road in Piccadilly Gardens, a boy not much older than me came up to me and demanded I give him £1. Scared, but nonetheless feeling safe in the crowd of city centre Saturday afternoon shoppers, I refused. As we crossed the road, he thumped me in the face with more power than I could ever remember feeling. I fell to the ground, almost being hit by an oncoming car in the process. I was physically okay but shaken and upset, and a kindly passer-by who had witnessed it all helped me up.

On another occasion when leaving Maine Road after a reserve match I held my small radio close to my ear. Some boys approached me, and I could immediately sense the danger. The large crowds associated with first-team fixtures were not around, so the small streets lined with terraced houses were relatively empty and felt more menacing. They tried to grab the radio, but I resisted, and somehow, I found an athletic sprint I did not know I possessed. I might have given the radio to them had it not been a present from my grandfather. It had been Gangan's pride and joy and I remembered how he had passed it to me like handing over a beloved heirloom. I ran until I found the safety of some workmen and then boarded the first bus that came along. Being something of an expert at keeping all things to myself, I did not tell anybody, fearing perhaps that if my parents found out they might have quite understandably stopped me going to the games.

In Leeds, I benefited from some wonderful experiences and made some special friendships. I liked the richness and variety of extra-curricular activities at school, the sports clubs, debating societies, school bands, and community work, and formed deep friendships around all of these. I developed my love of hiking through school excursions to the wonderful countryside to the north of Leeds and extending into the Yorkshire Dales, even going on several youth hostelling holidays with my school-mates David Gilpin and Paul Ellwood. Paul was a decent leg-spinner, and I would cycle for miles to watch him represent Horsforth CC Second XI at their home ground and in the outlying towns. We rarely spoke about our school life on those hiking trips. Paul and David were both high achievers academically so were in the upper stream and therefore were not as acutely aware of the worst of the bullying that took place within my class group. I am not sure that it mattered anyway as away from the school environment I preferred to lose myself in the sport or the hiking and not dwell on the more troubling aspects of life.

As a family, we were, of course, diehard attendees at our local Catholic church, St Joseph's where I served on the altar for nearly ten years. The church ran a vibrant amateur dramatics society, and most of my siblings and I took part in their productions of Christmas pantomimes and old-time music hall shows. The parish priest, Father Horkin, was not a man who was easy to warm to, but he and I built up a strong friendship, partly through football. He was an avid Leeds United supporter, forever lamenting their demise from the glory days of the 1960s and '70s. We even went to several games together at Elland Road.

Christmases were an especially joyful mix of the spiritual and the social celebration. Mum and Dad, ever conscious of those who might be alone for the festivities, would invite some of my father's international post-graduate students to our home to experience a traditional Christmas dinner. On more than one occasion we were joined by various Indians, Sri Lankans, Iraqis, Greeks, and Egyptians, thus causing Mum to worry about the religious sensitivities of serving turkey and pigs in blankets. We had holidays, and more exposure to 'approved culture' than we probably desired or could possibly appreciate. Occasionally we would even create bogus homework assignments to get out of our turn to go and see the English Opera North productions at Leeds Grand Theatre, for which my parents had bought season tickets that were far more likened to their own tastes than my Maine Road equivalent.

Like all siblings we did of course compete and argue, but we all knew we were there for each other. There were, and still are, 15 quite different individual relationships, each with their own dynamic and chemistry. Encouraged by my parents, we were varied in our interests, our ambitions, and our careers, and better collectively and as individuals because of that. Through this diversity, regardless of adoption, we shared a common blood, bond, and set of values that continue to pervade today.

We were also surrounded by good neighbours, long-standing family friends, and relatives. Most significantly for me, in Manchester, Nanna and Gangan indulged me as much as I indulged them. They were supportive and encouraging and while frequently exercising that grandparental privilege of neglecting the tough love they still told me when they thought I could be doing better. Gangan, especially, cared passionately about education. It had been his vocation and professional life, ultimately recognised and honoured with a certificate and medal awarded by Pope Paul XVI. He also craved attention, was opinionated, chauvinistic and conceited, and he always wanted to be involved with a childlike fear of 'missing out'. Most of all he loved his family, and I loved talking to him among the tomato plants in his backyard or in that tobacco-scented front room. Always Balkan Sobranie.

Much of the fear that had defined my school life in Leeds had, by my final mandated year, been replaced by benign acceptance. Standing up to my form teacher and confronting his behaviour had briefly been a liberating one, but it was not sustainable. Teachers were not likely to take you round to the back of the gym and assault you for telling them to 'fuck off', whereas fellow pupils were. Rightly or wrongly, I determined that my new way to stand up to them had to be different. I would try to ignore them and to show them that their verbal bullying did not affect me. I did not feel ready to do it overtly by taking on the ownership of the insult in the way that American Afro-Caribbean's adopted the n-word as their own, and the Gay Pride movement in the UK adopted and owned a plethora of intended smears, but at least I could put myself back in control by refusing to show that it hurt.

The perpetrators had also dwindled in number. Increased maturity, an appreciation that there were more important things out there like jobs, beer, and girls, combined with boredom as the novelty had finally worn off, meant they had moved on to other things and only a hardened few remained. But they were entrenched and resolute, fuelled by the coverage of the summer's race riots. My new form master was of the old-school variety. Mr Walsh was the mentor I could have done with much earlier. He was a strict disciplinarian, and nobody messed about in his lessons. He was also fair, honest, and witty, and treated the boys like the young men we now were. His specialisation was history and the classics, and he was knowledgeable and passionate about his subject. Driven by Mr Walsh's expectations for the class and the crucial O-levels looming ever closer I knew I had to get off to a decent start.

City returned for the new season full of confidence. Revitalised by John Bond's management, the FA Cup adventure, and finishing above United in the league for the first time in several seasons, there was belief that they could kick on in the new season. I still had my season ticket and at 15 I was in my last year as a Junior Blue. I continued to take my place in the Platt Lane Stand but had jettisoned sitting in my assigned seat with the juniors to mix among the adult supporters. I had not, however, abandoned the practice of visiting my grandparents before each game. Gangan wanted to know about school: could I be doing better; were my teachers good enough? What did I want to do for a career? He was desperate for one of his grandchildren to follow his own path of teaching.

Meanwhile, City had once more splashed the cash and signed England's Trevor Francis, scorer of the winning goal in a European Cup Final. Boosted by his undoubted class, progress was impressively consistent, and matchdays felt slightly different, with an unfamiliar air of relaxed expectancy. Previously it felt like any corner City won had been cheered ecstatically, as we might not see another for six months. Much as I loved winning, I did miss that feeling of shocked elation following a rare goal. I need not have worried; City would soon return to type.

There must be a time in every football fanatic's life when they finally let go of the deluded fantasy of becoming a professional player. Some are happy to remain as supporters, others lose their love of the game and go off chasing girls and music, some pursue wealth and various careers and if very lucky, a life in journalism covering the game. Many hang on to the delusion into young adulthood, only relinquishing the dream when they suddenly and tragically realise that they are now older than the players they are watching. Others just try to stay connected to the game in some other way. Then there are those who become referees.

It had only ever been at the back of my mind that I might try refereeing. Regularly, on Sunday mornings after Mass, breakfast, and dissection of the sports pages of the *Sunday Times*, I went with David to kick a ball about at the school behind our Pudsey Road house. After about an hour, we would have to leave the pitch, as from within the school would emerge the Sunday morning footballers. Some were slightly overweight and looked decidedly slow, already eyeing up the nippy young winger in the opposition team that they would be 'leaving a little something on' should he try any of his fancy stuff, like running past them. Some were walking hangovers, reeking of the stench of the previous night's beer, their faces showing the stubble strain of a few hours' sleep. *'Get through this and the pub will soon be open again for the hair of the dog.'* The older ones were accompanied by young children deposited upon them by their wives wanting a Sunday morning lie-in. They desperately looked around for a team-mate's girlfriend to take care of their infant charges before they returned home to 'fix those shelves'.

Our local team was Hough End Old Boys. Fortunately for me they rarely had a full complement of players, which often meant no substitutes, and nobody to run the line, the most unwanted job in Sunday football: assisting the league-appointed referee with throw-in and offside decisions. And so I volunteered. One volunteer, as they say, is worth ten conscripted men. My offer was immediately accepted, and a yellow or red flag was thrust into my eager young hands before I had a chance to change my mind. I barely knew what I was doing but nobody from the Old Boys cared if it meant they did not have to do it themselves. When somebody behind me shouted 'offside' I invariably stuck up my flag and the referee blew his whistle. The opposition called me a 'cheating little wanker' but I was used to much worse being thrown at me most days at school, and besides, I had a dozen of Hough End's biggest and hardest watching my back. For a short while it became a regular Sunday morning routine. They never knew my name and I never knew theirs, but they would greet me before the game:

'Hey young 'un, are you going to do the flag for us today?' It was nice to feel appreciated.

I didn't give the thought of refereeing any serious consideration until, at a school open day five-a-side competition, I somehow again ended up acting as a linesman. Mr Inns, (nicknamed 'Bernie' after the popular restaurant chain of the time, of course) was the referee. He was a senior maths teacher and an officially qualified referee with many seasons on the West Riding County FA circuit. He was rumoured to have once run the line at a game at Elland Road, but nobody could corroborate it. As we were walking off the pitch, he called me over.

'So do you want to be a referee, Denton?'

It had never occurred to me before, but given my love of football, the only logical answer seemed to be yes. He gave me the name of a colleague at the local Referees' Association to call. A few days later, putting on my most adult voice, I telephoned Jeff Ward. 'The timing is just right,' he said. They needed new referees and the next intake was being enrolled in a few weeks' time. The tutorials were to take place on a

Tuesday night in the players' lounge at Elland Road. Tuesday also happened to be Leeds Schools Senior Brass Band practice night. My parents would not want me to drop out of that, even though I possessed no natural ability as a very poor third euphonium. I calculated, nevertheless, that I could just about make it: I'd go from school to band practice in the city centre at 5.30pm, and then catch a bus to Elland Road to get to the referees' course at 7.30pm. Dad could then pick me up after the session.

Burdened by bag and brass, I stumbled into the smoky players' lounge on that first night. There were pictures of the Leeds United greats from yesteryear all around the walls: Billy Bremmer, Paul Madeley, Norman Hunter, and Allan Clarke. The room was already full with the course tutors, and 20 or so middle-aged Yorkshiremen. I stepped in, 15 years old but looking 12, St Michael's uniform still on, school bag in one hand and euphonium in the other.

'Is this the referees' course?' I asked, in full knowledge of the answer but unable to think of anything else to say.

'Has it really come to this?' I could feel them thinking it. 'Bloody kids wi' trumpets – are wi that bleedin' desperate?'

They accepted me, euphonium and all, and to a man they were very welcoming and generous with their knowledge, even when I would precociously try to answer every question put out to the group. Over the next eight weeks we worked through each of the Laws of the Game, starting with the basics, the playing area, the team, and the ball and progressing to explore the mysterious nuances of the offside law. I loved every minute of it, listening to these old, experienced guys telling me about all the games they had refereed. If only all studying was like this. If only I could apply myself to all subjects with the same dedication. Throughout the course I felt no fear about the exam or any trepidation of going out on my own to officiate after my inevitable qualification. It never occurred to me that I might fail. My inspirational first-form teacher Mr Laverty, who was also a qualified referee, found out about my interest, most likely because I went out of my way to tell him. He took me aside at breaks and tutored me, preparing me for the questions that might arise. It was over and above anything he had any obligation to do.

I sailed through the oral exam just before Christmas and became a qualified referee. I was presented with my certificate and badge, both at Elland Road and then on the stage at school assembly. I now had to find a referee's kit that would fit me. I am sure that my parents were a little conflicted – keen to encourage a worthy interest that would mature me, but concerned about another academic distraction. Nevertheless, they were supportive. After scouring every sports shop around Leeds we finally found a men's referee's kit that, with a bit of Mum's ingenious needlework, I could get into without looking like a character from a British Pathé newsreel film. Our assigned fixtures were mailed to us for the month ahead.

In January, the list came through. I would be officiating Pudsey Juniors v Horsforth St Margaret's on Sunday, 2 February, kicking off at 2pm. It was an under-12 fixture.

I initially felt a little disappointment as I had been expecting an adult game. In many ways I was more comfortable and at ease in the company of adults; the men who had adopted me as their linesman at Hough End Old Boys, and the referees' course. Most of the trouble I had encountered had come from other boys my own age. In reality it was the right decision as I would not have coped in the men's game where no countenance would be given for my youth. While the West Riding County FA and the Referees' Association had been superb in tutoring my qualification, and getting me on the list, I was on my own from here. There was no post-qualification support or mentoring programme for new referees.

Not wanting me to be late, Mum gave me a lift to that first game. I insisted that I get out of the car half a mile away once we had established the whereabouts of the club. I did not think it would look right and proper to have the match referee dropped off at the gates by his mother. I took a deep breath, puffed my chest out and tried to look like the man I was not. I walked into the clubhouse to introduce myself as R.M. Denton, the match referee. I just hoped they could not see that I was shaking with nerves.

Fortunately, Pudsey Juniors were, and remain, a very well-run junior club with teams for all age groups. Stuart McCall of Bradford City, Everton, and Rangers was a product of their system. A volunteer corps of parents and local coaches not only trained and organised the teams, but also instilled a sense of discipline and respect into the boys in their care. Consequently, my baptism was a relatively easy one, the only moment of controversy being a penalty I awarded against the home team. I picked up my £3 match fee and walked home satisfied with a job well done, confident that my climb up the ranks of the Football Association had got off to a solid start.

The refereeing was a big undertaking in my most critical academic year, but I do not think that it compromised the ominous trajectory of my results. I – and those around me – would be quite capable of doing that without the distraction of refereeing. While some long-distance athletes sprint to the finish line, head down and focussed, after five long years I was weaving and staggering like a marathon runner whose joints, full of lactic acid, cease to function normally. I just wanted to get it over and start again in sixth form, but it was never going to be that easy. I had not quite given up on my studies, but a few months' hard work would make little difference to what had preceded it. The situation was not helped by the 'hardcore' that were intending to squeeze out that last bit of fun at my expense.

Alban pointed to my school blazer over breakfast; there was something amiss with the back of it. I took it off and inspected it. The bottom flap was riddled with holes, each one framed with a charred black ring. They had been burned into the blazer by the end of a lit cigarette. I knew exactly by whom and when. The previous day I had sat with my back to a group of boys during a break. I ignored their usual anti-Paki jibes, but noticed their amusement regarding something else. I thought little of it at the time, but the source of their mirth was now apparent. Despite there being just a couple of months until the end of term, Mum was not going to have me going to school wearing something that resembled a sieve. She insisted I have a new one. I felt embarrassed to be going to school in a new blazer and guilty about the expense for my parents. I did, somehow, manage to dissuade them from writing a letter to complain, but I was not prepared to let it lie. At break-time I confronted the culprits. I knew that I would lose any physical battle and was prepared that the outcome of my actions might well result in harm, but they were going to be told how I felt. I controlled my emotions as I let them know that I knew they were responsible, and what I thought of them. I traded a few insults and expletives of my own about their ignorance, stupidity, and lack of job prospects. Then I walked away, their jeers and insults in my ears.

'Fuck off back to Paki land if you don't like it here, Denton.'

I walked away and left it at that. The next lesson was double maths entailing a geometry exercise. We were left to get on with the prescribed work, encouraged to work in pairs or threes, while the teacher got on with his own book-marking or lesson preparation. I was trying to understand why the angles on my triangles were not adding up to 180 degrees when a ringleader of my tormentors came over. At first, I assumed that he wanted to ask for help or possibly make peace. He sat next to me and opened his book. His geometry compass was inside it. Without speaking he calmly picked it up and pushed its inch-long point into my thigh. Then he got up and went back to his desk. Considering all I had been through, I was genuinely shocked. Too shocked to react or cry out. My pride also prevented it. The compass point was small in diameter so there was more pain than blood, but the message was sent. There was more from where that came from, so shut the fuck up. I resolved to just get through the term in one piece.

I finished my exams in June and enjoyed watching the coverage of the 1982 World Cup in Spain, Trevor Francis representing City in the England squad. I hiked the Cleveland Way, youth hostelling with my good friend Paul Ellwood, again avoiding any talk of school. All the time a dark cloud was hovering above the North Yorkshire moors. In August my O-level results would come out, and there would be no hiding from them. This was the one aspect of my school life that I would not be able to keep secret from anybody. They were public examinations so would even be published in the *Yorkshire Evening Post* newspaper!

Fellow one-time goalkeeper and present full-time Pope, John Paul II, visited the UK that summer and we went to celebrate Mass with him in Manchester's Heaton Park, but my fate was beyond even divine intervention. The results were released the same day as England's cricketers were playing Pakistan in the Headingley Test match. Lancashire's Graeme Fowler was set to make his England debut, and I was keen to go along. It would also delay having to discuss the results with my parents until I got home. I did not sleep much the night before, and my worst fears were pretty much confirmed in the morning. I passed just four: English Literature, English Language, Religious Education and, to everyone's surprise, Mathematics. It amounted to less than half the number of passes any of my older siblings had achieved, and, to make it worse, my cousin Richard, who was in the same academic year, passed nine or ten the same day. My mother had taken me to the school, so she already knew the results and would have told my father, but the walk home from Headingley that evening was a long and lonely one. I felt that I had let down myself, my parents, grandparents, and those teachers who had been so kind to me. I had some making up to do, not least to myself.

6

Rebuilding

THE BASELINE requirement for entering the sixth form at St Michael's College was four O-levels. I had scraped in by the skin of my teeth and an apprenticeship in the coal mines of Yorkshire or dark satanic mills of Lancashire could wait for a while yet. Ahead of me lay the difficult decision of which A-levels to choose. As the prerequisite was that the student must have passed the equivalent O-level, the decision was not in fact such a tricky one. I would go for English as well as pure mathematics and statistics. Economics and general studies were subjects introduced only in the sixth form and therefore exempt from the qualification criteria.

Harsh realities had also required City to make some tough decisions during the summer. The spending of the previous seasons had put the club in financial peril. Prize asset Trevor Francis was sold with part of his wages still owed and hopes were not high heading into the new season. Ever capable of delighting and disappointing their supporters in equal measure, City were top of the table after three games and an impressive second as the season moved into November. That was the delight. The disappointment would inevitably follow.

Back at St Michael's, with the fear of indiscriminate violence and abuse largely removed I felt able to apply myself more earnestly and consistently. The smaller number of pupils – all attending of their own choice – my increased maturity and that of those around me helped. When I did want to act the fool, I found a different audience, more interested in application than indulgence and I quickly got the message.

My refereeing career was also developing. I was being allocated regular games and older age groups to officiate as my confidence and competence developed. Not all the clubs were as well run and disciplined as Pudsey Juniors and there were some difficult moments with players, coaches and, especially, overzealous parents, but in a masochistic sort of way I enjoyed it and found it personally rewarding. The abuse was no worse, and a good deal less personal and hurtful than what had been dished out in the recent past, and quickly I learnt the knack of 'leaving it on the pitch' once the game was over. As a 'young' 16-year-old and the youngest sibling positions of authority and responsibility were quite alien to me. I naturally struggled to project the authority I barely felt myself.

My progress was better than I thought, however, and ironically it took a dressing-down from a senior referee to help me see it. Matches on the overused public pitches were subject to the vagaries of the West Yorkshire weather, often resulting in the end-of-season congestion that clubs and parents dreaded. Consequently, when the pitches were playable in the late winter and early spring the clubs would try to play as many games as possible on any given weekend. The manager of a team I had officiated on several occasions called me and asked if I minded bringing a fixture forward to just after lunchtime so that the club's under-14s could then play a cup game on the same pitch before the winter dusk drew in. I willingly obliged and the game went ahead without incident of note. That was until an angry, tracksuited figure accosted me while walking back to the clubhouse. It was the referee of the game that was to follow. He told me in no uncertain terms that I did not have the right to change a kick-off time without authorisation from the FA and that he would be reporting me as my action had damaged the pitch and delayed his kick-off. My initial reaction was that this was Cleckheaton Boys against Morley Colts, for fuck's sake, and not the European Cup Final. Rather than verbalise that, I apologised and went into the changing room wondering how I would explain my heinous action when hauled up in front of the FA. I sat there, annoyed and anxious, when the club manager walked in.

'What's that guy's name?' he asked me.

'You mean the other referee?' I replied.

'Yes, I do, if that's what he thinks he is. I heard what he said to you and he said the same to me. You are the best bloody referee we have had here this season and you have just had a great game and he talked to you like that. A bloody disgrace. Don't worry about him reporting you, I am going to report him.'

I felt flattered by his kind comments, bursting with pride as I headed home, but something was gnawing at me. Why did I need an informal conversation with a club manager reacting to an unconnected incident to tell me that? Why weren't the governing authorities giving me feedback? Referees were marked every game by both clubs so they would have known how I was performing, and they did also send their own assessors. As a very young and unsure referee it would have meant so much to have learnt that I was doing okay. To know that I had gained the respect of the clubs would have done so much to build my confidence.

A few weeks later my refereeing immaturity was evident when I made the decision to show my first red card. Even though my knowledge of laws of the game was consummate, I had much to learn about applying them with judgment. The under-13s team in question were losing by many and defending a corner on a cold, muddy afternoon. The heavy, wet ball broke to the penalty spot and was shot at pace past the goalkeeper. On the line the smallest boy on the field instinctively put up his hands to defend himself from the bloody nose that was inevitably coming his way. Technically and by the letter of the law I was compelled to award a penalty and a red card. I was less keen to send him off than he was to get off and into the warmth of the changing room. Reluctantly I reached into my top pocket and gingerly showed him the card. He walked off with his newly acquired notoriety and to the sympathy of the parents. Their boos and cries of 'shame on you' rang in my ears. I felt like the man who had just shot Bambi's mum.

The following week I received a summons from the West Riding County FA requiring me to attend a personal hearing about the incident. Convinced that I must have done wrong and was going to have my badge suspended, I waited anxiously to discover my fate, as the hearing was a month away. It turned out to be standard protocol for all cases of red cards in junior football. My report was read out, I was asked to confirm its veracity and was then told that I could leave. As I was leaving, an official pulled me aside and told me that it would have been acceptable for me to use some discretion in interpreting the law in that circumstance. At the end of the season, I was appointed to referee a senior boys' cup final so I must have been doing something right in the eyes of the authorities. Mum and my sister Kathy even came along to watch me for that match. Unappreciative of the gravitas of my position, and much to the bemusement of the other spectators, Kathy enthusiastically cheered every peep of her embarrassed younger brother's whistle as if he had just scored a winning goal.

It was too much to ask that all the stars in the firmament would align at any one time. Just as my scholastic endeavours and refereeing were going well, City took it upon themselves to spectacularly implode and John Bond resigned following an embarrassing 4-0 FA Cup defeat at Brighton. He had come to Manchester to manage a big club with big resources, but City were now a mid-table, seriously cash-stricken outfit, still paying for the profligacy of Malcolm Allison's experiment. Disillusioned with the lack of financial support, Bond felt he had taken the club as far as he could and walked away. He was replaced by his number two, John Benson, an able assistant but a man who had never before been in sole charge. The dip in form turned into a freefall plummet down the table. Going into the season's concluding game City were just one place and one point above the remaining relegation place, which happened to be occupied by their final-day opponents, Luton Town. A draw would ensure survival but only an unthinkable defeat could save Luton and relegate City.

I could not go to Maine Road as I was required to perform, in the loosest possible sense, as part of the school band at an open day concert. I took my place on the stage as inconspicuously as possible, nestling between the basses and the drums and out of the music teacher's eye line. The size of the brushed platinum euphonium resting on my lap meant that I could conceal the presence of the earphone wire leading from the radio secreted in my blazer pocket. I could hear that back in Manchester, City's performance was distinctly off key. Like the school band they were frequently hitting bum notes with no rhythm or cohesion.

As 'Radetzky March' staggered to its sorry conclusion the game was goalless and just five minutes stood between City and safety. Through the earphones I gleaned that Luton, sensing both opportunity and necessity, were pushing forward. They broke down the right and following a goalmouth scramble the ball ended up in the City net. As triangles tripped over trumpets and cornets collided with clarinets, the final clash of the cymbals marked the end of City's First Division tenure. Players and fans sank to their knees. We had no comedy clown-car music in our repertoire, as that would have been apt. Later, on *Match of the Day*, I saw how David Pleat, the Luton manager, had merrily danced his way across the Maine Road pitch celebrating his team's survival. Accompanied by the St Michaels's College band, he quick-stepped the same path that I too had trodden when leading out the ball boys. Dancing on my pitch. My

City. Relegated. City had flirted with relegation before and come good. Had it happened back then I would, in many ways, have been prepared for it. But this had happened so suddenly, almost without warning. Until April there were no danger signs. It felt like unexpectedly losing a loved one to an accident. Just the sudden realisation and shock but foremost the unerring certainty of it.

August duly came and with it the ignominy of relegation hit home. There was a strange sense of déjà vu as I enviously perused the First Division fixtures on the opening day of the season. It reminded me of how I felt when watching the third form 'upper' stream classes being led off after I had been relegated to the lower stream. For me it had represented a chance to shine in a less demanding 'division'. Could City cope better than I and bounce back? I was also curious to see Second Division football for the first time. There would be new local derbies against the likes of Oldham, Huddersfield, and Blackburn and old rivalries renewed in the shape of Newcastle and my old nemesis Leeds, who themselves had been relegated the previous year. They were all within manageable travelling distance. I could not openly admit it but I secretly looked forward to some aspects of the new experience. Of course, I foolishly foresaw City sweeping all before them on their glorious quest to instant promotion. Predictably changes had also been made to management and playing staff. Benson's reign as manager had lasted just 14 games and he was replaced by the no-nonsense Billy McNeill from Celtic. The free-spending days of Allison and Bond, and Swales's obsessive pursuit of United, would have to be put on hold for a little while.

I actually looked forward to going back to St Michael's for what would be my final year. Enthusiasm about school was an unfamiliar feeling. In error, I showed up for the new term a day late, probably indicative of how relaxed I felt about the restart. Previously the date would have preyed on my mind for weeks. My four O-levels had now been boosted to a princely seven, thanks to resitting the exams, and I felt good about my prospects of going to university. My interest in journalism remained but I possessed sufficient self-awareness to recognise that I did not have the hunger or aggression to survive in the cut-throat world of newspapers, so I hedged my bets by opting for the more generic subject of communication studies. But where?

In the sixth form common room, advice and discussion was abundant, if not particularly well-informed or supported by data. Prospectuses were laid out among the playing cards and ashtrays. Except for the elite Oxbridge set, academic course reviews and celebrated alumni were put aside. 'Nottingham has the highest proportion of female students to male'; 'Newcastle has a great night life'; 'Everyone smokes dope at Bath'. Life-changing decisions were made based on urban myth, apocryphal anecdote, and what somebody's older brother's friend might have got up to with some girl and a three-litre PET bottle of cider at a student party in Warwick. I concluded that I needed to get away from Leeds and home. Not so much because I did not like it, but more because I had seen through my older siblings that independence and self-sufficiency was an essential part of university life. I also wanted a town where football was played and one from which I could easily travel to see City, not every week, but when

I needed to. Liverpool University was my first choice and Sunderland Polytechnic my backup. In truth, I did not select them; they were the only two offers I received.

Home was also a quite different place by then. One by one my brothers and sisters had gone off to university: Elizabeth studying Medicine at Leicester; Kathy, French and Business at Birmingham; Rachel, Electronic Engineering at Newcastle where, much to her disapproval, Alban joined her a year later to embark on his Agriculture and Food Marketing degree. David was at home but rarely seen. He had opted not to go to university but to pursue a career in the hotel and hospitality industry in Leeds so was spending most of his evenings working. Number 282 Pudsey Road was much quieter with just three or four of us in the big house. There was no longer the need to negotiate and compromise over what we watched on the one television set and the structure and discipline that had been so necessary with six children growing up had been relaxed. My paternal grandfather, Poppa, who lived with us, had also taken to spending the summer months as guest of his daughter, my Auntie Ann, an ordained nun at the Poor Clare's Convent in Arundel, thus enabling my parents to take their first proper summer holidays together without worrying about leaving him alone. While the new environment afforded more space, comfort, and flexibility I did miss the chaos and collectiveness of the family unit and was happy to see my siblings return for weekends or descend en masse over Christmas. I am sure that my parents, especially Mum, felt the same way too – enjoying the new-found freedoms but desperately missing the dependence and presence of her children.

I was quick to exploit this new domestic world. I was 17, and although still short of confidence and bravado, girls and beer were very much on my radar if not my repertoire. More and more the conversation in the common room was migrating away from football, music, and TV shows and towards what the various groups of 'inbetweeners' had got up to over the past weekend and, more importantly, what the plans were for the coming Saturday night. I felt that my development and practical experience in this area was lagging my peer group so when I was invited to join one of the nightly excursions I jumped at the chance. It necessitated a quick visit to Top Man to upgrade my wardrobe and I then waited at the agreed meeting place. My two school mates were going to turn up with three girls they knew. How they knew them I did not know or care. They were girls and I had not encountered many in my football and refereeing circles. There were a couple in the Leeds Schools Senior Brass band but none of them were quite Tara Fitzgerald from the *Brassed Off* movie.

The plan was to have a few drinks in a bar and then go to the Bali Hi nightclub in the Merrion Centre. I waited nervously, rehearsing the feeble conversation that I had prepared. In time I saw them walking towards me. I nearly ran. These were not girls but women, and they scared the crap out of me. I had expected petite, sweet, and feminine but these, although I guess barely 18 themselves, looked to me to be about 30 and appeared scarily 'experienced'. I decided to stay but worse was yet to come. Full of bravado, having managed to gain entry into the swanky bar without being challenged about my age, I asked what they would like to drink. 'A pint of snakebite, please,' they all replied. So that was it, six pints of snakebite. The first round emptied my wallet. Having quickly exhausted my pre-prepared small talk, I went about downing my pint with indecent haste before heading back to the bar. The second round emptied my stomach. I made it on to the street, but much to my friends' amusement there was no way I would be going any further. Somehow, I managed to make it into a taxi and back home, vomiting out of the window while rummaging around to find the fare for the unimpressed driver. I got into the house and up to bed without being detected. For the time being at least I would stick to football.

With my siblings at universities around the country, I quickly saw the potential to get to more away games. I first suggested this as a 14-year-old when Elizabeth was in medical school and City were due to play Leicester at Filbert Street. I could go on the coach, stay overnight, and return the following day. To my surprise my request was granted, and Liz met me at Leicester Coach Station. With some of her medical student friends we went off to the game, a 1-1 draw. The next day I returned safely home. Leicester were relegated so that particular trip was short-lived but the following season I was off to Birmingham to see Kathy and take in Aston Villa away. I loved the away games, arriving in new cities and seeing different football grounds, ones that I had seen on *Match of the Day* and those that Peter Jones had described so vividly each time I turned on the radio. To see the different character of each one, the stands, and the architecture all telling its own story of past glories and failures. Understanding the ground in the context of their own cities and communities, something that radio or television could never convey, gave a new perspective. These windows on social history are becoming increasingly rare as they are now slowly being replaced by new, and albeit superb, stadia erected on greenfield sites outside city centres.

When the City team ran out, often in that famous black-and-red-striped away kit, it would just increase the sense of belonging, all in it together for the common cause. I especially loved being with the away fans. They were the most passionate and the less critical, the ones who had travelled from early morning and returned home, often tired and disappointed, late at night. The Second Division gave me a chance to do it in a more local and low-key environment. Of course, I went to the game at Elland Road, another City win, but that was with Father Horkin so the banter, songs and expletives were very much muted. From myself anyway. Father Horkin was not averse to taking the Lord's name in vain as he continued to lament Leeds' downfall. But there were away games against Huddersfield Town, Barnsley, and Sheffield Wednesday. I went to them all, standing in the away end, now truly one of the boys taking in the terrace wit where it existed but mostly, without the wit or originality, directing our tribal allegiances towards the 'Yorkshire Sheep-shaggers' in the home end. I would try to catch on as quickly as possible to the latest terrace song. Culture Club were number one in the charts with 'Karma Chameleon' and as City were challenging for promotion the song went:

Karma, karma, karma, karma, karma, come on City,
We're going up, we're going up.

Winning would be easy if your colours were like my team,
Red, white and blue, red, white and blue.

I never said it was good, but it was better than the Kippax's adaption of the St Winifred's School Choir's number one hit 'There's No One Quite Like Grandma' into a John Bond tribute, a few years earlier:

John Bond, we love you,
John Bond, we do,
John Bond, we love you,
John Bond, we do.

And on the day, we're champions,
We'll look at you and say,
There's no one quite like John Bond,
He has helped us on our way.

I am not sure which was more ridiculous, the song being sung by a burly terrace or the prospect of being champions.

The away game that had caught my eye that season was at Newcastle. City had not found it easy adjusting to life in the Second Division but were hanging on to the coat tails of the promotion hunt. Some emphatic victories had been interspersed with mediocre form. When the late-October fixture came about there were just four teams vying for the three places. Chelsea and Sheffield Wednesday were setting the pace and just behind were City and Newcastle. While Newcastle had not been in the First Division for some time, I was well aware of the fervent football culture in the north-east, and the bond between club and its community. They were now putting together a strong challenge spearheaded by their charismatic talisman Kevin Keegan. He had already announced that this was to be his last season and his year-long lap of honour was well and truly under way.

The fast east coast inter-city train line got me to Newcastle early and, by chance, I bumped into my brother Alban while wandering around the city centre killing time. A student at the university, he was still not into football, so after a brief chat I set off to the stadium on foot and was shocked to be there in just ten minutes. St James' Park was properly part of the city centre, the focal hub that can only exist in a one-club city. In front of me the famous Gallowgate End, run down and showing its age but nevertheless imposing and impressive, rose above the Georgian terraces. The occasion was all I hoped it would be and everything I felt football should be, apart from the result. I stood in the Leazes away end and watched Keegan, Chris Waddle, and Peter Beardsley rip City apart as Newcastle won 5-0. I could appreciate the atmosphere and the passion in that great stadium, but I could not enjoy the result as City were laid to waste.

The heavy trudge back to the station, accompanied by a police escort, through the now dark autumn night took me back to that first walk home from Old Trafford. This time, the Geordie fans good-naturedly waved five fingers at us from the illuminated buses heading out to Benwell, Byker, Felling, and other outlying villages. It had been a chastening afternoon but one I would go back for time and time again. The promotion push faded away in spring as the early season goals dried up. City would finish fourth, a distant ten points behind third-placed Newcastle.

At Christmas I also made the pragmatic decision to dump my maths A-level. Neither of my offers specified that I needed maths and I felt achieving another shock pass was not only beyond me but also would divert attention away from my other three subjects. If I could concentrate solely on the three, I could get into higher education. I enjoyed English and my A-level teacher, the flamboyant Mr Flynn, had a capacity for bringing the classics of literature to life. He was insistent that we live the experience of the books to the full, and in the school minibus we would head off to Manchester's Royal Exchange Theatre to see *Hamlet*, the Leeds Civic Theatre to see *Macbeth*, and to the village of Haworth to explore the Bronte Country of *Wuthering Heights*.

On one trip down the M1 from Leeds we were pulled over by the police. Our intent was innocent, to visit the Nottinghamshire villages around Eastwood that feature in D.H. Lawrence's *Sons and Lovers*, but the timing was unfortunate. Our little sortie was taking place at the time of the bitter and divisive miners' strike of 1984. The Nottinghamshire pits had refused to back Arthur Scargill and the National Union of Mineworkers in an all-out strike. Our unmarked minibus full of young males had been identified as a group of militant flying pickets heading south from Yorkshire to confront the Nottinghamshire miners. It probably did not help that one of our group had scribed the words 'NUM Passion Wagon' in the dirt on the back doors of the minibus. One look inside at the callow, clean-shaven occupants soon reassured the police, and we were on our way.

At least this time when the exams finally came around in June, I could feel that I had given it my best shot. We celebrated the end of exams and, with that, our school years, with a leaving party at the Leeds Irish Centre, pupils and some members of staff observing the significant rite of passage; this time I managed to handle my alcohol with a little more control. Now all I could do was wait until August and see what came along.

I decided to spend the summer of uncertainty in gainful employment as I awaited my results. I enquired at the Pudsey Job Centre and was duly dispatched to meet the landlord at The Beulah, a pub I knew well as I had passed it many times in the car on route to the M62 heading to Manchester. The role of barman was offered and immediately accepted; my enthusiasm undiminished by the distinct feeling that I was the only applicant. Once I had found my feet behind the bar, understanding how to pull the perfect pint of draught Tetley's Bitter (68 pence) and Tetley's Mild (66 pence), I revelled in the work. I especially enjoyed mixing with the array of interesting and different characters and opinions that frequented the pub. Before long they all knew my sporting allegiances and as the local Farnley Cricket Club used The Beulah as their post-match watering hole the piss-taking was sharp and good-natured. 'Oi, Lancashire, five pints of bitter please,' was the frequent call across the bar. It was the summer of 1984 and Ultravox's 'Dancing with Tears in My Eyes' was constantly on the jukebox, a song that still today fondly reminds me of warm summer nights in The Beulah.

As the days started to shorten and thoughts turned once more to the football season, A-level results loomed. I went to collect my results feeling cautiously confident, a stark contrast to the broken teenager of two years ago. There was disappointment again but this time not devastation. I had missed out on my first choice, Liverpool, but I had done enough to get into Sunderland Polytechnic. Haway the lads! I had now even increased my O-level count from a risible four to an almost respectable nine. That Thursday morning in August 1984 I walked out of St Michael's College Grammar School for the final time. I was ready to move on.

7

Away Games

THE MID-SEPTEMBER start to the polytechnic term gave me ample opportunity to assess City's promotion chances before heading to the north-east. When the time came for Dad to drive me up the A19 to Sunderland I had satisfied myself that we were nicely positioned for a return to the top flight.

While Liverpool University had been my first choice, the perceived lesser status of a polytechnic did not concern me. I was keen to embrace every aspect of the experience but still, nevertheless, felt nervous as I arrived. Much like the other 1,500 new students, I guess. My allocated accommodation was in the Polytechnic Precinct, a group of self-catering apartments on Chester Road, each housing ten students. Given my past experiences it was deeply ironic that I felt an initial sense of unease when the first four people introduced to me in Block 14 were all Asian – two Indians, a Malay, and a Hong Kongese. I went to my room wondering if I would be the only Englishman in the building. Unpacking my assorted bags and boxes took me about ten minutes. I then organised and rearranged my possessions that consisted of a paltry selection of clothes, an even paltrier selection of books and study aids, and most importantly my new radio, several times. It was probably more times than I organised them in whole of the ensuing year as I tried to convince myself that this was important work.

'What am I going to do?' I berated myself. 'Stay in my room for the next three years?'

I finally plucked up the courage to come out into the shared living area. A tall figure, looking every bit a mature student, was sat at the table reading the paper. He immediately looked up and gave me a warm smile. He was, in fact, just 18 months older than me. 'Ey up mate, fancy a brew?'

He introduced himself as St John Usher but quickly became known to all as 'Saint'. We had been thrown together in the strange new environment but soon found we had much in common. He too came from a large Catholic family and was from Yorkshire, albeit further south in Sheffield. He liked his sport and his beer. We were also different in many ways. His personality reflected his physical stature. He was 6ft 5in tall, athletic and with a moustache, in contrast to my 5ft 10in, skinny and clean-shaven appearance. The man, to me, the boy. He was confident, gregarious, and extrovert. He was Yorkshire to my Lancashire. He was rugby to my football. A microbiologist, he was the proper scientist to me, the social scientist. He also had a car. I had not even taken a driving lesson. He was more experienced in life and could certainly handle his beer. I was neither. In short, he was just what I needed.

We immediately chatted away, an easy conversation that has lasted for 35 years and counting. He was less enthusiastic than me about leaving Yorkshire and told me that he would 'give it three weeks and piss off home' if he didn't like it. He still lives in the area! I soon discovered that the emotional challenges of my childhood paled into insignificance compared to his physical challenges. Diagnosed with a malignant cancer at the age of ten, his parents had made the heart-rending decision that his left leg should be amputated above the knee. Despite the prosthetic limb he has used for the last 45 years he has never considered himself disabled, nor claimed 'disability' benefits or concessions, and continued to play many different sports at a very high level. Some fella.

We took ourselves off to the Student Union bar and then The Royalty, the adjoining pub that was to become our local. When we finally called it a night, we had decided that we would go to his home town and watch Sheffield United vs City together in November. Later that evening I also discovered that another of my new flat-mates was a City fan. It felt good to be among like minds.

My first year as a student at Sunderland was refreshingly typical. I tried to juggle the inconvenience of study as best I could, and mostly managed to not let it disrupt my social life. I spent most of my first term chasing after a Manchester girl for whom I had developed an infatuation, mainly on the basis that she actually talked to me in a pub. She was Catholic and her large family had once vaguely known my own when we lived in Stockport at the time of my birth, so I convinced myself that she was meant for me. After three years of amazing sex at Sunderland we would marry, have kids, all boys who would play for Manchester City and England, and live happily ever after. My shyness prevented me from ever asking her out and it went nowhere.

Despite having now spent more of my life in Yorkshire, I did, whenever asked, introduce myself as coming from Manchester. I then caused confusion every time I went back to Leeds in the holidays but self-identifying as being a Mancunian somehow seemed like the natural thing. I did not massively partake in student societies as I had my refereeing. I had continued to pursue that interest with the Wearside FA and it helped to have an interest outside the student 'bubble'. I took in First Division football at Sunderland and Newcastle, and when City made the journey north to Middlesbrough I took the short journey south, albeit ending in defeat. Two of my sixth form friends had ended up at Durham so occasionally we would get together. My youth hostelling and cricketing buddy Paul Ellwood was reading Chemistry at the university and Peter Kravos, a steady companion throughout St Michael's and the son of Slovenian immigrants, was studying in preparation for his ordination as a catholic priest at the nearby Ushaw Seminary.

We were typical students, living day to day on our meagre grants but somehow managing to scrape together enough for a pint before last orders were called at The Royalty. After some embarrassingly pathetic drinking efforts resulted in me throwing up outside the back of The Royalty, in Block 14, and just about anywhere else, I did slowly develop something of a drinking muscle. Saint and I decided we would share cooking duties and we managed to survive without poisoning ourselves. While not particularly healthy or nourishing, we got by. Most of our recipes will go to the grave with us, thankfully for all.

The trip to Sheffield United went ahead as agreed, with me meeting Saint's family for the first of many times. As Saint drove us down the A19 in his red Mini Clubman, we chatted about our flat-mates, our families and plans for the weekend. We were interrupted by a bang and a shudder as the Mini shook and veered sideways due to a blown-out front tyre. We promptly pulled over and jacked up the car. Another jolt told us that the jack had broken through the rusted chassis, and we were stranded in the dark in the middle of the North Yorkshire countryside. A kindly farmer and some bricks came to our rescue and we finally got the wheel changed. We returned to Sunderland on the train.

Communication studies, a mixture of media studies, sociology, and psychology, was interesting rather than intellectually challenging. I met the minimum academic requirements of the course and still enjoyed the full student experience with the independent living that it entailed. One of the features that defined the independent living was being away from siblings for the first time. Without the presence of David's distinctive colour, I was just another white boy from another white family. No explanations required or requested. I did not shy away from talking about David's ethnicity when family came up in conversation but neither did I go out of my way to signpost it. For a time, I wrestled with my feelings, a small pang of guilt that maybe I subconsciously welcomed the more comfortable environment of not standing out.

However, it was a student campaign that soon caused me to reflect on my own prejudices. The Student Union at

Sunderland was not a particularly militant or revolutionary one, but it had taken upon itself to withhold union affiliation to the polytechnic's Jewish Society. This position was based on the society's support of what was termed 'Zionism', which was perceived by the union to be a racist platform. Zionism was an unfamiliar concept to me and I was too lazy to investigate it for myself so was swept along by the older, more vocal, and politically motivated students who set out their opinions with force. The whole fiasco culminated in an emergency debate and a ballot that received national news coverage. Wearmouth Hall was packed as the few lone Jewish voices tried to present the argument to counterbalance the baying of the masses. The ballot was taken and passed; the Jewish Society's membership was denied. I voted for the motion. At the time I believed that it was the right thing but, just like many of the playground bullies, I had followed the mob. Not through any anti-Semitic sentiment but through a desire to fit in and a failure to question the facts for myself as they were presented. How quickly the persecuted can become the persecutor once the arithmetic changes. I had learnt a salient and lasting lesson that in time helped me to view some of the boys at St Michael's in a different way.

Despite the pleasant distractions of student life, City remained front of mind. Occasional trips home would inevitably be planned to coincide with Maine Road games, and I would always go the extra few miles to the ground, still visiting Nanna and Gangan before the match. The Easter holidays came along and City were occupying the third promotion place. True to type, some indifferent form followed, but with three games to go they were third with

Portsmouth, the next opponents, in hot pursuit. City made the long journey down to the south coast and came back with a vital win.

Three points from the last two games would secure promotion. Having missed out on attending the 1976 League Cup Final I was still impatiently waiting to see City win anything of note. Admittedly, third place in the Second Division was not how I would have previously defined success, but circumstances had changed and expectations recalibrated accordingly. I wanted to be there when promotion was secured. The penultimate game was away at struggling Notts County on May Bank Holiday. I went to the cashpoint machine inside Sunderland train station and checked the balance or, to be more accurate, the overdraft of my student bank account and immediately knew I could not afford the trip. I shut my eyes and took out the money anyway before going to the adjoining window and buying my ticket.

Via Newcastle and then Newark, I ended up in the beer garden of a pub close to the Meadow Lane ground. I did not know anybody but, in the spirit of the travelling supporter, no fellow fan is a stranger, and I immediately engaged in pre-match banter. My shyness miraculously disappeared in the company of the travelling congregation (and beer). I felt comfortable and at ease. With my credentials as an ex-ball boy, track record of followership, and general pedantic knowledge of all things City related I knew I could hold my own. A few pints of Shipstone's Bitter later we headed off to the game, singing our songs, full of end of season bravado on a beautiful May afternoon. As half-time approached, we were losing 3-0.

In all my time following City I had rarely been caught up in any of the football hooliganism that pervaded the game. Up to that point we had pretty much gone through the era without suffering the damage to reputation that had been the scourge of other notable clubs. Occasionally it was present, but having developed a good nose for sniffing it out I was adept at avoiding it. Today was to be a rare and unavoidable exception. Fuelled by the lunchtime refreshment and the anguish at the prospect of seeing promotion slipping away some fans took it upon themselves to express their frustration. The eight-foot metal fences between the supporters and the pitch were attacked and scaled. It quickly became evident that the structures were designed as an inconvenience rather than a formidable barrier to prevent anybody with serious intentions getting on the pitch. One by one they buckled under the weight of their assailants. The section of fence directly in front of me was not going to last beyond half-time and before long it limply fell towards me. I moved forward to stop it landing on the young boys that were underneath. I reached up to grab it as a police officer arrived on the scene – and that, m'lud, is the case for the defence! Stood there holding a piece of metal fence above my head amid the carnage and chaos, 'bang to rights' in the eyes of the constable who collared me.

The officer invited me to exit the stadium with unerring authority and a firm hand on my shoulder. Fortunately for myself and my fellow 'miscreants', the Nottingham Constabulary had been anticipating a fun-filled, good-natured afternoon. The thought that the relegation-bound home team might be three goals up at half-time and that this might in turn spark a riot had not occurred to them. Consequently, there was something of a disparity between the number of police officers on duty and City's travelling contingent. Having ejected me from the ground, my custodian swiftly turned on his heels and headed back inside to attend to more pressing matters than my arrest and incarceration. Relieved to have got away with one, I quickly made my escape.

As I headed back to the train station the second half restarted. City scored twice, but it was not enough to avert defeat. I arrived back at the Polytechnic Precinct late that night to tell my tale and suffer the inevitable piss-taking of my flat-mates. The drama of the farcical events and disappointing result dissipated as we sat up past midnight, along with 18 million other folks, watching the classic Dennis Taylor vs Steve Davis World Snooker Championship Final. It had been one of my more memorable sporting days.

As it was two years previously, the season would now come down to the last game with a place in the First Division the prize. Portsmouth had won while City had let themselves down on and off the Notts County pitch. Both teams were now level on points and only a vastly superior goal difference was keeping City in the third promotion place. We were to play Charlton at Maine Road. Undeterred by my costly personal debacle at Notts County, I nonetheless intended to be there. Thankful of my interest-free student overdraft I headed down to Leeds for a few days and persuaded Mum that she had not visited my grandparents for a while and therefore might wish to go over to Manchester that Saturday. Ever obliging, and turning a blind eye to the fact that most of my home visits tended to coincide with big football matches rather than filial affection, she agreed. David also decided to come along to the game and so we all headed off from Pudsey Road.

Shortly after departing, we saw cars turning off the M621 motorway in the direction of Bradford City's Valley Parade stadium. Purple-and-yellow scarves were trailing out of their windows. Bradford's hard work had been done and they were already Third Division champions. For them, the final day of the season was going to be one of coronation and celebration. How I envied them at that moment.

Nanna and Gangan, well into their late 80s but remaining mentally alert, were delighted to see me and we talked about life at Sunderland. Their interest in me was as keen as it ever had been during those first days of my visits. Much as I loved their company, I made my apologies a little earlier than they were used to, explaining that as the game was so important, we needed to get our place on the Kippax in good time. That was true in part, but a pre-match pint was now also part of my routine. For years I had walked past the Old House at Home, a pub next to 4 Brixton Avenue, without ever venturing inside. With David accompanying me I thought it would be a great chance to break my duck. We made our excuses and sneaked in a quick drink as we shared what we had both been up to in our increasingly separate lives. We didn't openly acknowledge it, but without the dark cloud of school life hanging over us, we were both more relaxed and at ease with young adulthood.

The mood on the Kippax was resolute and tense; 48,000 bodies were in the ground and every one of them was eager to bring back First Division football. The team would need them all as, ravaged by injuries, they were on their last legs. Fans or players need not have worried. The must-win approach that the situation necessitated had a positive effect and within ten minutes David Phillips and Andy May scored in front of the North Stand. Another three goals later and promotion was confirmed. The last 20 minutes was full of celebration and song. I passed on participating in the obligatory pitch invasion at the final whistle, not because of my exploits at Notts County, but because we were meeting Mum halfway along Yew Tree Road to head back home.

When we got to the car, Mum had her serious face on and immediately asked if we knew about the fire at Bradford. Stood on the Kippax, someone had said something about Bradford but that was all and I had not given it any more thought. Sat in front of the television in my grandparents' front room, Mum had watched the live pictures showing the inferno that had once been the Valley Parade main stand. A discarded cigarette had ignited loose paper and the flames had then ravaged through the old wooden structure. Within minutes the stand was no more. The car radio was on, *Sports Report* of course, and before we had departed the outskirts of Manchester three deaths had been confirmed. We had risen through the Pennines and into Yorkshire as we were informed of ten more. Silently we listened as we drove past the junction where, only a few hours earlier, we had seen the cars with scarves joyously trailing in the wind. The total was now 20-something and there was not a scarf to be seen. Twenty-plus of those supporters I had so envied just seven or eight hours earlier had now perished. We drove the last few miles home in silence as the numbers slowly increased. *Match of the Day* went ahead, but for once it began without the familiar theme tune. Jimmy Hill, sombre and dignified, informed the united football family that the number was now higher. They showed the City match, but it was a muted celebration as football came to terms with what had just happened.

By the morning, the death toll was in excess of 50 as the true human scale of the disaster was confirmed. And then early in the afternoon the telephone call came. As soon as it rang it occurred to me that it might be connected to Bradford. 'No,' I heard Mum gasp. 'No.' It was the headmaster of Thorn Park School for Deaf Children, the school where she had taught for the past ten years. The deputy head, Peter Greenwood, and his two sons Felix and Rupert were confirmed as among the victims.

I returned to Sunderland feeling numb. I knew that this would not diminish my love for football but up to that point the game, despite the on-pitch disappointments, had been a largely positive experience. It had been about life, not death. The triumph and the despair that it brought was transient and trivial. It had never occurred to me that football could bring real loss and grief. Two weeks later I sat with my flat-mates and watched, in silence and shock, as the Heysel Stadium tragedy played out in front of a European audience. Thirty-nine Juventus fans lost their lives that night following the collapse of a wall as they fled from Liverpool supporters. The actions that led up to it were not dissimilar to what had happened at Notts County in the first week of that tragic month of May 1985.

When I contemplated writing my story, I promised to myself that I would not use the internet to prompt my recollections of City's fortunes. If I could not recall anything unaided, then it could not be of sufficient importance to merit inclusion. For this reason, I am tempted to skip past the unremarkable 1985/86 season. However, given the infrequency with which they were to come about it would be remiss not to give a mention to the Wembley cup final that was valiantly contested. Tired of the passé pretentiousness of the FA Cup and League Cup, City exited both early in order to blaze a trail for the Full Members' Cup.

The European ban that had been imposed in the wake of the Heysel Stadium tragedy left a hole in the budgets of some clubs, so the Full Members' Cup was conceived by the chairmen to compensate for lost revenue. Such was the lack of public interest that, by the time City and Chelsea had sleep-walked their way to the final, playing in front of largely empty terraces, it was decided that the attendance was likely to be so pitifully low that the Wembley costs might not even be covered. But never did two such enterprising chairmen as Peter Swales and Chelsea's Ken Bates co-exist. Sensing that their success-starved fans might just enjoy a day out at Wembley, the two entrepreneurs allegedly offered to underwrite the cost, no doubt also hoping to make a quick buck or two for their clubs. And so just 24 hours after playing out a creditable draw in the Old Trafford derby, fighting back from a 2-0 deficit, City turned out at Wembley in front of a remarkable 67,000 people. We lost 5-4, no doubt knackered from the day before. That was the Full Members' Cup Final, and this is possibly the most that has ever been written about it. Whatever became of its first finalists, the perennially underachieving and financially struggling Manchester City and Chelsea?

My second year at Sunderland was thankfully more interesting than the football. I got by academically and excelled socially bringing my pre-vomit beer average up from 3.2 pints of Newcastle Exhibition to nearer 5.8 pints. Saint, I, and some friends had moved out of the polytechnic accommodation into our own digs at 1 Churchill Street and the bar at the Mowbray Park Hotel became our much-frequented local. Saint had also persuaded his girlfriend from Sheffield, Helen, to enlist on the biology degree course and through Helen's friends a strong social group emerged. A life-threatening fall off a two-inch curb (brought about while re-enacting a City goal for a disinterested audience) inconvenienced me somewhat early in the term as I sustained a broken ankle. It could have got worse as Helen's erratic control of an NHS wheelchair had my prostrate leg colliding with anything of a fixed nature at the Sunderland General Hospital. Plaster and crutches did not stop me getting to Maine Road during my mid-term break and I hobbled through Moss Side to see a 1-0 win against Newcastle, the comical sight of me limping along with plaster and crutches eliciting the friendly abuse of the Newcastle fans arriving in their coaches.

I did return home to make two cameo appearances at the altar of St Joseph's church with my long-standing on-stage partner, Father Horkin. Happily, my oldest sister Elizabeth, fellow survivor of the Kop at Elland Road, got married to a fellow doctor, Ben. Sadly Poppa, my paternal grandfather, passed away. He had lived with us for 14 years and watched us all grow up while never quite recovering from the loss of his own wife, my grandmother, and leaving his beloved

Northampton. His death, however, was not without its own story. Poppa held a suspicion of many things. Not least of these was yoghurt. 'No good can come of it,' he would insist, 'live bacteria.' Feeling ill and laid up in bed, my father had enquired if he would like anything to eat. Poppa's disdain for yoghurt was bizarrely matched by his penchant for an over-ripe banana cut up and served in some milk. I can only think it is a war thing. Scouring the kitchen, my father could find no banana, never mind a fetid one, but in the fridge, there sat a banana yoghurt. 'The old boy will never notice,' may not have been Dad's exact words but they were possibly his thoughts as he put the yoghurt, banana pieces and all, into a bowl and left it by Poppa's bed. Twenty minutes later he returned to find the bowl half-eaten and Poppa taking his last breaths. He passed away in Dad's arms just minutes after consuming his first yoghurt. He was a man who liked to be proven right. Although the routine post-mortem later revealed natural causes, I have viewed all yoghurt with deep suspicion ever since.

It must have been the fun times and the ease I felt in the company I kept that my time at Sunderland seemed to fly by. What had seemed like interminably long academic years at St Michael's appeared fleetingly brief at Sunderland. We finished that term watching England reinvent themselves mid-tournament in the 1986 Mexico World Cup, courtesy of a benign bar manager allowing us countless lock-ins at the Mowbray. Inspired by Reid, Lineker, and Beardsley and undone by Maradona's 'Hand of God', England succumbed at the quarter-final stage. Before I knew it my third and final year was upon me and beyond that employment and the real world.

In truth, I very nearly did not make it back to Sunderland. I had continued to supplement my student grant by working at The Beulah during the holidays. The money was useful, it got me out of the house, and I liked the work as well as the social aspect of it. I would occasionally hang around with David and some of his friends who worked in the hospitality industry, and I enjoyed the social life that seemed to go with the work. I was competent and, even though the landlord had changed, my duties had expanded beyond just pulling the pints and collecting the glasses to cellar work, cashing up, and various other tasks. I was starting to give serious consideration to a career in the industry, so when an opportunity arose to, albeit briefly, step into a management role it was not to be turned down. Landlord Albert decided he wanted to take his wife off to Tenerife for a well-deserved holiday and asked me to deputise. I happily accepted. Two weeks as 'mine host' at The Beulah seemed to be a good way to kick off my summer holidays. Albert duly showed me the ropes including a couple of 'tricks of the trade' down in the cellar. Nothing illegal or fraudulent but just how to maximise profit and minimise wastage. The two weeks went smoothly with one or two glitches, but nothing too serious. I would strut around the bar full of self-importance, introducing myself to customers who were not regulars as 'the landlord' and then take umbrage when they registered my youthful appearance, lightweight in every sense, with understandable incredulity.

My penultimate shift finally arrived, and I was knackered. The long hours and the responsibility had started to get me. As a student the whole notion of hard work was an unfamiliar one. One more lunchtime to get through and then Albert would be back. Having called time and closed the bar, I went to the cellar. Albert had shown me how to replace lager that had been pulled through the pipes, but not served, back into the 50-litre pressurised kegs. One job left to do. I took my bucket of lager downstairs and picked up the bespoke spanner that would allow me to remove the 'spear', a metal tube that extended from the opening to the base of the keg and through which the lager was dispensed under pressure. I went to work, unscrewing the securing bolt, thinking about what I would be spending my wages on.

I do not recall if I felt or heard the almighty 'whooossshhh' first. I fell back on to the stone floor as the metal spear flew out of the keg. It crashed with a thud into the beamed ceiling, leaving a two-inch dent, and dropped with a deafening clatter. It had missed my skull by millimetres and left the slightest nick on my forehead. Relaxed and demob happy, I had committed the cardinal error of forgetting to depressurise the keg before opening it. The metal spear, once unsecured, had flown out, propelled by enough pressure to power a small rocket. Had my head been just another inch forward I certainly would not be here to talk about it and Albert would have returned from his two weeks in Tenerife to find his barman's brains scattered liberally around his cellar. Someone, somewhere, was looking out for me that day.

When not working at The Beulah, much of that summer was spent down the road in Sheffield with Saint, enjoying the hospitality of his family. His mother, Doreen, was ever prepared for impromptu house guests descending at a minute's notice courtesy of Saint and his brothers. I frequently tested her tolerance through my legendary inability to hold my alcohol. On one infamous hungover morning as she was giving me a lift back to the train station, I asked her to pull over the car not two minutes after we left the house. I stuck my head out of the passenger door and threw up before sheepishly returning to the passenger seat. 'St John did tell me that you suffered from car sickness,' she sympathised, not wishing to prolong my embarrassment. My good friend had the nickname, but Doreen was the real saint in so many ways. The nature of Saint's microbiology course meant that his third year was an outplacement work assignment and, consistent with one of his principal interests, he had secured a position at the Whitbread Exchange Brewery in Sheffield. I would be returning to Sunderland without my buddy but as Helen was still in town I knew that his visits would be frequent.

City had made an indifferent start to the 1986/87 season and it would get worse. The squad was now a mixture of youth and experience with little in between. The youth was promising but too young and the experience was, to put it bluntly, too old. City were bottom of the table and heading towards relegation, but I could at least take solace in the fact that United were not doing much better. Hope briefly surfaced when two back-to-back wins were recorded at the beginning of November, a feat made all the sweeter as United had just suffered successive defeats under their struggling new manager who seemed doomed to fail, the hapless Alex Ferguson.

I listened to the second of these City wins, against Charlton, on a bus as I travelled back from a match I had officiated that afternoon. Having recovered from my broken ankle I quickly resumed my refereeing career and promptly enrolled on the list for the Hetton Youth League. This was a proper league, well run and competitive. The teams were under-16 to under-18 and full of man-boys. Tough, strong, committed, and passionate. The football was real and intense, an integral part of the community as I had ever witnessed. The refereeing was hard and required 100 per cent concentration, and the abuse was, to put it mildly, 'frank' both from the pitch and sidelines. When the final whistle blew, we all respectfully shook hands and moved on, accepting it for what it was and what it meant to us all. I would catch the bus out from Sunderland town centre to the outlying towns built on coal mining and decimated by the 1984 strike and the subsequent pit closures: Herrington, Murton, Hetton-le-Hole, Houghton-le-Spring, and Easington. They were wonderful experiences. I have been lucky to touch and encounter football in so many ways, on so many levels. These remain some of my most powerful and most loved memories. Those whose only exposure is via TV are missing out on so much.

Despite all the fun I was having, in the back of my mind I knew that finding employment would be made somewhat easier if I successfully graduated. My degree required that I submit a dissertation on an approved subject of my choice. As a media or television career was my preferred career route, I chose to bring my cerebral insight to 'Wogan – the Production and Popularity of the Television Chat Show'. Terry Wogan was the Graham Norton of his day, preceding Norton's 'camp' with the charm and blarney of the Irish. Celebrities, be they genuine royalty or Hollywood royalty, would be queuing up to appear on this thrice-weekly early evening show. In short, he was the main man of television. He was both Ant and Dec. I wrote to the BBC and was invited down to London to observe the live broadcast of the show. Henri Mancini, Elaine Stritch, and Johnny Mathis were his guests. Afterwards, in the green room I met them and then was introduced to Wogan himself. He kindly gave me some quotes for my dissertation. But, much fun as it might be, none of this was helping me to get a job. Once Christmas had come and gone both City and I needed to up our game and take control of our short-term futures.

There was a day before Sky TV existed. Before the countless news, sports, shopping, lifestyle, and quiz show channels. That world of not such a long time ago was the world in which I sought employment. Four terrestrial channels – BBC1, BBC2, ITV, and Channel 4 – and realistically fewer than 20 potential employers in an attractive industry for aspiring communication studies graduates. I had my work cut out. I wrote to them all, several times, and I got the 'Thank you for your interest but ...' letters in return. I did get invited to Tyne Tees for a discussion that felt more like an open day and, with more hope than expectation, I applied to the BBC Graduate Scheme optimistically thinking that my Wogan dissertation and evening spent rubbing shoulders with the famous would give me an advantage. The rejection letters arrived promptly. In truth, I had not put in the same hard legwork as many of my fellow applicants in an ultra-competitive industry. I had not done the polytechnic radio thing or got myself involved in student newspapers, not through laziness but because of other time-consuming activities such as refereeing. I did get an interview at Tyne

Tees for the position of trainee television journalist. One position and 1,500 applicants. I did well to get the interview and opened the rejection letter with knowing and benign acceptance.

City's relegation, confirmed with two games to go, was greeted with similar equanimity. While feeling gutted, I did not have the same sense of despair and shock that I had felt when it had happened before. There had been a certain inevitability about it ever since the return to the First Division. A lack of investment in the team and over-reliance on youth had meant the squad was totally inadequate to cope with the challenges of the First Division. Manager Billy McNeill had, most tellingly, sensed the inevitable and jumped ship to join Aston Villa after only a few games of the season. Villa were also relegated, leaving McNeill with the unenviable 'accolade' of having managed two clubs to relegation in the same season. His assistant, the veteran Jimmy Frizzell, oversaw City's demise and was then put out to pasture.

I graduated with my 2(ii) BA (hons) Communication Studies and in the summer of 1987, 21 years old, I left Sunderland and full-time education to go and make my mark in the world. I did not return to Pudsey Road as my parents, liberated in their choices by Poppa's passing, had traded in the large old family house that had served the growing family so well for a more manageable, modern property in the nearby village of Birstall. One of our last family gatherings in Pudsey Road, around that old dining room table, was the celebration of my 21st birthday with family and student friends.

8

Trading Places

AS MUCH as the job thing did not unduly concern me, I am not sure that everyone in the family shared my youthful confidence. I would continue to pursue my media interest until the end of the summer and then, if nothing was forthcoming, I would try my hand elsewhere. After all, Harry Enfield's 'Loadsamoney' kept telling us that the economy was strong, especially for plasterers. I considered myself to be willing and intelligent so felt confident that opportunities would present themselves. I had moved back home and, with Mum and Dad still working full time, there were plenty of 'paid' jobs that needed doing around the new house. I did not have the craft and DIY skills of my father but I could turn my hand to any number of mundane tasks, allowing him to swoop in at the end and add the 'puffery'. I applied the plaster to the walls of the Sistine Chapel, and he was Michelangelo.

While money was tight, I nevertheless managed to get to many of the City games, taking advantage of the relative proximity to Maine Road and the multiple away fixtures that were on my doorstep. My parents' move had meant that

Manchester was now more accessible, with the train journey from Dewsbury or Huddersfield getting me into the city in less than an hour. It was good to also spend regular time with Nanna and Gangan again, now into their 60th year of marriage and increasingly reliant on family and friends for day-to-day needs. I had time on my hands, plenty of it, and I was happy to share it around.

Meagre money for unremarkable talent was also the new operating model in Manchester. The ability to attract the best players with the prospect of high wages and glorious achievement was a thing of the distant past. The same applied to City's ability to attract the top managers and Mel Machin was duly appointed. Machin was a highly rated young coach, but unproven in the managerial role. I did get to see a win at Bradford, the first away victory in over two years, and a performance that gave hope of great things to come from the youngsters who were now the core of the team. The supporters did not let the occasion pass without laying a floral tribute outside the rebuilt main stand, scene of that tragic fire.

Ever keen to use my spare time productively and extend my football interest in new ways, I took my FA coaching badges at Carnegie College in Leeds. I enjoyed the course but found it challenging. Designed for ex-professional footballers wanting to prolong their careers in the game, it required a level of technical ability that I simply did not possess. I struggled with trivial details like nearly all the practical pieces; unable to demonstrate many of the basic skills that I would be required to teach. My faith in the system and the credibility of the qualification was upheld when they quite rightly failed me. It would have been a travesty to put the future of the country's young footballing talent in my hands.

November came, and I still had not found employment, but at least City's young players, now very much my contemporaries, were starting to make better use of their talents than I was of mine. Two home games scheduled in the same week gave me a bit of a dilemma. I could not afford to go to both so would have to choose between a Wednesday night fixture against Middlesbrough or Huddersfield on the Saturday. I went to the midweek game, a keenly fought draw against a Middlesbrough side who would ultimately earn promotion. Three days later and with my pockets now empty I listened to the radio as the first match report came through from the Huddersfield game. Against the run of play, City had scored and led 1-0. At half-time, with City 4-0 up, I wondered if I had made the wrong choice a few days earlier. This suspicion was confirmed when numbers five, six and seven were scored. Eight and nine were interrupted by a Huddersfield penalty and with the last kicks of the game David White went around the visiting goalkeeper, who by now did not know whether it was Pancake Tuesday or Sheffield Wednesday. City had won 10-1 and I had missed it all. Remarkably, I had never seen a City player score a hat-trick, but that afternoon David White, Paul Stewart, and Tony Adcock each claimed three goals to add to Neil McNab's opener. My only consolation was that Granada had covered the game and it would be on TV in the evening. I recorded it and still have that overplayed, grainy VHS video. I called Gangan to share the moment with him. City had scored ten, unheard of in modern times and not repeated at Football League level since. The historic victory did not mark the dawn of a new era but it did give a glimmer of the potential that lay within the club.

Eighteen months earlier City had won the FA Youth Cup with a team of largely Manchester-born players. But the fortunes of football, and those who ply their trade in the sport, hang by so many delicate threads. Injury, the right environment, the senior players they mix and train with, club stability, the coaching and management are all pivotal. With my sky blue-tinted glasses on, I would contend that City's Class of '86 had the potential and ability to match anything that United's future famed Class of '92 later went on to achieve. Steve Redmond was the captain, a natural and strong leader, mature beyond his age, his timing of a tackle making up for his lack of pace. Andy Hinchcliffe was an intelligent and adept defender with great dead-ball and crossing ability who, with a bit more luck avoiding injury, could have challenged Stuart Pearce for the England left-back slot. Ian Brightwell had the stamina and sporting pedigree you would expect of the son of Olympians Ann Packer and Robbie Brightwell. He was tenacious, energetic, and versatile, with an eye for goal. David White was raw talent, using pace and aggression to tear past defenders, and also a prolific goal scorer. He was equally at home on the wing or down the middle and on his day was unplayable. Paul Moulden's claim to fame is there for all to see in *The Guinness Book of Records* – 289 goals in 40 games during one season for Bolton Lads Club, predatory finishing ability that took him into City's first team. Finally, there was the prince of them all, Paul Lake. Lake made playing football look as easy and natural as he himself said it felt. I saw him play in just about every position for City and he was among the best regardless of where he was asked to play. More than that he was one of ours, City through and through. I am convinced he would have been one of the greats, not just of City but also for England.

It was not to be, however. Not for the group, nor for the individuals. Some were unlucky with injury, failed by a club where poor leadership and financial constraints meant they did not receive the best medical care. Not many years later, Manchester United's feted Class of '92 emerged into a squad whose members already consisted of Schmeichel, Bruce, Robson, Cantona, and Hughes to name a few. Not a bad group to pick up the odd bit of friendly advice from. With all due respect to Kenny Clements, John Gidman, Imre Varadi, and Neil McNab, all fine professionals, they lacked the stature of their counterparts across the city. The comparisons are stark. The Class of '92 matured as Alex Ferguson, his authority established by a Premier League and FA Cup victory, had stabilised the club and was on the way to shaping it in his image. Who knows what might have been had they traded places. In 1988 when, Ian Brightwell, the last of the Class of '86, departed he had played under nine different managers and three chairmen. Ability aside, they never really had a chance. The false dawn was evident when, later in the season, City played the return fixture against Huddersfield and lost 1-0.

The closest I got to being a journalist was to be offered a job as a junior reporter on the *Batley News*. Batley was the neighbouring town to Birstall, where my parents now lived. I went for an interview and remarkably, despite the fact I could not yet drive, was offered the position. The fact that the editor suggested that I could cycle to wherever I might be required told me all I needed to know about the scope of the role. It would be some time before I reported on the G7, or even what was happening nine miles away in Leeds. My parents tried to persuade me to take the position. I think my mother was filled with the romantic images of junior reporters from another era, as brought to life in Evelyn Waugh's *Scoop*, which was being serialised on television. My not so romantic images were of still cycling around Batley aged 40, notebook in basket, reporting on the latest civic dignitary to be buried in a church graveyard. There was that and the fact that the pay was crap. My head was also turned by a career in business, although what sort of career and whose business I did not know or really care. Those questions were answered by an advert in the *Sunday Times*. A company called Nacanco was launching a graduate training scheme and invited interested candidates to apply. I had seen my siblings Alban and Kathy progress through similar schemes at Marks & Spencer and Boots, so this seemed a good way into the world of industry. I attended interviews in the glamour towns of Skelmersdale and Luton before being offered the role of graduate trainee, commencing in January 1988, at an annual salary of £8,000. I accepted the offer despite not being entirely sure what line of business Nacanco was in, but, true to my word, I had found a job before the year was out, if only just. The human resources manager who hired me also happened to support City.

I received instructions to report for duty at the Skelmersdale factory as the programme was structured so that all graduate trainees would spend their first month on the shop floor learning the core business. I soon discovered that Nacanco was an acronym for North American Can Company and that I was now, in the industry vernacular, a 'metal basher'. My employers made beverage cans, to be filled by the likes of Coca-Cola, Pepsi, and the UK's many breweries by bashing them out of sheets of aluminium coil. After my first day on the factory floor as a working man I did go back to my hotel and think, 'Is this really it for the rest of my life?' but I soon became comfortable in my new environment.

The town of Skelmersdale, developed to cope with the post-war Liverpool overspill, was not the prettiest place, but it was full of the friendliest people. It helped that I liked my football and did not support United as the factory floor was very much an extension of the Anfield and Goodison Park terraces. City, enjoying a bit of a League Cup run, had been drawn at Everton in the quarter-finals. A couple of my work-mates offered to take me along, but I had been assigned to the night shift. I went to see the plant manager, but not wanting to make an exception for the graduate trainee, he understandably declined my request. Given that my purpose was more 'ornament than function' around the factory, I was not in the best mood as I reported for work that evening. The shift supervisor pointed to a ladder on the side of an industrial oven that cured the cans once they had been sprayed with an internal protective lacquer. 'Get up there kidda and I'll see yous in the morn'n,' he said to me in thick Scouse. I climbed on top of the oven, feeling its warmth through the piercing January night. Laid out before me was a radio, a pillow, two meat pies, and the biggest pile of jaw-dropping porn I had ever seen. I listened to City lose 2-0, embarked on some light reading, and drifted off to sleep. When I came down in the morning my eyes were watering. I felt light-headed and dizzy. 'Jesus, that is some porn,' I thought to myself. The supervisor pointed out to me that I had not worn the protective face mask that was also there and, as I slept, I had been breathing in the fumes from the solvent-based lacquers being cured in the oven below me. My month of service on the shop floor was nearly done and I was ready for head office before I caused further self-harm.

Up until then, I was a mongrel northerner – Manchester, Leeds, Sunderland and, briefly, Skelmersdale. Moving to head office would take me to the leafy Home Counties and Bedfordshire. What little I knew about Luton was predictably through football, and I did not particularly like it. I could forgive their club's part in City's relegation in 1983; David Pleat was a young, enterprising manager and his team played good football. Against any other side that day I would have been cheering for Luton. Pleat had moved on and, in my opinion, so had Luton's footballing soul. They had invested in an artificial plastic pitch that had changed the sporting dynamic of the game. It had been the green, natural grass of the pitch that had first awed me and captured my attention. To see football played on a synthetic carpet just did not seem right. Worse than that, their answer to the question of hooliganism had been to introduce a membership scheme designed to prevent any visiting supporters attending their games. I did not agree with much that Peter Swales had done, but his principled stand in refusing to attend City games at Kenilworth Road was the right one. If no visiting supporters were allowed, then no visiting directors would be there. Worse for Luton was that many people felt that their chairman was not doing this for the good of football or the town but as a publicity stunt for his own political ambitions. I did not meet a single Luton supporter who agreed with the ban on away fans. Luton, in my opinion, was anti-football, but otherwise I moved to my new town with genuine enthusiasm.

My job in head office was as an internal sales correspondent. I was responsible for managing customers' requirements, arranging delivery schedules, and liaising with production planners to organise the next run of Strongbow Cider or Skol Lager cans. It soon became apparent that in this industry there was more demand than supply and Nacanco quickly became known as the 'No Can Co'. Each Thursday, customers would confirm their requirements for the following week. We would then batten down the hatches as we fended off irate brewery supply directors and soft drinks company executives wanting to know why they could not have the cans they had ordered six weeks ago. In the afternoon, the temperature increased a notch as the brewery chiefs, still operating in a world where a liquid lunch in the tap room was the accepted norm, became more verbose and forthright. They were not averse to throwing the odd 'fuck', 'twat', and 'arsehole' (and worse) into the conversation. By 5pm the last of us left standing felt like the Welsh Guards at Rorkes Drift. All that was missing was a rousing chorus of 'Men of Harlech' from the sales office choir. It was a lot of fun really.

The attritional environment that fostered a real sense of bonding was also an invaluable education, but I quickly realised that I did not want to spend all my career in that office. One major barrier stood in the way of my progress and removing it could also unlock other opportunities: I needed to learn to drive. There had previously been no great incentive for me to pass my driving test. I did not need it for my work, and I could not afford a car anyway. I had taken, and failed, the test while living in Birstall, but applied myself properly in Luton and at the third time of asking I passed and was, finally, independently mobile. The breweries, soft drinks companies, and more importantly, football stadia of the country awaited me.

The season that had promised much in the autumn had once more delivered little in the spring. Another cup run, in the FA Cup, briefly offered hope but the all-conquering Liverpool side of Beardsley and Barnes had quickly snuffed out any lingering dreams. But I was not to be deterred and had ambitious new plans. With my driving licence secured, I loaned the money from Dad to buy a 1969 VW Beetle and convinced myself that supporter and club were now going places. I did not set my sights too high and the first of those places would be the city of Hull; a new season beckoned.

I ventured eastwards in the Beetle along a part of the much-travelled M62 that I had not travelled down before. With time to kill I parked up near the ground and headed into town, buying myself a smart new Adidas jacket. As I tried it on and admired myself, I decided to wear it to the game. Being in Hull it would have been churlish of me not to partake of the local fish and chips so refreshed and sated I headed to Boothferry Park. The old ground had been newly smartened up in preparation for the season. That summer facelift, and specifically the new lick of paint on the crash

176

barriers in the away end, looked so smart and fresh that it might have been only completed that morning.

The damning evidence was the horizontal red stripe that every visiting City fan acquired across their chests and arms once they had leant on the not-yet-dry crash barrier. Strike One. 'Well, one brand-new Adidas jacket ruined is not going to spoil my day,' I consoled myself. 'Only something like Andy Dibble dropping a cross into the City net could do that.' Dibble read my mind and duly obliged for the game's only goal. Strike Two. Mightily frustrated, I got in the car and headed back out of Hull and towards the motorway. As I approached a junction, I let myself get distracted by a couple of local girls displaying all their late-summer finery. I did not see the traffic lights change to red and drove my cherished Beetle straight into the back of the car that had stopped in front. Strike Three! This independent travel was not quite turning out to be everything it was cracked up to be. Slowly things did get better and after a few weeks the new squad and old car had both repaired themselves and started to live up to expectations. Of course, true to type, there would be a twist or two before the end of the season. There would also be a lot of fun.

Many theories have been expounded as to why the hooliganism that had been such a scourge of football in the 1970s and the 1980s slowly died away. Sociologists and behaviourists will tell you that it needed to be viewed in the context of a bigger issue and the problem was not football's but society's. Economists have linked it to the revival of the UK's economic fortunes. Others will talk about the middle-class gentrification of football brought about through the establishment of the Premier League. Some will see the introduction of all-seater stadia as a crucial point of inflection. I am sure that all these hypotheses have credence, but rarely does 'banana aggro' get a mention.

It had started the previous season. There are different versions of when and how but the connection seems to go back to City's recruitment of Imre Varadi in 1987. At an away game the fans started chanting to bring on the substitute, 'Imre Banana', and the name stuck. Soon a six-foot inflatable yellow Fyfe's banana appeared on the Kippax. Slowly more and more followed and by the start of the 1988 season it had become an essential matchday accessory. Literally hundreds of inflatable bananas bouncing up and down. Soon it expanded from the humble banana. Animals featured strongly, both real and mythical, from land, sea, and sky; sheep, sharks, and swans. The best was saved for away games. A giant Loch Ness Monster made it all the way down south to Plymouth and, at West Brom, Godzilla waged mighty war on Frankenstein, vociferously urged on by the support in the City end. Home crowds around the country watched, perplexed and amused as the inflatable menagerie went on its travels. Anything that could be inflated was by now welcomed into the family. An oversized Newcastle Brown Ale can appeared at Ipswich to chants of 'You dirty Geordie bastard' when, with no provocation, it attacked a demure blow-up doll and exposed her questionable modesty. At Leicester, an inflatable Ansell's beer can placed by sponsors in the centre circle was savaged by banana-wielding City fans. The police laughed, and the home crowd jeered as the good-natured assailants were led away. It was the most fun I can ever remember having at a football game. The craze spread beyond City, famously to West Ham with their inflatable hammers, Stoke with their Pink Panthers and on a memorable FA Cup weekend Grimsby Town with a shoal of haddocks. And then like all great underground movements it went away as quickly as it had arrived. But boy was it enjoyable while it lasted.

Do I really think that it changed the way people behaved at football grounds? Not in itself, no I do not, but I do think it was symptomatic of a bigger movement that was emerging. Supporters were fed up with the damage that the thugs with no interest in football were doing to the game. They were also fed up with the equally inept and ill-judged responses from the authorities and career politicians. They were taking football back for themselves. They would set the rules and redefine the supporter experience and if that meant waving a plastic banana above their heads then so be it.

Banana aggro also coincided with another supporter movement: the fanzine. At last, there was an alternative to the formulaic, City-produced *Match Day Magazine* pushing the official club message with its predictable ghost-written manager's notes, 'off the shelf' away team summaries and player profiles. *Match Day Magazine* finally had competition on the streets around the grounds, with material written by the supporters, for the supporters. They would be vocal and honest about their club's shortcomings on and off the pitch. The content was irreverent, witty, and cynical. The writing was intelligent and insightful and discussed the things that mattered to fans. They were not afraid to mix football with other popular cultures and even politics. City had *King of the Kippax* and *Bert Trautmann's Helmet* and Brighton fans with a touch of pathos named theirs *And Smith Must Score* after Peter Jones's commentary at the end of the 1983 FA Cup Final. Celtic had an excellent and cuttingly witty fanzine, including a 'They Disgraced the Hoops' feature as an antidote to the usual bland player profiles. In February 1990, Stoke City's publication, *The Oatcake*, celebrated Nelson Mandela's release after 27 years of incarceration with a front cover featuring the South African taking his final walk to freedom, the speech bubble coming out of his mouth enquiring, 'Have Stoke won owt yet chuck?' Football fans were starting to be heard but not before it was too late.

A few months later, it was the afternoon of 15 April 1989. I potted the black ball and finished the remainder of my pint of Bombardier bitter before leaving Dunstable Snooker Club. The time was just before 3pm and there were six games of the season left. City were in second place and promotion beckoned. As they were due to play at third-placed Blackburn that afternoon, I wanted to get home before the match started. I got in the Beetle and turned on the radio. The pre-match build-up was from the FA Cup semi-final at Hillsborough between Nottingham Forest and Liverpool. Summariser Jimmy Armfield remarked that the ground was filling up nicely and that, in particular, an area on the Leppings Lane terrace looked very full. Before I had completed the ten-minute drive to my lodgings, over 90 of those Liverpool supporters would be dead, crushed between the weight of the crowd behind them and the barriers in front.

I watched the horror unfold on TV. The abandonment of the match, the confusion, the panic as totally unprepared ground staff were again having to deal with death and not football. I saw the anger and the anguish on the faces of frightened and desperate Liverpool fans wandering, in a daze, around the Hillsborough pitch. Then, like on that car journey from Manchester listening to the Bradford tragedy, the numbers kept coming. As dusk closed in the full scale of the tragedy was apparent. I had not left my seat in front of the television. While all this had been going on the rest of the football programme had gone ahead. Everton had won the other semi-final against Norwich, but their supporters' joy quickly evaporated when the news from Hillsborough came through. Many would have had friends and family at the Sheffield venue. City had crashed 4-0 at Blackburn but that did not seem to matter. Mum called me, anxious to check that I had not gone to the game. As it happened, I had been offered a ticket in a pub the night before. I reassured her and she asked me how I felt about it. 'They will blame the fans,' I told her. 'They will blame the fans.'

The eminent Home Office pathologist for South Yorkshire, Professor Alan Usher – who also happened to be Saint's father – led the post-mortems the following day. 'Traumatic asphyxia' was the verdict in the overwhelming number of cases. Most of the victims were younger supporters, several of them girls, who had got into the ground early to secure a place near the front. Consequently, when the crush came, they had nowhere to go. Behind them the life-sapping force of the massed crowd; in front of them the six-foot steel fence that stood between themselves and the oxygen of the pitch. Expectant fans had turned up at a football match full of hope only to have their dreams and bodies crushed on the terraces of Hillsborough.

Like most supporters, I felt the tragedy as keenly as if it had happened to my own club. Notwithstanding the ability to reach an FA Cup semi-final, it could so easily have happened to us. Like many, I also did not know how to react; football had to go on hadn't it? It did not feel right to be playing and watching football but by the same token it did not feel right to pack it all in. Bradford and Heysel had both happened at the end of the season, the final game in both cases. The clubs and the wider football community had been afforded time to grieve, to come to terms with what had happened and to recalibrate before the start of the next season. Hillsborough had taken place as the season was still in progress and about to reach its climax. After a respectful pause, the league programme resumed. City won just one of those last six games, that solitary victory overcoming a 2-0 deficit at Oxford. Typically, they surrendered a 3-0 lead at home to Bournemouth in the penultimate game but limped back into the First Division with a scrappy draw at Bradford. For a few minutes we forgot about Hillsborough and celebrated our restored status. Liverpool went on to an emotional victory against Everton in the delayed FA Cup Final and then lost the title on goals scored to Arsenal. Michael Thomas scored an injury-time winner that inspired Nick Hornby to write his book, *Fever Pitch*, and a generation of supporters became aspiring authors.

The summer saw football stadia across the country rapidly modified to ensure that spectators were no longer trapped in confined terraces and the towering fences were removed or adapted. What City needed now was a gentle reintroduction into the tough environment of the First Division. When the fixture computer came up with Liverpool away followed by Spurs, United, and Arsenal it did not bode well for a triumphant return. City duly lost the opener 3-1 at Anfield as the Kop rediscovered its roar. United were due to come to Maine Road for the seventh game and with just one win recorded, First Division survival already looked perilous.

Hope sprung from the fact that United, still trophyless under Alex Ferguson, were going through their own transition troubles. A new and expensively assembled squad had not yet gelled and they looked short of confidence and cohesion. City's young, largely homegrown team seized the initiative and ripped into United from the start, going 2-0 up in the first ten minutes and adding a third before the break courtesy of Ian Bishop's spectacular diving header. United pulled one back with a classic Mark Hughes volley, prompting City to go up the other end a score a fourth. The crowning glory was saved until last. Bishop, at his creative best, sprayed the ball out to the marauding David White on the right wing. Without breaking stride White clipped his cross to the far post where left-back Andy Hinchcliffe had steamed into the penalty area and powered his header into the roof of the net. Hinchcliffe and Lake's five-fingered salutes to the fans, both United and City, became the iconic image of the game. Fifteen years would pass before City would score their next winning goal in a Manchester derby, so it was a fitting one to savour. Ferguson recalled that he went home that night and 'put his head under a pillow for hours'. For him things would get marginally better. For City's Class of '86, this was to be as good as it would ever get.

The win provided the confidence boost and impetus to string together some positive results, but the inconsistency prevailed. Going forward City always looked like scoring, but defensively they were disorganised and at times chaotic. I had moved to Finchley to share a flat with my brother Alban, who was rapidly making his way up the ranks of the food retail industry. As December approached, I dragged him along to Highbury and we stood in the Clock End as Arsenal hit four. Derby then swept in six at the Baseball Ground. Peter Swales lost his nerve and Mel Machin lost his job. The chairman, ironically oblivious to his own greatest shortcoming, cited the manager's 'inability to relate to the supporters' as being the key reason. Most of the football world was surprised by the quality of his replacement. Timing favoured City on this occasion and Howard Kendall, who had led Everton to two titles before being lured away by the Spanish peso, had just been sacked by Athletic Bilbao. Swales moved quickly and got his man. As with John Bond seasons before, the experienced manager immediately identified the issues and made the changes that he deemed to be necessary, notably bringing in the experienced midfielder Peter Reid from Everton.

I received a well-deserved promotion to the position of junior account manager just before Christmas. It came with a small salary increase, but more importantly a company car. I would now be on the road visiting customers, rather than tied to the office. Positive career move as it was, I could think only of the opportunities to get to more games with petrol and hotel expenses paid.

On the first day of April, I drove my newly acquired Vauxhall Astra to Villa Park. My companion for this away-day was Nick, a colleague at Nacanco and a fellow obsessive with whom I would spend some of my most enjoyable football moments over the years to come. Under Kendall's stewardship the results had improved and slowly City had crept up the table but were still hovering just above the relegation places. Aston Villa, under England-bound Graham Taylor, were embarking on one of their sporadic but ultimately futile challenges for the title. City had not won an away game all season. In fact, it had been four years since we had last won any top-flight away game. City won the match 2-1 despite conceding an early goal. An organised and mature performance suggested that Kendall's team had finally found their mettle. Peter Reid's goal ten minutes from time sent the following behind the goal into rapture, but that is not my abiding memory of the match. Stood behind that goal in Villa Park's North Stand I first heard 'Blue Moon' sung. City had no anthem at this time, not the way Liverpool had adopted 'You'll Never Walk Alone'. A few of the fans singing it were familiar with the words. Quickly more and more joined in. I listened carefully, trying to catch the lyrics and not make a complete arse of myself before I gave it a go.

Blue Moon, you saw me standing alone,
Without a dream in my heart,
Without a love of my own.

Soulful lyrics that resonated and a good tune to accompany it. An apt length for the average Joe to remember and a melody range and pace well suited to terrace tenors. Why it came about or from whom I do not know, but it felt right that day at Villa Park and it has felt right every day since.

The tune still in our heads and content, having seen a fine match, Nick and I headed back down south. Being a similar age, Nick had also shared many of the same boyhood experiences of football on the radio so naturally we tuned into Radio 2. As the news ended the BBC were sad to report that sports commentator Peter Jones had died. He had collapsed the previous day while aboard the BBC launch, commentating on the University Boat Race. Nick and I looked at each other both feeling the loss in our own way. I had never met Peter, corresponded with him, or seen him. To this day I do not know what he looked like. He had, nevertheless, been a big part of my life. He had helped to shape the person I had become and the passions I pursued. When I got home, I sat down and tried to remember his voice, the authority, warmth, and clarity, ensuring that the occasion, and not he, was the centre of attention. Through the triumph of English European nights to the tragedy of Hillsborough he had brought it all to the nation and, I felt, to me personally. He had done it with dignity and brilliance, never failing to find the right words for the moment. Thank you, Peter Jones.

City progressed from the Villa win to finish impressively and, more importantly, clear of the relegation places. There seemed to be an uncharacteristic stability as the season concluded. Work was going well; I had my car and a job I enjoyed. Remarkably, the England team were also thriving as, like the rest of the nation, I revelled in the euphoria that was Italia '90. The summer was coming and there was much to look forward to.

9

Loss, Love, and Lager

BIG, FANCY, foreign holidays were not my thing. At the age of 24 I had never set foot on an airplane. My football team had not exactly given me any incentive with forays into European competition and watching City always seemed the best reason to venture abroad. Consequently, I spent time off work in and around the UK with my friends. Saint had discovered that unoccupied university halls of residence were a cheap and decent source of accommodation, so a group of us – Saint, Helen, his brother Adrian, and assorted friends from polytechnic days – took advantage of the facilities at Lancaster University, Stirling, and East Anglia.

In the summer of 1990, post-World Cup ecstasy and agony and with the last strains of 'Nessun Dorma' fading away, the happy group headed off north of the border to Stirling. On the second evening we made our way from the student bar and, passing a telephone kiosk, I checked in with Mum and Dad who had just returned home from their own vacation. It was a timely, but ultimately tardy, call as that morning Gangan had passed away in Manchester's Withington Hospital. I was aware that he had been ill, but that had been the case many times and he had somehow always managed to pull through. He had recently been fitted with a pacemaker and, invigorated by what he considered to be a new immortality, had got to the top of his stairs only to collapse and fall. This time there would be no great recovery.

I had seen him a few months earlier, visiting 4 Brixton Avenue, as City played their Easter fixtures and performed the same well-practised chores, and then some more. His mind was as alert and alive as ever. We had talked about the usual things, about me first, how was I doing, how was work. He never quite understood what I did, but then again some of the time neither did I. Then we would talk cricket, football, family and, of course, go into the garden to admire his beloved tomato plants. Whether I wanted it or not, he would leave me with a gem of wisdom to take away and ponder over. He was there for me during my darkest days, and I regretted that I could not be there for him at the end. Most of all I felt profound sadness that my 91-year-old friend had left me.

Saint and my holiday companions provided great support and I cut short the break before returning to Leeds ahead of the funeral. We had a family dinner, fondly remembering him. There were no tears. I recalled Poppa's funeral and said, 'I don't want him to be wheeled down the aisle like a dessert trolley.' I hated the sight of the funeral directors placing Poppa's coffin on the bier and pushing him out of the church. So we agreed that six of his grandsons, and there were after all 12 of us to choose from, would carry him on our shoulders.

The service was in St Cuthbert's Church, attached to the school where he had served as headmaster for so long. Former teachers and pupils mixed with family. I read the bidding prayers, just about keeping it together, and then we laid him to rest at a beautiful spot in Manchester's Southern Cemetery. A willow tree overhangs the grave. Eighteen months later we would reunite him with Nanna when she too passed away. There is room for one more in that plot, H1876, and I cannot think of many better places to end up when my time comes.

After the funeral we went back to the Withington house to sort out a few things for Nanna, who was moving into a care home, but most of all to say goodbye to the memories that lay within. I went into the small back garden and inspected the orphan tomatoes, wondering what would become of them. They had not been watered for a while so were drooping in the summer heat, heads respectfully bowed in mourning. I attended to them and then walked through to the kitchen; the old Aga, provider-in-chief at so many Saturday lunchtimes, now sat silent and cold. Finally, I went into the lounge; Gangan's big armchair, his throne from which he had pontificated with equal verve on matters of importance and (more often) irrelevance, never looked emptier. I looked around at the busy, tobacco-stained walls, closed my eyes and breathed in the air one last time. Always, always Balkan Sobranie. And then at last I wept.

Returning to Manchester for the new season without the physical presence of my grandparents in the background was a strange feeling. Alban had moved to Scotland, but fortunately for me he still contributed to the bulk of the mortgage, so I continued to live way beyond my means in the Finchley flat.

It meant that the journey north was a long one. I missed having the convenience of a staging post at which to stop off as well as, of course, their company. Howard Kendall had acted with decisiveness in the summer in strengthening the squad but his boldest move was an internal one. With an eye on the future, Kendall made Paul Lake the club's new captain and centre-half. He adapted to both the new position and the responsibility with consummate ease. For two and half games, Lake was a commanding presence, a young leader through example, as graceful as he was powerful. In game three he landed awkwardly, twisted his knee, and left Maine Road on a stretcher. The next day the club reported that he would be out for two or three weeks. The fans held their breath and waited. Then waited and waited some more.

While we all impatiently looked forward to Lake's return City continued to progress with an impressive run of unbeaten results, but November proved to be the month for 'blue on blue' changes at the top. The cruel nature of both politics and football is that loyalty beyond the supporter base is a rare commodity. While most of the nation was gripped with the battle for the Conservative party and country's leadership, as John Major unceremoniously ousted Margaret Thatcher, I was more concerned with equally underhand 'blue on blue' leadership changes that were taking place 200 miles north of Westminster. While City were on the up, Everton were on the slide. The Goodison board dispensed of the services of their manager Colin Harvey and picked up the phone to Peter Swales, but not before sounding out Howard Kendall. Swales was powerless to prevent the inevitable as the manager's heart was set on return to Merseyside, swapping the blue of City for the blue of Everton, Kendall described his time at Maine Road as an 'affair' with City while still being 'married' to Everton. The fans did not take kindly to being Kendall's 'bit on the side' and it felt like the club had been used and dumped. Despite the humiliating nature of his departure, there was no denying that the roll in the hay with Kendall had been good for City and he left a club in immeasurably better shape. Peter Reid was swiftly appointed as player-manager and guided the side to a creditable fifth place, one above Manchester United. The Paul Lake comeback never materialised, and he did not play again all season.

For a single guy in his mid-20s, I had a pretty good job. It was not the best paid but it came with a company car; my portfolio of accounts was liberally scattered around the country and the customers were keen to give me business. Those customers were also predominately in the beer industry. Being the junior on the team I was given the lesser accounts, which meant working with smaller breweries or cider producers. Better for me as there was less pressure, and I could build up business from a low base. I would be happily despatched to the Cornish Brewery at Redruth, Taunton Cider in Somerset and Bulmer's in Herefordshire, Greene King at Bury St Edmunds and Faversham's Shepherd Neame. When there was a midweek home game, I would coincidentally find myself in Thwaite's at Blackburn and JW Lees in Oldham. The meetings would usually consist of a discussion about future requirements, service issues, and the supply of cans. We only got dirty and discussed prices once a year. The business of the day over, we would adjourn to the taproom and sample the product. I felt comfortable in the environment. Being a male-dominated industry, the conversation would often migrate to sport and despite my relatively young age I could hold my own in any company on that subject, albeit I did struggle with the rugby union obsession of Wales and the cider-producing counties in the south-west.

Before the control of the breweries got taken over by the chief financial officers and the marketing directors, the head brewer was the main man, and I encountered all sorts of weird and wonderful characters. I turned up at the Felinfoel Brewery in Llanelli early one morning to meet with the head brewer. He leaned across his desk and asked, 'Want some breakfast do ya?' Envisaging a plump bacon butty or the Welsh equivalent of the full English, I replied in the affirmative. He reached behind his chair into a sack of malted barley and put a handful in front of me. 'There ya'are. Keep you going all day, that will, and put hairs on ya chest too.'

Such was the compatibility between my work and my real passion that I somehow managed to persuade my boss it would be a good idea to take customers to Maine Road, in appreciation of their business. I promptly secured the best seats in the ground followed by dinner on Rusholme's celebrated curry mile, known affectionately as 'Curry Nation Street' after the long-running Granada soap opera. I am not sure that the customers enjoyed it as much as I did – they tended to politely decline a second invitation. I suspect they were envious of their colleagues and competitors who were being wined and dined at Anfield or Old Trafford's lavish 'prawn sandwich suites', enjoying considerable better fayre both on and off the pitch.

On only one occasion was there any conflict in the symbiotic harmony of this beautiful relationship between work and play. I returned to my hotel room after a night out with colleagues. The beer had been flowing, followed by an Indian meal washed down with cheap curry-house wine. As I stumbled into bed, I suddenly recalled that City had been playing that evening. It must have been an unimportant fixture, most likely in the Full Members' Cup or whatever its latest incarnation was. I switched on the TV and drunkenly fumbled with the remote control but was unable to find the result on Teletext. Cursing that the internet had not yet been invented, I reached for the phone and dialled 0898 121191, the indelibly memorised number for City Clubcall, the premium-rate telephone service for all things Manchester City. My next conscious memory was of waking up a few hours later with a dull head and a nasal Mancunian voice in my ear, 'And Niall Quinn rose at the far post to make it 2-1.' I quickly slammed down the phone, but not before confirming the result, and tried to sleep through my throbbing hangover in dread of the phone charge that would appear on my room bill in the morning. It came to more than £150 and I decided that my best policy was to come clean and tell my boss the truth. Fortunately, he also enjoyed his football and let it go with a few choice words. He knew me well, and had it not been such a ridiculously plausible story, I am sure he would have suspected me of availing myself of an altogether different kind of premium phone service.

Saturday, 24 August 1991 was a day to remember in the Denton household. City went to the top of the league for the first time in many years. I had moved from Finchley to the

Bedfordshire town of Flitwick and shared a flat with Clive, a colleague and ardent Liverpool supporter. I arrived home after travelling up to Manchester where I had witnessed a nail-biting win against Crystal Palace and Clive had left me a scrawled message. My parents had phoned shortly after the game's conclusion and seemed eager that I should call home. I rang them back immediately and I could sense the happiness and energy in their voice.

'Isn't it wonderful news? We are so thrilled and proud,' Mum said. I was surprised as they did not usually share such enthusiasm about my football obsession, and I tempered her excitement, 'Yes, I know, it's great but we are only three games into the season, and anything can happen. And we didn't actually play that well.'

'No,' she replied with exasperation, 'Liz has given birth to a baby boy! You're an uncle.'

Ed was the first of my many nephews and nieces to be born and when my sister, and brother-in-law Ben, asked me to be his godfather I felt immense pride and joy. Within days I had given him the only christening present I could think of. I enrolled him as a Junior Blue. I was equally happy and proud when, ten years later, he told me that he supported Leicester City. Ed was born in Leicester, raised in Leicester, and went to school in Leicester. That is his team, and like me, many years ago, he had found his own identity and football was part of it.

Peter Reid's first full season coincided with the last year of the old Football League First Division. As predicted to Mum, City's form tailed off but a fifth-place finish for the second year running was a solid achievement. The battle for the title was fought out between my two nemeses of Leeds and

Manchester United. I consoled myself with the knowledge that at least one set of supporters would be thoroughly hacked off at the end of the season as their antipathy towards each other exceeded even my own. Leeds ultimately won, Alex Ferguson went back to his pillows, and the rest of us awaited the launch of the Premier League.

The opening weekend of the new era was widely welcomed with curiosity and intrigue. The First Division chairmen, envisaging the riches to come, had gone into their hotel huddles and conceived the notion of a lucrative breakaway from the Football League. They had then sold the idea to the rest of the Football League clubs with all the subtlety of a steamroller careering down a steep hill. In reality, they had no choice, 'fait accompli' – if you do not vote for it, we will do it anyway. But this average football fan had his doubts. Not so much suspicious as just not sure what would be different. The pitches would be the same size and the ball would still be round. There would be more televised matches thanks to the Sky deal but what would it all mean to anybody who attended live games?

The Premier League kicked off on a late-August Saturday, so nothing different there, but City did not join the party until two days later. While the nation waited eagerly for the overhyped *Monday Night Football* from Maine Road, the home crowd had another thing on their minds, and it wasn't Sky with their cheerleaders and skydiving mascots. Paul Lake would finally be making his long-awaited comeback. He had been missing for almost two years. I had not been there when Colin Bell had made his emotionally charged return from injury on Boxing Day 1977, but I had, of course, heard all about it. It represented a part of Manchester City folklore as essential as Bert Trautmann's broken neck and Denis Law's back-heel. I had heard all about the whispers going round the ground at half-time as the news that he was coming on as second-half substitute circulated, and I had heard of the tumultuous roar as he ran on to the pitch. I had heard stories of grown men crying and how, inspired by Bell, City went on to score four goals in the second half. Those who had been there were making the comparison.

In many ways it was unfair to both Bell and Lake. Bell had fulfilled his potential when he was struck down. Lake was all about promise, lots of it. Bell had 48 England caps in his locker. Lake had plenty at the junior levels but, although included in England squads, was yet to be capped at senior level. Bell was 32 at the time of his comeback; Lake was just 23. Nevertheless, there was a feeling that with a fit Lake, City could go better than their successive fifth-place finishes. The last game he played had Lake as a centre-half. Typical of his supreme versatility he made his comeback as a centre-forward. He played a crucial role in the opening goal that was then cancelled out by QPR's equaliser. A draw was a disappointing start but at least 'Lakey' was back. Then just ten minutes into the next game, a defeat at Middlesbrough, Lake's knee ligament snapped for the third time. He was to battle bravely for the next five years, against pain, medical science and, saddest of all, the club's negligence, but was never to play professional football again. Despite having played just 110 games, he was inducted in the City Hall of Fame in 2004, taking his rightful place among the club's greats.

The recovering Lake was a fan as much as he was a player, and he was only able to watch from the sidelines, sharing the frustration and anguish of every supporter, as Manchester's two football clubs moved inexorably in opposite directions. United would finish as champions of the first Premier League season and their Class of '92 were about to make their indelible mark on the game, just as the pride of City's Class of '86 hobbled off the stage.

City would fall dramatically off the pace during the next year. Reid was unable to build on his impressive start and the foundations that Kendall had put in place. The newspapers reported that his relationship with Peter Swales was becoming more fractious with each passing month. After a less-than-convincing opening to the 1993 season Swales appointed the little-known John Maddock as general manager. The idea was that the ex-*Daily Mail* journalist would act as a go-between for Reid and the chairman. It quickly looked as if the writing was on the wall for the manager. The extent of Maddock's vaunted man-management and mediation skills was to immediately recommend that Reid be dismissed. Swales duly obliged and started the search for what would be the 11th and ultimately final manager under his chairmanship. The speculation was that Maddock had been brought in to insulate Swales from the increasing wrath of the supporters and the derision of the media.

Managerial changes were also afoot in Bedfordshire. On a visit to one of my customers, the Whitbread Beer Company, I spotted a vacancy on the staff noticeboard. Nacanco had been good to me but it was time for a change. From supplier to customer. Given that my new employers also had breweries at Salmesbury, near Preston, and more significantly Boddingtons in Manchester, I knew that attendance at City home games would not be compromised. They also had some pretty cool beer brands.

My new role required me to liaise with key packaging suppliers. I was required at a meeting in Chester and, during the pre-meeting dinner, a softly spoken manager from the Continental Can Company leaned over towards me. 'You like your football don't you Dickie?' He pulled out a photograph of a skinny, long-haired blond teenager wearing a Manchester United shirt. 'This lad's going to be a proper footballer,' he told me, the parental pride clearly evident. His name was Colin Savage and his son was Robbie, a graduate of United's Class of '92, who went on to have a successful top-flight career with Leicester City, Birmingham City, and Blackburn Rovers before becoming a popular broadcaster.

Having, in effect, sacked Reid, Maddock was then given the job of finding his successor. If the appointment of the general manager, a role and individual now regarded with deep suspicion by the fans, had shocked football world then the name of Reid's successor would be a bigger surprise. Prior to the announcement of the new manager, *The Independent* had speculated on the leading candidates: 'Steve Coppell, the former Crystal Palace manager, Joe Royle, the Oldham boss who has turned Swales down in the past, Rodney Marsh, once the hero of the Kippax End, and Terry Venables, who Swales has admitted wanting to take to the club in the summer, are among the candidates to succeed Reid.'

Maddock duly convinced Swales to appoint, er, Brian Horton. The 'Brian Who?' nickname that Horton immediately acquired was somewhat unfair. He had been an accomplished midfielder first at Port Vale and Brighton and then as captain of Luton, accumulating more than 600 games in the process. City fans had good cause to remember him as David Pleat had jumped into his arms following his merry dance across the Maine Road pitch after the relegation dramatically inflicted by Luton. As a manager, Horton's curriculum vitae listed only Hull City and Oxford United. The new man struggled from the start at a club whose leadership structure was starting to spiral out of control, and whose supporters were at best ambivalent about his appointment. Results on the pitch were inconsistent and his demeanour, wide-eyed as if caught in the headlights and with an uncanny ability to answer every question with another – 'isn't it ?'; 'aren't they ?'; 'didn't we ?' – did not help him to establish credibility with the media, the supporters and, I suspect, a dressing room of senior professionals.

If Horton was having challenges in asserting his authority, that ship had long since sailed for Swales. Following the whole Maddock debacle (the ex-journalist resigned shortly after Reid's departure), the fans had endured enough and made it known at the ground, in the papers, and on local radio. In 20 years, Swales had brought to City 11 managers, two relegations, and one trophy. Even that piece of silverware was a distant memory of 18 seasons past. Despite his position on various FA boards, he was also regarded as a figure of ridicule both within City and the football community. His diminutive height was offset by his penchant for patent leather Cuban heels and the true nature of his hair – combover or toupee? – was a mystery for all. It all betokened vanity, egotism, and ultimately an insecurity that was manifest in his leadership style. The campaign to remove him started and quickly accelerated. Like all great crusades, the worthy cause received spiritual blessing when even the local vicar publicly preached against Swales's tenure. With God on board, all that was now needed was someone to replace the lame duck chairman. Step forward Francis Lee.

Legend had it that Lee, a third of City's most celebrated triumvirate of Bell, Lee, and Summerbee, had made his millions in bog roll and waste management. The truth was that his business interests were wider than that, but the obvious associations of toilet paper and Manchester City provided the better newspaper copy. The 'Forward with Franny' campaign was up and running, swept along on a populist wave, and powered by desperation, militancy, and blind optimism. The levels of enthusiasm for the iconic Lee's cabal exceeded any real financial substance that the group could bring to the club. After an increasingly bitter campaign he assumed control as a minority shareholder with his priority to ensure that that he was still controlling a Premier League club at the season's end. In March, with City once more hovering dangerously around the relegation places, Horton made a move into the transfer market. The signings of Peter Beagrie, Paul Walsh, and particularly the unknown East German Uwe Rösler proved to be inspirational, bringing the goals and energy into the side that ensured survival. The final home fixture, a 2-2 draw against Chelsea, marked the last game to be played in front of the Kippax Road terrace. Following Hillsborough and the Taylor Report it would be demolished and replaced by a new all-seater, hospitality-friendly stand.

Relaxed in the knowledge that Premier League football was guaranteed the fans partied on the Kippax, celebrating the great memories that the old terrace held. The odd inflatable banana was even seen to make a comeback.

Popular convention would have it that the rambling memoirs of a man just short of his 30th birthday should, by this point, have included some recall of romantic liaisons, or failing that, just carnal liaisons. It is not out of consideration to other parties that I have omitted any such detail. Such episodes occurred but they were few and of short duration. My natural shyness proved a challenge and the fact that this was often coupled with an inconvenient tendency to embark on random stress-induced spells of projectile vomiting meant that I wasn't always the best catch for a romantic night out. Well, not a second one anyway.

Close friends have frequently reminded me about the rather special meal I once prepared for a female colleague. The young lady was considered the 'office catch' so the date itself was regarded as something of a coup. I had gone to great lengths to prepare a gourmet experience that was as exquisite as it was intimate: melon balls served with prawns followed by chicken sautéed in a tarragon sauce. The ginger nut roll with whipped cream was the dessert rather than any proposed after-dinner activity. Unfortunately, she, or to be more accurate her mother, called me late in the afternoon to cancel, citing a spurious illness or accident. As the food was already prepared and the champagne chilled, I considered that it would have been wasteful not to consume it. All of it. I dressed, took my seat at the dining table, and serenaded by *The Best of Barry White*, I set about demolishing the culinary feast on my own, bubbly and all. My friends are able to recall it because their abiding memory of the evening was one of talking to me, in my inebriated stupor, as I telephoned them one by one to lament about the cruel nature of true love.

Had that night gone to plan I am sure that it would ultimately have ended up the same way it did with Sarah, a lady I met when, at 29, I was a little older. I was introduced to Sarah at a Flitwick house party held in a colleague's home. She was studying a post-graduate diploma at a local college, and we started seeing each other for a while. From Lincolnshire farming stock, she had no interest in football and consequently found my obsession somewhat baffling and often frustrating. I liked her very much and tried my best to be attentive. I would occasionally give up a Saturday afternoon to take her on a country walk around the Bedfordshire countryside, sometimes making the ultimate sacrifice of leaving my pocket radio at home. We would wander, hand in hand, through a picture-postcard village and as she was admiring the pretty cottages and the historic church, I would be desperately looking for a red telephone box. Once one had been located, I would dive straight in there, dialling my trusted 0898 121191 to obtain the latest live updates. Whereas most of her friends might have worried about their boyfriends sneaking off to call other women, I furtively made excuses to call my football club. Sarah just about tolerated that, but it did all come to a head shortly after she had graduated and returned to live with her parents in the Wolds. She would continue to visit me every couple of weekends and with careful planning I could combine my football activities around her visit, ensuring she received the attention she deserved.

One weekend Sarah had the romantic notion of paying a surprise visit. Sweet as the idea was, it also proved problematic as I had prior commitments. We enjoyed a quiet Friday night together and then some of Saturday morning, but in the afternoon, City were playing so I set off to the match. It had never occurred to me to take her along and she entertained herself alone. I arrived back home in time to go out for dinner, but she was a little disappointed when I suggested we could do coffee at home as I did not want to miss *Match of the Day*. At this point in my life, I also happened to be playing regular Sunday-morning football, so as we lay in bed the next day, I had to explain that her plans for a lie-in followed by a drive out for a nice country pub lunch were not entirely compatible with the activities of Fidus Boddingtons French Horn FC and their dodgy goalkeeper. I did make the concession of only having one post-match pint and returned to a beautifully clean house and the smell of a roast dinner. We dozed through the afternoon, me watching the live game on Sky and nodding off and she, well I am not too sure to be honest, but I suspect making plans for the evening. At some point the washing-up fairy also paid a visit as when I woke up the kitchen was pristine to a standard beyond my capability and quite frankly my comfort. It must have been about six o'clock when I got up off the sofa and went upstairs, returning a few minutes later with my kitbag.

'Do you need that washing?' she asked.

Unbeknown to her I had recently joined a Sunday night five-a-side league at the local leisure centre. I explained that the games were only 15 minutes long and I would most likely be back within the hour, but I could sense that I had probably pushed it a bit too far this time. She was not a temperamental person; it would probably have been easier if she had thrown the immaculately clean frying pan at me.

'Richard,' she said quietly. She was a bit posh like that and did not like to call me 'Dickie'. 'You know I sometimes think that you care about Man City more than you care about me.'

My reply was crass and not even that original: 'I think I probably care about Man United more than I care about you'.

I went to the five-a-side and when I returned her car was no longer outside my house. The choices we make in life. As somebody else more famously remarked at the time, 'There were three of us in the relationship and it felt a bit crowded.'

I did not intend my clumsy response to be hurtful and I genuinely was sorry to lose Sarah from my life, but it did also betoken an involuntary honesty. Notwithstanding the Manchester United comment, football in general had been my constant for so long. On a wider level it had never let me down, I knew what to expect, and there was a relationship of mutuality. It was reliable, consistent, and not too demanding of me. In many ways I did love football more than any relationship and I knew that to commit myself to a relationship properly would mean I would compromise on football and that would always be a choice that would be lurking in the dark shadows. I was not ready to let go.

And then there was 'Merv'. Merv was not her real name and for these purposes we will call her Doris. She was a lovely girl I saw for a couple of months during the summer of Italia '90. She was originally from southern Europe; Greece, I think. As sometimes betokens ladies from this region, she did have a slight but detectable adornment on her upper lip. I made the schoolboy error of telling my friends this. Unfortunately, the Australian Test cricket team were touring England at the time. The significance of this fact is that the Australians had within their number the splendidly moustached Merv Hughes. Doris was the antithesis of the larger-than-life Merv Hughes, apart from that one minor detail; she was cultured, petite, and placid. I was far too gentlemanly or maybe cowardly to tell her why my friends kept referring to her as Merv so we went our separate ways.

The single life did not unduly concern me. I saw it as a reasonable trade-off that enabled me to pursue my lifelong passion without the constraints that I perceived a committed relationship would present. Nevertheless, I envied and admired friends who had seemingly managed to strike that balance and settle into a family life. Foremost among these was Saint, who finally tied the knot with Helen. I was hugely honoured to be asked to be his best man and surprised nobody when I turned up for the wedding unaccompanied. I did feel some regret that my bachelor status was looking increasingly like a permanent state of affairs and briefly reappraised my priorities as Saint and Helen embarked on their new, fully rounded life together. However, theirs was a late-July wedding and the new season was only a few weeks away so too much reappraisal and contemplation would have to wait for another day.

Franny Lee's early leadership contrasted sharply with the previous regime as he tried to replace Swales's authoritarian ways with a more inclusive and open style. This manifested itself with the new policy of inviting a City fan to sit on the board. The *King of the Kippax* editor, Dave Wallace, was asked to attend certain parts of board meetings. It proved to be an ill-founded and unworkable concept, but an interesting experiment, exciting and optimistic while it lasted. The fans' representative was excluded from some of the more sensitive (and revealing) aspects of the board's discussions and therefore felt unable to contribute or influence effectively. In contrast, where the open style was far more manifest was on the pitch. Horton had stumbled upon something with his recruits and started the new season playing attractive, expansive football. The Maine Road game against Spurs in October saw City run out 5-2 winners in an early Premier League classic. Less than a month later this carefree, attacking football was exposed in a 5-0 mauling at Old Trafford. City's season was never to recover and by Easter the battle for survival was once again a very real one. Horton ultimately steered the ship to safety, but his appointment, which had been the final chaotic act of the Swales era, felt doomed to end in dismissal from the start. Lee, who had always been suspected of wanting to put his own man in the job, duly fired the unlucky manager.

When the chairman did make his first managerial appointment, he found a man in his own likeness as he chose a long-standing friend. Alan Ball and Francis Lee were born within 20 miles of each other, almost exactly a year apart. They had both learnt their football and had their greatest successes with Lancashire clubs and then England. Both were diminutive in height but large in personality. Neither lacked self-confidence or opinion. It is said that at Ball's first team talk with the City squad he was not shy of referring to his World Cup winner's medal of a distant and nostalgic past and that this was a continuing theme throughout his tenure. There is no doubt that it set the tone for a difficult relationship with many of his senior professionals.

The results indicated that this was not a happy camp. City were winless and bottom of the table in November 1995. With just two points scored, relegation was looking like a certainty, but a brief revival spearheaded by a talent so unique to anything before seen at City gave some hope. On the eve of the season Lee and Ball had followed up on a tip-off from a hopeful agent and signed Georgi Kinkladze from Dinamo Tbilisi for a bargain £2m. Kinkladze had recently starred against Wales for his national team, Georgia, but in truth few of us had ever heard of him or knew what to expect. He was in same physical mould of Ball and Lee, but he also possessed, by way of his mother's obsession with ballet and her true ambitions for his career choice, a remarkable nimbleness and quickness of feet. He took a few weeks to settle into his new surroundings but as he improved, so did the results and he quickly became the new hero and hope. When he was dancing past opponents, he was electrifying to watch and whatever they might have had across the city at Old Trafford, they certainly didn't have anything like Kinkladze.

Into the late winter, City had at least given themselves some hope of escaping from the dire early season run. Along with Kinkladze's flair there were signs of real fight, with an industrious young midfield of Garry Flitcroft and Steve Lomas making up for Kinkladze's undoubted defensive deficiencies. For all his artistry, tracking back was just not his thing. The next game I could get to was Newcastle at home. How would Kinkladze fare against Kevin Keegan's title-chasing, free-scoring Magpies? I drove up only to find the game was ticket-only and sold out. I was not going to waste the petrol money so bought a vastly overpriced ticket from a tout outside the ground. City did not win, the game ended 3-3, but it was worth every penny spent. Kinkladze ran the show with his jinking runs, creative passing, and mesmerising dribbling. City took the lead three times and were pegged back each time. Two weeks later, Kinkladze tip-toed through the Southampton defence and scored his signature goal. I watched it at home and immediately I knew I wanted to see more. The time had come to get a season ticket once again. The only question was what division would I be watching my football in?

With three games to go City were still in the bottom three, but all was not yet lost. I was seated in the newly opened Kippax Stand to see a nervy 1-0 home win against Sheffield Wednesday and the following week drove to Villa Park knowing that if results conspired against City, relegation could be confirmed that day. City won 1-0. At least, if we went down, we would go down fighting. One game remained and one relegation place was yet to be decided. City were on 37 points, along with Coventry and Southampton. Hope still existed, but City's inferior goal difference plus the final opponents being Liverpool meant the odds were not stacked in our favour.

In the week leading up to the match, Peter Swales died. There is no doubt that the bitter battle for control of the club had cost him both his health and his purpose. His leadership style and decisions were questionable, but I do still think he acted with what he believed were best interests of the club at the time. Without City, it seemed he just lost the will to go on. Debates raged during the week as to whether the circumstances that had led to Sunday's decider were of his making or Lee's but it was too late for a meaningless blame game. Prior to the match a minute's silence was perfectly observed and it felt like the supporters and the former chairman had at last made their peace.

A very different kind of silence was soon to engulf proceedings. If City fans were hoping for a favour from a Liverpool side with the imminent FA Cup Final against United on their minds, we were in for a rude awakening. Within the first 15 minutes Liverpool had scored twice. It was not as if they were carving us apart; the first was a deflection, the second an own goal. With 20 minutes to go it remained 2-0 and relegation looked a certainty. A City penalty converted by Rösler gave some belief, then Kit Symons pounced on the loose ball from a corner to volley home for 2-2. This would now be sufficient if Southampton or Coventry were to lose. As the clock moved into injury time the scores remained level. A spurt of frantic activity on the City bench indicated that perhaps there had been a crucial goal elsewhere. Word went from the management to the players that Southampton were losing and a draw would now be sufficient. Steve Lomas walked the ball into the Platt Lane corner to use up valuable seconds. Suddenly, Niall Quinn, substituted, showered, and dressed in his trademark disco pants, leapt from the bench and chased down Lomas, alone in the corner. The news from Southampton had been misinformation – they were still level, and City needed a winning goal. The final whistle went and City were again relegated, this time while 'protecting' their doomed position.

Only one club, my club, could go down in such bizarre circumstances.

I watched the game from the luxury of the new executive boxes in the rebuilt Kippax. My sister Kathy, ever considerate of her brother's passion, had made a fortunate marriage choice. My brother-in-law, Chris, was a director of a company whose chief executive was a long-standing City supporter and had taken a season-long subscription to one of the facilities. Wined and dined, we watched the debacle unfold from the detached splendour of the hospitality box with the unsavoury backdrop of United winning the league being shown on the in-suite television. I felt like an observer rather than a participant as I longed to be in among the passion and pain of the fans in the seats below me. Later that evening I watched Niall Quinn give an honest and frank interview about the shortcomings of the City team and offer a heartfelt apology. A man to face up the cameras, he looked as if he too was feeling the pain every bit as much as the supporters. He had played his last game for City. Who else would leave in the summer? Would the vultures swoop for Kinkladze? One of the motivations for buying my season ticket had been to see Kinkladze. I would be watching second-tier football, and would he even stick around?

One week later it got worse as the same Liverpool side, proudly wearing their infamous white suits but meekly waving white flags, surrendered in the FA Cup Final. United were winners of the Double and City had been relegated. I watched the final, supporting Liverpool of course, with some friends in Flitwick, where I had now bought my first house. Afterwards we went to the local pub. Several pints into the evening a group of red-shirted United fans came in, stopping off for a celebratory drink on their way north. I turned to my friends and told them, 'I am not putting up with this.' I got up and walked to my home across the road. I went upstairs, defiantly put on my sky blue City shirt and returned to the pub. Just how much City would be needing me and every other one of their supporters I could not imagine, but this was not a time for hiding my colours.

10

Rolling with It

NEWCASTLE'S SPECTACULAR implosion to gift United the Premier League meant the only trophy adorned with black and white ribbons that summer was the one won by Germany. It was the heady summer of Euro '96 and football was coming home. Finally, for the first time since the year of my birth, England was hosting an international tournament. It was a temporary but welcome respite from the disappointment of relegation, but also one that came with an annoying side effect. The occupants of workplaces up and down the country all suddenly started to believe that they were football experts. Authorities on all things technical and tactical. My Luton office was no exception. Overnight, assistant brand managers and inventory planners shared opinions on whether Terry Venables should go with the 'Christmas tree' or 'diamond' formation. Given that I predominately worked with marketers, that was one whole lot of inflated opinion. It did not, however, deter me from putting my football snobbery aside and ingratiating myself a couple of the company 'higher-ups' to blag corporate tickets whenever I could.

I managed to avoid sobriety for nearly 24 hours courtesy of the Queen's Club corporate hospitality tent at tennis's Stella Artois Championships one sunny Friday. This was followed by England vs Scotland at Wembley the next afternoon. I had intended to go home to Flitwick in between but never made it as the two events merged, briefly interrupted by a few hours' sleep in Hyde Park. The only 'sassenach' among hundreds of good-natured Scots. I delicately made my way to Wembley a little 'tired and emotional' but that all quickly evaporated in the special atmosphere of the occasion. An international encounter that felt more like The Rose and Crown vs The Auld Hoose. There was no better cure for tired and emotional than the delirium of witnessing two of the most exhilarating minutes of football unfold before me. David Seaman's penalty save was immediately followed by Gazza's wonder goal and 'dentist's chair' celebration. A week later I returned to watch England's cathartic penalty shoot-out win against Spain, with Stuart Pearce's 'psycho drama' daring the nation to dream once more. I was back in the pub, in Flitwick, as England lost to Germany in the semi-final.

The disappointment, as it had been with Italia '90, was real but it was also short-lived. I would have loved to see England win the tournament but club football, and City, was a bigger priority for me. I am not embarrassed to say that I felt a much closer affinity to my club and its supporters than I did to the national team. Maybe that was partly because of my first experience at an England international, just a few months before Euro '96. The occasion would go down in infamy, a fixture against the Republic of Ireland in Dublin that was abandoned after 20 minutes following a riot by so-called England fans. A guest of Murphy's Brewery, I was the only Englishman among our party. My embarrassment for both my country and my hosts ran deep and was a sorry reminder of the nationalistic ignorance of my schooldays. But tragically, unlike the playground at St Michael's, most of the perpetrators were grown, mature men, some no doubt parents and professionals. My hosts saw me safely back to my hotel room after the match had been curtailed, conscious that an English accent amid an angry and insulted Dublin could have serious repercussions for my safety.

Given the choice of England winning Euro '96 or City getting promoted I would have chosen promotion any day. Maybe it is because of people like me, and a common attitude of parochialism throughout all levels of the game, that England has failed to address its shortcoming, as a national team with a consistent unified approach. But as the choice was not a binary one, I stood right behind England during those weeks and was belting out 'football's coming home' with all the gusto of the next man. It was still being sung on the opening day at Maine Road as I took my place in the Kippax for the new season, this time with the words optimistically altered, 'We're going up, we're going up, City's going up.'

Football fans rarely learn from past failure and the popular view on the Kippax was that we would indeed go straight back up. This was now considered more likely as the gap between the Premier League clubs and the First Division – as it had been renamed – was starting to emerge on so many levels, meaning that City should have a financial advantage, in the short term at least. We had also held on to Kinkladze and he would surely dance through second-tier defences at will. Inevitably, things did not go to plan.

After just four games Alan Ball saved his long-time friend from having to make an uncomfortable decision. He resigned. The fans had made their feelings known and a poor start to the season brought forward what many had seen as inevitable for many months. Ball's last act was to prove a significant one, the acquisition of Arsenal reserve forward Paul Dickov, a player in the Ball and Lee mould. Lee went looking for his next manager and City settled into mid-table mediocrity. Kinkladze struggled to cope with the man-marking strategy that most teams deployed. In many games, it was more of a case of 'men' marking. For a club with little money, an average squad, and a track record of boardroom mismanagement the list of managers linked with the role was surprisingly ambitious. Dave Bassett discussed the role and declined; George Graham got in his car and started heading north but by the time he reached Watford Gap got cold feet and turned around. Joe Royle was (again) courted but also turned it down. When, finally, Steve Coppell was appointed, I was quite pleasantly satisfied. He projected an articulate and intelligent persona and had previously developed a very good Crystal Palace side. I could get past my aversion that an ex-United player was taking charge, especially as it appeared that nobody else wanted the job.

Prior to Coppell's arrival, City had a formidable cup tie to negotiate. In their rich and glorious history City had never lost a two-legged match by more than two goals. This history included meetings with not just the elite of England but also some of Europe's biggest names, such as AC Milan and

Juventus. Enter Third Division Lincoln City in the League Cup. City took an early lead in the first leg before Lincoln went on to score five without reply. The season was already looking like a long and troubled one.

Coppell brought a degree of organisation to the team and the signs were encouraging that a promotion push might yet be on the cards. Then, out of the blue, he too departed. Leaving the office for a lunchtime pint, I heard the news on the radio: 'After just 33 days in charge, Steve Coppell has resigned as manager of Manchester City due to ill health.' Ill health? What did that mean? Was he dying? When I got home, I watched Sky News as he explained that his doctors had advised him that the stress of managing City was seriously affecting his wellbeing and he should quit before it did irrevocable damage. You could not have made it up. Manchester City, the club that came with its own medically certified health warning.

There was no denying that he did not look a well man, ashen and gaunt. Francis Lee, sat next to him, did not look too good either. Confused and embarrassed, he projected the image of the caricatured self-made northerner trying to fathom out why a man could quit football because of mental health. Lee was trying his best to put a brave front on it, wondering where his next manager would be coming from, but his face said it all. His bewilderment, and that of many supporters, would turn to anger and then incredulity when Coppell, looking every bit the picture of good health, would return to Crystal Palace a few months later and lead them to promotion.

In many ways the haggard Coppell made him the ideal man for the City job: tired, stressed, and with the look of a man carrying the forlorn hopes of a systemically failing club on his shoulders. It was increasingly becoming the 'in' look for the fans, now living on the distant memory of a single trophy back in 1976. That is the thing with managers and players – as Coppell, and previously Kendall, demonstrated, they can walk out whenever they want, be it 33 days or longer. For the fans it is different. There is no walking away. Although you may occasionally think you have left it behind in pursuit of other, more rational and reliable interests, 'it' keeps sucking you back in. Stressed after 33 days, Stevie? Try 20 years then see how you feel. To be honest you get used to it. I believe they call it Stockholm Syndrome.

So, while the rest of the league's clubs were participants in the Manager of the Month competition, City were more interested in their manager *for* the month. Control of the stumbling jalopy was handed over to Coppell's assistant, Phil Neal. Neal had never really recovered from the stigma of his association with Graham Taylor's failed England regime and the derision that ensued. The City job was not one that he was going to be given full-time and was also one he probably did not want. He stepped in and performed with honesty and dignity but was facing too many obstacles both on and off the pitch. Results reflected the chaos and at the season's halfway point the third tier was a more likely prospect than a return to the top one. My glorious comeback as a season ticket holder was descending into farce.

After a predictably joyless Christmas, Lee, who was now accumulating managers at a rate that exceeded the boundless profligacy of Peter Swales, finally got his man. Well, at least he found someone who was willing to take on the job. Frank

Clark had established a reputation at Leyton Orient and had then stepped into Brian Clough's significant shoes and taken Nottingham Forest back into the Premier League and then into Europe. It represented as good an appointment as Lee could have hoped for. At the season's third attempt, City got a 'bounce' from the new manager. A few loan signings gave the team a better balance and Kinkladze was switched from his midfield role and the freedom and flair came back to his play, as did the goals. For a moment the play-offs looked like they might just be within reach, but the calamities of the early season were too much to overcome. The contrast in styles between the two men in charge at the start and end of the season could not have been greater. The campaign began with Ball belligerently waving his World Cup winner's medal and ended with the laid-back, rock 'n' roll-loving Clark literally strumming his guitar to his first-team squad at impromptu gatherings.

There was a time in every summer when I would let go of the season past and start to cross off the days before the start of the new campaign. I expect that for everyone it is different but for me, during all the 1990s, that time was cricket tour. Dr Harding's Touring XI was founded in 1955 by an eminent doctor who had been a member of the Sheffield University Cricket Club before retiring to the Wiltshire village of Whiteparish. Keen to maintain his links with Sheffield and cricket, he had invited the university team to come south and play against his new village cricket side. Professor Alan Usher, Saint's father, was one of those first tourists. For the next three decades the tour carried on in various guises and drew its touring members from various interested cricket bodies around Sheffield.

As the 1990s dawned, Dr Harding was long deceased and most of the original connections had been severed. The tour was struggling to pull in the required numbers needed for both the cricket and the vibrant socialising that went hand in hand. In danger of dying on its feet, it required fresh impetus. In stepped Saint and his brothers. The tour was reinvented, maintaining a core of medics through Saint's older brother, Alan junior, and introducing members of the Metropolitan Police cricket team through younger brother Adrian, a serving officer. Saint and I provided the contingent from the drinks industry, as Saint was now a qualified brewer and brewery owner. The Professor assumed the worthy position of club president, a role befitting a man of his stature. Dr Harding's Touring XI had re-formed itself into an explosive cocktail of medics, police officers, and alcohol industry professionals and generally behaved as might be expected when young professionals are let loose, free of responsibilities, for a long weekend in Wiltshire. In short, we upheld the good name and reputation of all touring teams. Football was my first love, but the cricket tour was a big part of my life for many summers and provided me with the laddish camaraderie and belonging that I valued. I was in my early 30s and I remained single, I had little responsibility at work or at home, and touring cricket played beautifully into my lifestyle, helping to pass the long close-season.

Our weekend of larks and lubrication was nicely staged in early July, midway between the football seasons. Sleep-deprived and nursing hangovers, we would emerge from our beds in the Fountain Inn and push our full English breakfasts around our plates while we waited for one of the younger tourists to go and collect the morning papers from the village shop. The papers were the red-tops of course and the front page would get a cursory glance. We would have an ongoing wager as to which celebrity of the day might meet their end while we were on tour. The Queen Mother regularly defied the odds and remained 'not out' while Marlon Brando, Luther Vandross, and Barry White all spectacularly lost their middle stumps.

All eyes would then turn to the sports pages. The Test match scores first and then the close-season transfer speculation. Lying in the beer garden of the Fountain, I read that City had signed Lee Bradbury for £3.6m. We had signed players who I'd never heard of before but that had been for about £300,000. Bradbury's transfer fee was more than double City's previous record. The new star striker was on the back page of *The Sun*, resplendent in the recently launched, garish Kappa kit that the Gallagher brothers of Oasis notoriety had modelled a few weeks earlier. I turned to my fellow tourists, most of whom also had a football interest. Nobody had heard of him. Francis Lee later admitted that he had not even heard of him when the manager requested the funds. He gave Clark the go-ahead, allegedly telling him, 'You had better be right as it's the last of the money.' Within five minutes of seeing Bradbury in a pre-season friendly, Lee felt his worst fears would be confirmed.

In Bradbury's defence, he did not set the fee and he had been a regular scorer for Portsmouth the previous season. But £3.6m! I do not know whether he had been strumming on the guitar too much or hanging round with his rock 'n' roll buddies but something happened to Clark that summer.

Maybe, just maybe, he had been on a cricket tour himself and come back a changed man. A few pints of the scrumpy can do that to you.

The previous season had ended on a high and optimism was abundant. Kinkladze's rediscovered form and his decision to sign a contract extension were great endorsements that maybe things were, after all, heading in the right direction. There was the cool Kappa kit, modelled by the Gallagher brothers, giving the club a modern take on the newly elected Tony Blair's 'Cool Britannia'. Britpop, Manchester City-style on the Maine Road pitch. It only felt right that I should turn up at Maine Road on that first day strutting along Platt Lane as if I had walked straight off an Oasis CD cover. But from day one all the progress that Clark had made evaporated. Kinkladze was restored to the deeper midfield role that so obviously did not use him to optimum advantage. The new signings took time to settle. In the case of Bradbury, who quickly assumed the unfortunate nickname of 'Lee Bad Buy', he did not settle at all. If my first year as a reborn season ticket holder had been a debacle then my second one was turning into an unmitigated shambles.

Amid a string of pitiful performances City did manage to pull out a 6-0 win against Swindon Town in November. As luck would have it, I missed that one. I happened to be in Zimbabwe at the time, my first venture outside of Europe. I was there with Colin, a work colleague and fellow cricket tourist, and Stephen, another colleague on a job transfer from a sister brewery in New Zealand. In two nerve-jangling weeks, we survived canoe safaris interrupted by recalcitrant hippos, snake pits, the vagaries of Zimbabwean motorists and ensuing police justice systems, and the hallucinogenic effects caused by an over enthusiastic dose of the anti-malaria drug, Larium. It all made watching City seem a bit like an afternoon tea party with mother. As City scored the sixth goal against Swindon, I was plummeting, head first, towards the Zambezi attached to the end of a bungee cord. Despite that welcome anomaly of a result, City were ominously descending towards the bottom of the division at similar speed. Luckily, my bungee held good, and I was able to bounce back to tell the story. City's bungee was about to snap snap and there would be no bounce back. After relegation from the Premier League Franny Lee had promised to get the club out of the First Division but surely the third tier was not what he had in mind.

That same November, City played bottom side Huddersfield Town at Maine Road. It was, by miserable coincidence, a decade to the day since that once-in-a-lifetime 10-1 victory. Full of youthful hope, the Class of '86 had swept the Yorkshiremen aside with the promise of so much more to come. A decade on, we lost by a single goal, hardly registering a shot, in a game as short of quality as most of those present had ever seen. The strains of 'You're not fit to wear the shirt' could be heard around the ground as the players left the pitch. Of course, the real issues behind ten wasted years lay far beyond the current team.

It had been the cruellest of winters, and when, in spring, the green shoots of a recovery failed to emerge on the Maine Road pitch, Clarke was fired. Immediately, and with uncharacteristic efficiency, the oft-courted Joe Royle was installed in his place. He had 14 games to save City from the ultimate humiliation. Royle acted fast by bringing in combative midfielder Jamie Pollock from Middlesbrough and, for a tenth of the Bradbury fee, the little-known Shaun Goater. Any initial improvement was marginal and City were staring into the abyss with two games remaining. The unthinkable second relegation could happen.

The season's penultimate game was at home to QPR, with the west London side just a point above City. I parked up and walked from the car to Maine Road, past those familiar red-brick terraces. The mood was sombre, and a sense of foreboding hung heavy in the air. Heads were bowed in contemplative thought, few words exchanged. The Moss Side residents stood on their doorsteps and watched with macabre fascination the cortège of fans shuffling past. Resembling mourners, it felt like we were on the way to our own funeral. The walking dead. Any hope of resurrection lay in the unlikely possibility that City could defy their dismal season-long form.

After just two minutes the gloom was briefly lifted, and the Kippax roared. Kinkladze had been left out by Royle for a couple of games, preferring to stake the future of the club on graft and grit. It had not worked and, restored to the team, the Georgian showed imagination in his head as well as his feet to curl a quickly taken free kick into the back of the QPR net. There were sighs of relief all round.

'We can get out of this.'

What then followed was a whole new chapter in City's capacity for cock-ups. Goalkeeper Martyn Margetson needlessly handled a back-pass in the penalty area; free kick to QPR. Rather than hanging on to the ball and arranging his defensive wall Margetson meekly handed it back to the QPR players who promptly took the set piece and calmly passed the ball into the empty net for 1-1. It had taken just five minutes to surrender the precious lead but that was merely the appetiser. My seat in the Kippax was about 20 rows from the front, level with the penalty spot at the North Stand end. If any perspective on what happened next could be described as the 'best seat' I certainly had claim to it. When Jamie Pollock, running at pace towards his own goal, intercepted a bouncing ball midway inside the City half I had the perfect view. His first touch took it away from the QPR midfielder, his second touch teed it up with poise and precision and his third touch, a deft header, lobbed the ball beyond the onrushing goalkeeper and into the net, making the score 2-1 to QPR. It was the kind of thing that Matthew Le Tissier was doing regularly for Southampton at the time, but always at the right end. It is a goal that is regularly featured in any YouTube list of top ten own goals. City fans looked at each other, a paradox of disbelief and knowing acceptance. The QPR supporters later voted for Jamie Pollock as 'The Most Significant Man of the 20th Century'. Bradbury later equalised but the result meant that QPR were safe, and City would go to the final game at Stoke occupying one of the relegation places.

City promptly rose to the occasion with a resounding 5-2 win, but the occasion refused to rise to City. Port Vale and Portsmouth recorded unlikely away wins and City were down. Officially called the Second Division under the post-Premier League rebranding, as far as every fan was concerned it was really the Third Division. As the team trooped off the

Britannia Stadium pitch, Kinkladze threw his shirt and boots into the away end. We all knew we had seen the last of this enigmatic, skilful but inconsistent midfielder and, in our hearts, we also knew that his inevitable departure was right thing for both him and the club. He had been our greatest hope and at the same time our greatest liability.

While Kinkladze stayed until the bitter end, Lee had not. Having stated at an earlier AGM that he would 'jump from the Kippax stand' should City go down he did not last long enough as chairman to make good his promise. Unable to implement the financial restructuring required and with his own credibility undermined by the managerial merry-go-round, Lee stepped aside relinquishing the chairmanship to the little-known David Bernstein. Bernstein's first public act was to issue an unequivocal and heartfelt apology to the supporters. The healing process had begun.

According to the film *Love Story*, true love means never having to say you are sorry. The significance of Bernstein's apology was never about the words or about admitting culpability, but it did acknowledge the special relationship between club and supporter. While chairmen, managers and especially players might come and go, the fans were there for the duration. However, for many the prospect of local derbies against Bury and Macclesfield Town felt like one humiliation too far. There comes a time when everybody has cause to assess the key relationships in their lives and many, including myself, were now going through that process. It had had started out as pure infatuation, an unconditional love. My sweetheart in sky blue could do no wrong – how could they when I was telling anybody who cared to listen to me that they were the best? It never occurred to me that I could be mistaken. The 1976 League Cup had proved to me that they *were* the best and I was sure that soon there would be many more trophies to follow.

Despite the odd hiccup with the Junior Blues, my love was reciprocated with letters from Joe Corrigan, my discounted season ticket, and then my appointment as ball boy. We were in it together. Life partners. The generally indifferent form and the heartbreaking 1981 FA Cup Final defeat had done nothing to diminish the feeling. As in all relationships though, there comes a point when you are able to recognise and admit that the other party has some faults and is maybe not the paragon of perfection you had told yourself for so long. That reality probably struck me around my 16th birthday. Growing up and wising up, I reluctantly started to accept that City came along with a host of imperfections. It was difficult at first, but I came to embrace the idiosyncrasies and foibles that made City what they were. They became endearing characteristics. Each failure and calamity on and off the pitch, and each gloriously unexpected triumph represented just another wrinkle line on the face of a loved one. I learnt to see it for what it was: character and personality. Every now and again, after a humiliating defeat, I would ask myself why? But I never once asked myself 'Who else?' I would unfailingly come back for more because it simply was and is who I am. It is me. It is immutable.

When searching for identity in a new school in a new town, City gave me that identity. When the pain of the bullying was crushing my self-esteem, City gave me my pride and purpose. What's more, they gave me hope, something to look forward to when it felt like there was nothing. When I did not have the mental courage to say 'I am a Paki lover' I would find the strength to proclaim my love for City and take everything that came with it. When I needed to escape from the trials and challenges of growing up, City was my refuge and my shelter. Inside Maine Road I would feel at home, with my second family. I belonged there. So, while I might be frustrated and angry, and from time to time feel used and let down, I never once considered walking away. Especially not at this lowest point. Besides, if I did then what had it all been for in the first place? The end of the journey would be so much sweeter for what had preceded it. City had been there for me and I would be there for City.

I had once discussed with my father, a renowned scientist and academic, the subject of faith and in particular his Catholicism. 'How could it be,' I asked him, 'that a man whose professional reputation relied on data, fact, and intrinsic proof of the theories that he was espousing could maintain such a strong belief in a God and religious doctrine for which there was no compelling scientific explanation?' He told me that it was precisely because of faith. Something that he valued as much as all the academic papers he had written and read. Faith was something so powerful that it transcended all the evidence and data. It did not require proof, it required belief. In the absence of hard evidence, it was subject to persecution, ridicule, and doubt but still it prevailed. A belief and trust in something so powerful that it defied all the data, all the evidence, and all reason. I suppose my relationship with City was one of faith and until the glorious second coming I would continue to believe and follow.

The ultimate relegation was, in many ways, a cathartic moment. It had to be. Surely it could not get any worse. The release of anger and frustration took place during the summer when the fixture list was published and the impending prospect of away trips to York, Lincoln, and Wrexham became reality. Royle had stayed on and Kinkladze, as expected, had not. While little-known in football circles, Bernstein came with a reputation as a formidable business leader. For a City chairman, he seemed uncharacteristically understated and was keen to play down expectations. He talked with refreshing clarity and honesty about the challenges that lay ahead. The return for the season's opener at Maine Road against Blackpool was greeted with a sense of acceptance and a little curiosity. The previous day, I had attended the funeral of Saint's father, the Professor, who had passed away after an illness. A range of family, senior academics, and high-ranking police officers mixed with people of all ages and from all walks of life, among them many cricket tourists. It was a fitting send-off that reflected his ability to engage with all characters, regardless of age, status, or position and gave great perspective to the relative insignificance of the season about to start.

The one constant at City, throughout all the turmoil, was the support. That the loyal fans would turn up in their numbers there was no question. A crowd of 32,000 attended the opening fixture and would continue to do so throughout the season. The irony today of hearing opposition crowds taunting City fans with choruses of 'where were you when you were shit?' is never lost on veterans of that era. Accepting the situation did not, however, countenance the prospect of anything other than a fleeting, one season ducking in the icy waters of the third tier. That belief was immediately affirmed with a comfortable 3-0 victory. A week later a reverse by the same score at Fulham suggested that things might not be quite as simple. The novelty of a new kind of football and never-visited stadia quickly wore off. Turning up at Wycombe, Lincoln, and York and deriding their 'Subbuteo' stands was fun for a few minutes but the joke quickly turned sour on the back of chastening defeats.

I had the dubious honour of presenting the match ball to the captains in the centre circle prior to the kick-off at Northampton Town. My old mate Nick, who did business with an ex-Northampton captain, had arranged it. Me having this responsibility amused my Northampton-born father no end as we talked about how my grandfather, Poppa, would have been proud. But leading the team out in front of 50,000 at Maine Road it was not. Nick, ever the willing and curious travel companion, accompanied me to Bournemouth to see nine-man City hang on desperately for a 0-0 draw after Jamie Pollock and then Kevin Horlock, for an offence the referee described as aggressive walking, had been sent off. None of the mediocrity put me off taking advantage of the freedom afforded by my job and using any opportunity to combine business with questionable pleasure. The geographical location of the stadia in the new division meant that potential beer packaging suppliers had to be found in far-off places where, coincidentally, factory audits and technical meetings coincided with City's arrival in town. Visits to the Boddingtons and Salmesbury breweries in Manchester and Preston continued to be a regular Friday afternoon feature unless of course City had a midweek home game, in which case I was suddenly 'required' to be in the north-west on a Wednesday. However, there was no getting away from the fact that we were struggling to find our feet in a poor league, against poor opposition with poor referees. Heading to Christmas we were not much more than a poor mid-table third-tier side. A desperate situation called for a major move into the transfer market. A new Kinkladze had to be found.

Andy Morrison's forearms were wider than the Georgian's thighs. The barrel-chested centre-half with anger management issues arrived from Huddersfield Town for just £80,000 and looked more like one of the draymen who delivered the kegs to The Beulah. The piano tuner had been replaced by the piano shifter. Morrison turned out to be one of the most important signings that City ever made. His deceptively quick mind and movement did not go unnoticed but what was most apparent from the first moment was his leadership. In a team that lacked on-field cojones and a division that demanded physical and mental presence, he brought both. Royle quickly appointed Morrison as his captain and the effect was immediate on both his team-mates and opposing players. City would no longer be bullied in the Second Division playground. Royle later described him as the 'man for the job and the division'. Royle had also spoken of City being an oil tanker that would take time to turn around but, once the turn had been completed, the sheer weight of force would keep it moving inexorably forwards. Like many others, I can look back and pinpoint the moment the tanker started to turn.

I had spent early December 'Down Under' with Saint; the ever-understanding Helen once more disproving my theory that marriage and being a passionate sports fan were incompatible. Along with his brother Adrian and cricket tour companion 'The Whippet', we had taken ourselves on a long-promised trip to see England play Australia in the Ashes. Following the Ashes opener at Brisbane's 'Gabba' ground we had toured the Gold Coast. We returned from the antipodean sun just before Christmas to a cold and wet England. City's form was as gloomy as the weather. The two previous results had been a defeat at York and a hard-fought Boxing Day win at Wrexham. Stoke, the early season leaders, were the visitors at Maine Road. If City were to push for promotion then they had to make their move. The players left the Maine Road pitch to half-time jeers. Losing 1-0, the performance had been lethargic and listless. Were the faithful finally losing their patience? Only the players and the management team know what was said at half-time, but legend has it that frank and robust words were exchanged. With the boos still ringing in their ears, uncomfortable home truths were spelt out and nothing was left unsaid. The City team that emerged after half-time was a different one. There was a new intensity and purpose. Within five minutes of the restart Paul Dickov had equalised and belief visibly spread through the team. When Gareth Taylor scored the late winner, the tanker had started its slow turn.

While City wrestled with their inconsistency in the first half of the season, Fulham and Walsall had taken control of the automatic promotion places. The lottery of the play-offs was the best that could be hoped for and on the back of an impressive second half, play-off qualification was achieved with comfort and, more importantly, confidence. It might have only been Wigan, and it might have only been the Second Division play-off semi-final, but the Maine Road crowd was ready to blow off the last lingering cobwebs of malaise. After all, we were just one step from Wembley. I took the afternoon off work and drove north up the M6, joining other City cars trailing scarves on the way. It could have been as if we were heading in the opposite direction to Wembley itself for a 'proper' cup final. The match was tight and Shaun Goater's goal was scrappy as he bundled the ball across the line from about a yard. All Wigan supporters will, of course, tell you that it was his arm that propelled the ball.

The final whistle was greeted with more relief that triumph. One game stood between promotion to the First Division. While the pitch invasion was probably not consistent with the scale of achievement, to see happy, smiling, singing faces at Maine Road, was a welcome change.

Wem-ber-lee, Wem-ber-lee,
It's a shitty place in London that we're never going to see.
Suddenly the lyrics needed to be altered. Now all I needed to do was get my ticket.

There had been a long-standing joke on the Kippax that it was a good thing City didn't get to any cup finals as the ticket office would only screw up the allocation. The joke was not without an element of truth, based on the frustrations of many fans trying to navigate their way around bizarre ticket allocation systems for the bigger games. After phone calls and faxes desperately explaining why I should not have to go all the way from Bedfordshire to Manchester to present myself in person in order to collect my ticket, the envelope finally landed on my doormat. I recognised it immediately as I had received many tickets via the post, but none for a Wembley final. I opened it with every bit of excitement as when receiving my childhood letters from Joe Corrigan. No signed letter from Joe in this envelope, just a small piece of paper with words the 'Wembley Stadium' and 'Manchester City Football Club' next to each other. In 33 years I had never seen that combination of words on a ticket.

That same evening, United scored two goals in the final three minutes of the Champions League Final to defeat Bayern Munich and complete an historic Premier League, FA Cup, and European Cup treble. By contrast, on Sunday, City would play Gillingham for the right to play in the second tier of English football. As Ole Gunnar Solskjaer prodded home United's winner, I turned the television off and went to bed with a resigned groan. I had more important things than trebles to dream about.

My Wembley day was mapped out to the last detail. The train from Flitwick to West Hampstead. A couple of pints in West Hampstead – there were bound to be fellow fans hanging around there – and then the rest of the journey on the tube. I got to the ground early, by 2pm, completing a circuit of the old stadium as I savoured the atmosphere. The fans of both teams, lapping up this rare occasion, were in good voice. Morrison, as he had been most of the season, was an injury concern but he was declared fit and able to lead the team. City were in the bright yellow and blue away strip but who cared – the much-vaunted blue Kappa home kit had brought little luck over the last two seasons.

The first half was unmemorable. I cannot recall anything that happened on the pitch, other than feeling tense and uneasy throughout. City did not look like they were in any danger, but neither did they look like scoring. The expectant enthusiasm of the support was now subdued. The longer it stayed 0-0 the more the nerves would spread, and the second half continued in the same vein. None of the players were taking any risks – no one wanted to make the error that would cost the game and wipe out a season's endeavour.

Ten minutes to go and there are still no goals. Extra time beckons. Then a rare moment of quality. A pass is threaded through the City midfield and Carl Asaba outpaces the defence to shoot under goalkeeper Weaver. The Gillingham end of the stadium, quiet until now, explodes in celebration. Before City can launch another attack, Gillingham break and score again. It's 2-0. Their supporters and players are in dreamland; with eight minutes to go the game is as good as done. City do not make a habit of coming back from 2-0 down.

For the next eight minutes I stand in silence. Leaning against one of the famous Wembley stanchions, I stare blankly into space. On the pitch is a blur of City yellow and Gillingham blue. Is it the tear in my eye that is creating the blur? I am thinking about another season of journeys to the godforsaken 'Subbuteo' grounds of the third tier. I am thinking about United winning the Treble and parading the trophies around Manchester. Most of all I am wondering again why I give so much of myself only to be rewarded like this. I had been so sure we could not screw it up this time. Surely not against Gillingham. I look at the scoreboard to check that I am not imagining this. The brightly lit 'GILLINGHAM 2 MANCHESTER CITY 0' says it all. If I need any more confirmation, I only need to look at the exits. Hundreds of City fans are streaming away, tired, hurt, and unable to stay to the end of another disappointment. The match is not yet over but I consider joining them. Goater breaks into the penalty area but is tackled before he can get his shot away. The loose ball breaks to Kevin Horlock who drills it, left-footed and low into the Gillingham net; 2-1.

What I do not need right now is hope. As every football fan knows, it is the hope that kills you. Still, while City are out there, hope exists. After all, United scored twice in the final minutes five days earlier. But they are United, and this is City.

The added time board goes up. Five minutes. A groan from the Gillingham end and pleasantly bemused looks from the City fans wondering where the five minutes have come from. City pump long balls forward to Goater and Gareth Taylor but Gillingham are holding out. One minute left. Wiekens from deep inside the City half goes long again, and this time Taylor wins the header. The ball falls to Goater and he manages to poke it forward. Paul Dickov, Alan Ball's parting gift, takes one touch and then fires the ball past the goalkeeper and high into the roof of the Gillingham net. The City end goes crazy. I grab the nearest person to me; anybody, I don't care. We hug and dance and we laugh and cry. Joy, but most of all relief. And yet it is only 2-2. The final whistle has gone and like the players we must gather our composure for extra time.

We are slowly working our way through the gamut of emotions this afternoon. The excitement and hope as we made our way to Wembley soon to be replaced by the sickening nerves as the importance of the occasion sank in. Then the abject agony and desperation followed briefly by relief and ecstasy. There is no room to feel triumphant just yet, but there is an electric giddiness among the fans, sparked by what they have just witnessed.

The momentum is with City on the pitch and, just as importantly, the belief is with City on the terraces. Both teams slug out extra time, reserves of energy all expended. There are a few wild hopeful swings but no killer blows. Penalties it shall be. Referee Mark Halsey doubles down on his generous five minutes of injury time by deciding that the penalty shoot-out will take place at the City end. Horlock goes first; 1-0 City. Paul Smith picks up the ball for Gillingham and makes that slow walk to the penalty spot. The City whistles and hoots start slowly but by the time he puts down the ball and turns the noise is deafening, a crescendo of hostility and distraction. I am not sure how anybody could block that out. He does well to even get the ball to the goal, but it is a weak effort and Nicky Weaver's trailing leg does enough to stop it. Still 1-0 City.

Goal hero Dickov goes next and hits both posts but not the back of the next. Still 1-0.

Gillingham's Adrian Pennock blasts the next one high into the north London sky. Four penalties and three misses, but it remains advantage City.

Terry Cooke steps up and scores as does John Hodge for Gillingham; 2-1 to City.

Richard Edghill, who has never scored a goal, places number four firmly into the net with all the aplomb of a seasoned marksman before kissing his badge; 3-1 City.

Gillingham have two penalties left. If they miss either one, City are promoted.

Guy Butters shoots hard but straight at the falling Weaver who is able to readjust and parry the ball.

As City fans dance in the stands Weaver takes off on a deranged run around the Wembley pitch pursued by his delirious team-mates. And now, finally, there is jubilation. Never in my wildest nightmares had I imagined that my first taste of glory would be winning the Second Division play-off final, but did it matter? Did it hell. United could keep their Treble. This was real, this was City, and this was ecstasy.

Andy Morrison hauled his beer-barrelled torso up the Wembley steps and for the first time I saw a City captain hold a trophy aloft. The players and supporters celebrated long and hard together, both acknowledging each other's part. Joe Royle looked physically and mentally exhausted, wasted, as he took his leave down the tunnel while acknowledging the fans with a measured wave and a clap. He knew there was more work to be done.

I decided against having a celebratory pint in West Hampstead, eager to get home and watch every minute of the match on video. Like Royle, I also looked and felt knackered. Just a few hours previously I had walked the short distance from my small two-up, two-down house to the train station. The residents of Flitwick had been going in and out of the shops and the children had been playing in the park opposite. I retraced my steps of the morning, and the children were still playing in the park. Oblivious to my crazy day, the people of this small leafy Bedfordshire town were going about their business as if nothing of any note had been going on elsewhere. A picture of suburban order. It felt like I had been in a parallel universe for the day.

Those of a certain age may remember a gentleman by the name of Mr Benn (not the politician). As the eponymous hero of a 1970s children's cartoon series, the sober Mr Benn, resplendent in suit and bowler hat, would leave his house at 52 Festive Road and take the short walk to a costume shop. On the way there he would pass the children playing in the park and the adults going about their daily business. Once in the costumiers the mysterious shop owner would appear 'as if by magic' and suggest an outfit for Mr Benn to try on. He would change his clothes and then step out into a magical other world appropriate to the costume of the day. There he would embark on an intriguingly bizarre adventure in which good invariably prevails over evil. The modestly triumphant Mr Benn then miraculously reappears back in the shop where he changes back into his civvies and retraces his steps to 52 Festive Road. As he nears his home the same children are playing, and the same adults are still doing whatever they happened to be doing. Of course, they are completely oblivious to Mr Benn's surreal day. As I walked down Coniston Road, I pondered my own day and observed my neighbours, still absorbed in their own activities. I nodded in deference to my fellow adventurer. Since the age of nine I had wondered what it would feel like when City won at Wembley. Now I knew. It felt like Mr Benn.

11

Upwardly Mobile

AS UNITED paraded their three tin pots around the streets of Stretford, Joe Royle was planning for City's new season. In the immediate euphoria of Wembley there had been talk of an open-top bus parade. Royle had instantly declined the suggestion, bringing a sense of honest perspective to the club's achievement. Nobody disagreed with him. For once this fan was looking forward to the coming campaign with a rare sense of pragmatism. After the last few years, a season of dull consolidation would be welcome, but Royle was having none of it. He had maintained that once the tanker had turned around there would be no stopping it. He wanted back-to-back promotions.

A home defeat in the opening game against Wolves was more in line with the fans' expectations than Royle's. This was followed by a goalless draw at Fulham in a game more memorable for Andy Morrison's red card, awarded for the offence of licking Stan Collymore's nose. When we thought the afternoon could not get any more bizarre, Nick and I rounded it off by sharing post-match pints in a west London pub in the company of Noel Gallagher. The third game, a resounding 6-0 win at home to Sheffield United, finally got the season going. I was present of course, still making the drive up from Bedfordshire and, when I could, manipulating my modest contributions to Whitbread's beer business around midweek matches. By Christmas things would change, and my matchday commute and expectations for the season would increase significantly. We were both upwardly mobile.

My career as an unspectacular marketing operations manager had been stagnating. Whitbread was a good company, one where I had been fortunate to forge some great friendships, and the work enabled me to indulge my passion in a convenient way, but I needed a new challenge. I looked around at a few jobs and was invited for an interview at Diageo's Technical Centre in Bishop's Stortford. The company seemed a good fit. I had spent a career working my way up the value chain in the drinks industry, from pulling pints in The Beulah to selling beer cans at Nacanco and then on to working with great beer brands. Diageo, owners of Smirnoff, Johnnie Walker, Guinness, and Baileys, seemed the next logical move. I joined the company in December 1999 and in my first week was asked if I was interested in a move to the USA office. I thought about it for approximately 30 seconds and agreed. Twenty-five of those seconds were spent thinking about the implications it entailed for following City. The other five were frittered away on trivial things such as health insurance, accommodation, money, and security.

At Maine Road, progress had also been dramatic, justifying Royle's pre-season confidence. I left for Connecticut in the first week of the new millennium with City second in the First Division and hopeful of a Premier League return. Royle had given the team the self-belief to push on. He was not going to be cowed by the trauma and shambolic events of past seasons the way the fans, or at least some of us, were occasionally disposed to be. The last game I saw before I jetted off was at home to Fulham. City won 4-0 and Shaun Goater scored a hat-trick. It was the first time I heard his song:

Feed the Goat,
Feed the Goat,
Feed the Goat and he will score.

It was the best possible send-off; City and supporters in good voice.

The game was a convenient stop-off on the way back from the Lake District to Heathrow Airport. I was returning from Windermere where I had been to celebrate my brother Alban's wedding to Alison. Four of my siblings were now married and my sister Rachel had committed herself to a life of religious devotion (as a nun, teacher, and later a hermit) so I was alone in having no relationship ties. I continued to see it as an acceptable trade-off and part of my life choices. It afforded me the freedom to embrace opportunities like the United States but saying goodbye to an ever-increasing extended family of in-laws, nieces, and nephews was a wrench. However, I was now in my 30s, had only recently left Europe for the first time, and, having caught the travel bug, was keen to make up for lost time.

Life in Stamford, Connecticut, was a new and exciting experience. The heady exhilaration of New York City was an hour away by train and in the other direction was the beautiful countryside and coastline of New England. The job was a lot of fun and my employers were paying for my accommodation, so life was comfortable. I did not even have to worry about making new friends as Colin, a close friend and colleague from my Whitbread days, as well as cricketing and Zimbabwe touring companion, had also moved to Stamford as the North American brand director for Boddingtons. It only seemed logical that we share both accommodation and our new adventure together. We came from similar northern backgrounds and shared common values and were determined to make the most of the opportunity that had presented itself.

The biggest adjustment I needed to make was in how I kept up with City's fortunes. Most significantly, there was the time difference. Most games still kicked off at the traditional 3pm so that meant 10am Connecticut time. Previously I had not had much use for this new gimmick called the internet but now it became indispensable. Nothing like as sophisticated as it is today, and City did not yet have their own website, but pages such as sportinglife.com kept me in touch. For midweek matches I quickly mastered the happy knack of pretending to be earnestly working at my desk during the afternoon while following the action on my laptop.

Live English football on television was just not an option. The Premier League was only just on the peripheries of the US sports channels and the lesser First Division was way behind women's minor league lacrosse in terms of local television coverage. I first fell in love with football through attending a live match; radio had then given me a different experience, taking me to so many different footballing occasions through vivid description. Television had laid it all out in front of me, bringing the iconic names and faces into my living room. Now the fledgling internet was completely different. Instead of voices and pictures there were words and numbers live on the screen. No intonation, no action, no passionate commentator describing evocative images. I needed to fill in the gaps for myself. It wasn't ideal, but I was 3,000 miles away and it was keeping me in touch regardless of whether in Connecticut, Chicago, or Colorado.

In Manchester, the impressive form was maintained into the spring and automatic promotion remained a real possibility. Over the Easter break Charlton made a decisive move, leaving City and Ipswich to contest the final place. With two games to go City led by two points. A win at home to Birmingham on a Friday night in May would put us on the cusp. The play-offs would be a creditable achievement but, much as last season's Wembley drama had been an uplifting and unforgettable day, nobody wanted to live through it again.

I tried to persuade my boss, also a Brit and ironically a United fan, that I needed to be back in the UK for a meeting. He agreed. Life was full of pleasant surprises. As the British Airways flight departed the eastern seaboard and rose above the descending sun I stretched out in the business-class seat and sipped my gin and tonic while perusing the menu. I thought about the money scraped up for my economy coach trips to Manchester and the endless rides on the number 48 bus and I raised my glass, thankful for my good fortune.

I landed in Manchester, did the obligatory family visit and the non-obligatory but reassuringly restful visit to Gangan and Nanna's grave, before I made my way to Maine Road. A beautiful late-spring evening befitted the sense of renewal and optimism that pervaded the occasion. To see so many smiling, genuinely hopeful faces heading down those familiar streets towards the old ground was a wonderful sight. The game was no classic and most City fans, never mind anybody else, would struggle to recall any of the action apart from Robert Taylor's goal on the stroke of half-time. The assured defence did its job and the fans again swarmed on to the pitch at the final whistle. The players went to the directors' box to celebrate in front of the supporters, knowing that victory the following week would guarantee promotion. For the fourth time in the past five years City's fate would be decided in the season's final game, away to Blackburn.

I knew that there would be little chance of getting a ticket, and I was right. I did delay my return to Connecticut so that I could watch it on TV. Blackburn dominated the first half. They scored one goal and hit the woodwork on multiple occasions. Weaver was leading a charmed life in goal just to keep City in the game. Elsewhere, fourth-placed Ipswich were 1-0 up and as things stood would be promoted ahead of City. With nothing at stake, the home team were playing expansive, liberated football while City were looking clueless, and the second half continued in the same vein. Blackburn hit the bar. The ball could have bounced anywhere but luckily it landed in Weaver's hands. They hit the post and the ball ran out of play. We badly needed a break. Then Horlock and Kennedy combined down the left and the Goat was fed. Horlock's curving, inviting low cross was met at the far post and Goater was not going to turn up the opportunity to score his 29th goal of the season. It proved to be the catalyst that was needed. Before the chorus of 'Feed the Goat' had died down, City were in the lead thanks to a punt downfield and a Christian Daily own goal. I could almost touch the Premier League, the promised land, and a place at football's top table once again. By the time Kennedy and Dickov added further goals, the City following at Ewood Park had already started to conga around the stadium.

After four long, tortuous, and chaotic years we were back. Royle, the manager Swales had relentlessly pursued, had assembled and led his team of lower-division journeymen to deliver above and beyond the sum of their parts. In the background the understated but shrewd chairmanship of David Bernstein had given the boardroom a stability that had been lacking for so long. We were no longer the laughing stock of English football. I drove to Heathrow the next day, stopping in the British Airways lounge to read all the papers, and headed back to Connecticut for a summer of excited speculation. After the much-needed recent austerity surely the purse strings could be loosened a little as the big money of the Premier League was now returning. Who would we buy? I could not wait to find out.

My new life called for a new kind of celebration, although in truth any celebration was a novel and exciting experience. The internet had not only helped me to keep in touch with City's fortunes, it had also enabled me to meet other fans in the area. Two weeks after City's fans had painted Blackburn blue and white our small group met up in Manhattan and embarked on a celebratory booze cruise around New York's west harbour and then headed to the bars of the city.

Appropriately we ended up in The Manchester, a pub on Second Avenue, entertaining the bemused locals with choruses of 'Blue Moon' and 'Feed the Goat'. The conversation quickly moved from celebration of the previous season to speculation about the coming one and opinion as to how Royle might strengthen the squad. Would he risk upsetting the collective spirit and unity that had been such a vital ingredient of the success so far? There was no hiding from the fact that the squad lacked quality. The right balance needed to be found.

The signatures of Steve Howey and Alf-Inge Håland, two solid and seasoned Premier League campaigners, suggested that Royle's priority would be to bring in proven experience. I was walking down a street in Orlando when I heard about a double swoop for the enigmatic Paulo Wanchope and a former FIFA World Player of the Year, George Weah. This represented much more of a gamble and only time would tell. Nothing was going to keep me away from City's return to the big time, not even the Atlantic Ocean. It felt like a bit of an anticlimax that the first game was not a glamour fixture but a repeat of an encounter from the previous season, Charlton Athletic away. I touched down at Heathrow and headed straight to south London, that mixture of opening-day nerves and groundless optimism still undiminished. It lasted until about ten minutes after kick-off. Charlton looked like a Premier League club and City looked like they were stuck not in the First Division but back in the third tier. The 4-0 defeat was flattering; it could have been eight. City did respond immediately, and I got up to Manchester to see both Wanchope and Weah score on their victorious home debuts against Sunderland, but that was as good as it got.

Within a few weeks Weah was on his way, citing differences of opinion with Royle, and Wanchope's maverick style proved incompatible to the structure and discipline that Royle had instilled. Any amount of industry and effort could not make up for the paucity of quality. Relegation looked like a possibility by the autumn and a probability by the new year.

I had returned to the UK again to watch the much-awaited Manchester derby in October, decided by a David Beckham free kick. When the return fixture against United loomed in April relegation was a certainty. There was the unthinkable outcome that a United win could both confirm them as champions and relegate City. It did not quite work out that way, and the 1-1 draw was best remembered for Roy Keane's knee-crunching tackle on Håland. But City's fate was sealed a few days later. I watched it in a bar in Manhattan, raising a defiant chorus of 'Blue Moon' upon the final whistle.

Royle was sacked a week later. The relationship between Bernstein and Royle had been key to the club's significant progress, but Bernstein was also a ruthless man, with the best interests of City at heart. It felt harsh on Royle who had, as much as anything, changed the culture and self-belief of the club both in the changing room and on the terraces. He had inherited a disorganised playing squad and club structure and out of the chaos had created a solid if unspectacular unit. The last season had been a step too far. Maybe he was a victim of his own success with back-to-back promotions. Maybe that season of consolidation in the First Division would have served him and the club better but that was not Royle's style. He had been responsible for some wonderful moments and, most significantly, in turning around the big ship sailing on the Ally-Ally-Oh he had given the club back its belief.

Bernstein's decisiveness and forward thinking was a contrast to the chairmen of the past. He did not dispense of Royle's services without having a replacement lined up and within days Kevin Keegan was installed in the manager's office. Years earlier, when I was a ball boy, Keegan had signed my book. In those few moments he was welcoming, warm, and friendly. It was easy to sense that he was a 'people' person and his subsequent management spells had revealed someone who relied more on his interpersonal skills and passion rather than deep-founded tactical and technical discipline. He was possibly well suited to City, an emotional basket case of a football club.

My American adventure was turning out to be an enriching one. My work with Diageo took me across the whole of the country and I relished every moment of it, but I missed family and friends and of course I missed seeing City. Much as I loved the life I was living, whenever the job presented an opportunity to get home and go to a game I would be there, and sometimes I even visited my now-retired parents in Yorkshire. Likewise, if anything remotely City-related happened in America then I would also be there. When Miami Fuse played the New York Metro Stars at the Giants Stadium in New Jersey the local City contingent turned up en masse just to cheer the Fuse's Ian Bishop. The ex-City player was missing us too as he was straight over to the stands to talk and mix with the blue-shirted group.

There had been a few opportunities to see City on TV, a ritual that invariably involved an Irish pub, several pints of

Guinness and the full breakfast all before noon. Relegation put an end to that, but the internet was rapidly evolving, and even though live streaming was some way off I did manage to somehow catch most of the highlights and, with Keegan in charge, there were plenty to choose from. The new manager had added the grit of Stuart Pearce and footballing intelligence of Eyal Berkovic to the squad and the season had started off with predictable inconsistency as goals flew in at both ends, culminating in bizarrely contrasting results from week to week.

The month of September 2001 started in the Playwright pub in Stamford. I had befriended an avid Chelsea supporter from Hertfordshire who also happened to be the *Daily Mirror*'s correspondent for the USA. Why Andy Lines, now the *Mirror*'s chief reporter, chose to base himself in Stamford I never quite understood but we hit it off straight away as fellow expat football nuts. A group of friends including Colin and his American fiancée Liz, Andy and I got together in the Playwright and partied all afternoon as first Sven-Göran Eriksson's England thrashed Germany 5-1 in Munich, and the Republic of Ireland then beat the Netherlands 1-0. Both countries were on their way to qualifying for the 2002 World Cup finals. The matches might have been the other way round; the memories are lost in a haze of Guinness and celebration.

Three days later I departed for Peru to hike the Inca Trail, the ultimate destination being Machu Picchu. I was part of an organised trekking tour and following a few days of acclimatisation in the historic town of Cuzco we started our hike on a beautiful Tuesday morning, struggling manfully with the altitude but taking in the stunning Andean scenery. We were camping but hardly roughing it, our bags being carried by the local porters and camp set up in advance of our arrival at each stop. There are two ways to get to Machu Picchu; one is the strenuous walking route that we had chosen and the other is via the more sedate passage courtesy of the train to the local town of Aguas Calientes. Invariably tourists taking either route congregate at the Sun Gate, the dramatic elevated entrance to Machu Picchu that marks the end of the Inca Trail and provides the iconic photo opportunities. Stood there, admiring the spectacular view, I met an English gentleman who had arrived on that morning's train. We exchanged pleasantries and he was interested in my trek. As we were about to go our separate ways, he casually asked me my opinion on the events of the last few days. Instinctively I thought of City, but they were only playing West Brom and that could hardly be considered newsworthy in darkest Peru.

'What events?' I asked.

My access to any media since we had set off on the Inca Trail on 11 September had been non-existent. The time shown on my digital photograph as we took the first steps of our trek was 8.45am, approximately the same time that the first airplane crashed into the World Trade Center. The contrast was hard to reconcile. In this beautiful, mysteriously spiritual setting, suspended in cloud and time, my acquaintance regaled me with the horrors of 9/11. Four days had passed after the attack, and it felt like he had discovered one of the last people in the world ignorant of its occurrence. Without knowing the full details, my mind turned to the colleagues and friends who were constantly flying in and out of New

York – were they okay? I had not told my parents the details of my trip and they would not have heard from me for nearly a week. What might they be thinking? I continued my tour of the Inca settlement, eager to absorb every moment of it, but full of confused emotions and keen to connect with the suffering outside world once again.

I returned to New York on the following Tuesday, one week after 9/11, the stricken city still shrouded in a cloud of dust. On a clear day, from the end of the road where my apartment stood, I could have seen the towers of the WTC rising above the Manhattan skyline across Long Island Sound. At home, catching up on my inbox I lived the dramatic events of that tragic morning, all taking place while I had basked in my Andean oblivion. I opened emails from colleagues, friends, and families telling first of shock and horror, then later concern and sorrow as events unfolded on television screens across the world. The last one sent in the early afternoon of 11 September was from a senior president of my employers. The final sentences read, 'Please now go home, shut down your laptops and turn off your televisions, if only for a few minutes. Check on your neighbours, hug your partners and be strong for your family. Tell your children that this day is not a true reflection of humanity, and it is what we do when the sun rises tomorrow and not what happened as the sun sets this evening that will define us.'

I did not know the City fan who had died in the Twin Towers at all well I believe he had been present on our celebratory tour of Manhattan the previous summer, but we all felt his loss keenly.

Sometime during those few days City's most significant act of the season, the signing of Ali Benarbia, had taken place. In the wider context of what was happening, it was an irrelevance, but Benarbia was Keegan's masterstroke. The midfield playmaker had played all his football in France and was largely unknown beyond Ligue 1. He left the field on his debut to a standing ovation from the Maine Road faithful and the appreciative applause did not abate all season. Dovetailing perfectly with Berkovic, they formed an unlikely Jewish-Muslim alliance at the heart of Moss Side. With such creativity all that was now needed were some goalscorers, and in Goater, Huckerby, and the revitalised Wanchope, we had the firepower. City became the great entertainers across all divisions; 108 goals were scored. This was, after all, a Kevin Keegan side so there were also 11 defeats. For once things did not go to the last day of the season and promotion was confirmed with games to spare. From Stateside it seemed like I might be missing out on a whole lot of fun. I was ready to head back home to reunite with one old friend and bid farewell to another.

While in America the internet had been indispensable in keeping me in touch with City. Through it I had met new friends, and the City community in New York. Unexpectedly, I also reunited with an old friend. The fanzine phenomena that emerged in the 1990s had now moved online, via websites and chat rooms. Browsing through one of these, I came across an article by my old St Aidan's pal Paul Burns, the boy who had persuaded me to be a City supporter when we were much younger. He was still very much a Blue. Like me, he had travelled, spending some time in Japan, but now he was back in Manchester. We exchanged emails and agreed to meet when the new season began.

The old friend that I needed to say goodbye to was Maine Road itself. Chairman Bernstein had seized the opportunity to move the club to a brand-new stadium across Manchester. Maine Road had been state of the art in its day, but that day was the 1920s and long gone. The tired old ground, full of so many memories, was now showing its age. Manchester's bid to host the 2002 Commonwealth Games had been contingent on there being an ongoing use for the stadium that was to be built in the neglected east of the city. Bernstein negotiated a deal with the council that would see the football club relocate to the City of Manchester Stadium after the Games. It would be hard to leave Maine Road, but it was the right decision.

The immediate task in hand was to ensure that City moved to their new home as a Premier League club. For each one of the past five seasons we had switched divisions so to retain top-tier status would be no formality. Recognising the importance of the forthcoming season Bernstein allowed Keegan to spend lavishly, and for the most part he did so wisely, notably bringing in a proven top-flight goal scorer in Nicolas Anelka. A few eyebrows were raised when Peter Schmeichel was acquired on a free transfer, but his physical and mental presence soon won over the doubters. As much as ingrained tribal allegiances dictated how I irrationally felt about United, I saw no problem if their ex-players wanted to come across the city. I also still considered myself a goalkeeper and therefore took an avid interest in studying the great Dane and his style. In his final season before retirement, he projected a colossal presence, backed up by age-defying agility. It was an inspired signing.

After what seemed like a generation of nail-biting chaos a season of relative calm was welcome. Changes were made to team and tactics following an initial adjustment to life in the Premier League. Relegation, or the danger of it, was never an issue. There was the little matter of the final Manchester derby at Maine Road, a fixture that City had not won since the 5-1 massacre of United back in 1989. The respective clubs' fortunes had diverged in starkly contrasting directions since that day but here was a last chance to at least inflict a flesh wound. The Kippax rocked and City rolled. Anelka, representing the new guard, opened the scoring only for Ole Gunnar Solskjaer to equalise minutes later. The 'old guard' then assumed control. Wiekens brilliantly marshalled the defence and Gary Neville 'fed the Goat', needlessly allowing himself to be dispossessed on the goal line and then watched helplessly as Goater fired home. Midway through the second half the Goat scored his 100th City goal to wrap up the points. It felt good to be back home and to give the Kippax one last glorious moment in the sun.

The final game at Maine Road was always going to be one of mixed emotions. A celebration of what had been; the great memories on and off the pitch and the lasting friendships made. But also the sadness at letting go of an old friend. Fittingly I met up with Paul and his parents. Through his family I had become a Junior Blue and in turn my love of City had turned into something manifest and real. It felt right to see them again and acknowledge their culpable role in my life's obsession.

Before my final visit to Maine Road, I had one final pilgrimage to make on foot. I left my car outside my grandparents' former house on Brixton Avenue and took that well-trodden path of my childhood. I walked up Yew Tree Road, so much of it intrinsically unchanged, recalling the excitement and impatience of that very first journey. I crossed Platt Lane and emerged at the back of the Kippax. In place of the famous terrace of my childhood was now the all-seater stand towering above the pitch. I did not go straight in but took one last circuit of the ground, past the North Stand and out on to the forecourt in front of the Main Stand. The crowd was gathering at the entrance, on the lookout for the numerous celebrities, past and present, that would also be coming to say their goodbyes. Then I went down to the Platt Lane entrance. The old stand, with its wooden bench seats that I had so proudly occupied, had been replaced in the early 1990s but the brick-walled entrance remained. I remembered my nervous excitement as I fumbled with that first season ticket, not believing I would be allowed in the ground until I was physically in my seat. In 1979 that season ticket had cost me just £4, a pound less than I had just spent on the 36-page Maine Road souvenir brochure.

Inside, the party had begun with heroes of the past parading around the pitch, savouring their own memories and indulging in one last chance to receive the adulation of the crowd. John Bond was there, as was Dennis Tueart and a well-fed Georgi Kinkladze. While moving on was undoubtedly the right thing it also felt appropriate to indulge in some nostalgia and a little regret. I recalled the great goals, the all-too-rare wins, the heartaches, and the comedic football, but most of all I recalled a place where I felt safe and welcomed. When being battered in the winds of teenage turmoil, Maine Road had been my shelter. It had been my constant and comfort, my escape from the world outside. As a ball boy I had been privileged to be allowed into that sacred inner sanctum of any football ground, the players' area. I looked around; how many of these had been that lucky? Then again, each one of us had our own, personal and defining relationship with the stadium and, more importantly, we had our own memories. And those unique memories were the only ones that really mattered. They were our truth, our lived experience, and our reality. Each seat within the four incongruously individual stands – Main Stand, Platt Lane, North Stand, and most poignantly the Kippax – told a thousand stories. I had once led out the ball boys and the team on to that same pitch in front of 50,000 spectators, 15,000 more than were in attendance on this day, but so many of them would be the same people. In a few minutes Shaun Goater, captain for the day in his last game for the club, would take that same walk down the tunnel and on to the sunlit pitch and for one last time the Maine Road crowd would rise to welcome City, our City.

Ever disrespectful of an occasion, City lost 1-0 to Southampton, but that did not dampen the mood as the fans flowed on to the pitch and partied into the evening, acquiring all manner of souvenirs as they departed. The next day the only ball to be seen at Maine Road was a wrecking ball and within weeks the stadium was no more.

With my older brothers Alban and David. Someone has just told me that I get to support City

My first communion and the obligatory siblings photo. Alban, Rachel, Elizabeth, Kathy, David.

Joe Corrigan, my first footballing hero

Paul Burns, myself and his mum with the 1976 League Cup

St Michael's College, Leeds, where I spent my formative years

Walter and Annie Clift (or Nanna and Gangan) on their 50th wedding anniversary

In the back garden of 4 Brixton Avenue

Ricky Villa crushes my dreams in 1981

The confirmed football bachelor, with Saint on his wedding day to Helen.

Enjoying the Andean scenery at Machu Picchu, ten minutes before being told about 9-11

Against Gillingham in the 1999 play-off final. Dickov shoots and City's future changes.

2003. Nearly 30 years later, friends reunited, Paul, his mum and I recreate that picture

City lost to Southampton and the next day the bulldozers moved in and Maine Road was no more.

Michael and Anne Denton (or Mum and Dad). The epitome of love, life and belonging.

2011 FA Cup. Finally after 35 years a trophy.

One more chance. Aguero shoots and Singapore holds its breath.

12

Home Truths

I SWIPED my brand new 'Citycard' against the digital reader. The pristine electronic gate turned and gave an efficient buzz to signal my entry into our shiny new home. It was a stark contrast to the heavy clunk of the rusty, manually operated turnstiles that had confirmed my admission to Maine Road many years ago. I told myself that this was a good thing, and that I would not become wrapped up in a sense of nostalgia and a yearning for the past. Especially as that past had so often disappointed. I had listened to too many fans from other clubs who had made similar moves, complaining about concrete, sterile stadia in out-of-town locations, that lacked the perceived character of their previous homes. In many cases the worst fears had become self-fulfilling prophecies and they themselves had failed to create an atmosphere and sense of belonging. This was the new, progressive future and it had to be embraced.

Significant financial benefits aside, the new ground had everything that could be asked for. The location served me less well, adding time to my journey; however, it was not stuck on a greenfield site in the outskirts of the city but within a short walk of the centre, and felt part of Manchester's industrial fabric. It had a sterility about it for sure, but the facilities and design could not be faulted. Character is woven into the structure of stadia over time, not created in an architect's studio. The only thing that it did not have was a name and an identity. Some referred to it as the 'City of Manchester Stadium' and others as 'Eastlands'. The lasting name and indelible identity would be forged in time through unimaginable events both on and off the pitch. Barcelona came for the pre-season opening and obligingly let City claim victory in the stadium's first game. Star striker Ronaldinho was enthusiastically cheered every time he touched the ball, in tribal appreciation of his decision not to join United in the summer.

On the pitch the football mirrored the new surroundings in many ways. Nice to look at and functional but not particularly spectacular or with personality. Keegan had strengthened the squad during the summer and for the first half of the season the inconsistent results that defined the old stadium were distant memories. The Maine Road match experience that we had left behind in many ways had reflected the ground: each way you turned you saw a different aspect in the four contrasting stands. Behind every patched-up terrace, blocked toilet, and comically malfunctioning scoreboard there was a story and a memory, a triumph and a disaster. The inadequacy of the facilities could be forgiven and overlooked because its strength and soul were not in its physical construct but in its history and relationship with people and place. At the City of Manchester Stadium, there was no lengthy tapestry of memories to fall back on but there was functionality, efficiency, and for the most part competence. In the absence of a stadium with a rich history we were craving for the promise of a bright new successful future that could not come quickly enough.

The season did have its moments of note that made the new ground come spectacularly to life. The stadium's first Manchester derby ended in a resounding 4-1 win, and, as form dipped alarmingly towards the end of the campaign, a Paulo Wanchope winner against Newcastle to secure survival was greeted with a roar of elation and relief worthy of the Kippax. But the best moment was saved for away from home and the FA Cup, City proudly reverting to type in the craziest of ways.

I had a ticket for the FA Cup fourth round replay at Spurs and, having repatriated to Royston in Hertfordshire, White Hart Lane was only an hour away. I recall having a bad day at work. What was so bad about it I cannot remember, but it must have unavoidably detained me as I did not go to the game. I got home just before kick-off and the match was on Sky so at least I could watch it live. The decision not to go seemed to be a good one at half-time with City 3-0 down. The best hope of a comeback, Nicolas Anelka, had limped off injured and Joey Barton had been sent off. No star striker, ten men and three goals to the bad. There was only one thing to lean back on: Spurs had long held the ability to indulge in the same mix of comic failure and glorious triumph as City. They did this to the extent that they had often been referred to as the 'Manchester City of the South'. To be fair to Spurs, they had occasionally converted their glorious inconsistency into a proper trophy or two rather than the lower-division tin pots that City had acquired. Any hope of redemption lay not in the ten men in sky blue but in the 11 men in white. Cometh the hour, cometh the Spurs. Sylvain Distin headed a seemingly meaningless consolation goal and Paul Bosvelt made things interesting ten minutes later, reducing the deficit to one. When Shaun Wright-Phillips's little dink rolled into the net I gave a rueful glance to the unused match ticket that was on my coffee table and poured myself another glass of wine.

The best I thought we could now hope for was extra time, believing that with ten tired men, the only realistic chance lay in a penalty shoot-out. Then Steve McManaman picked up play and fed the ball out to Michael Tarnat on the left. Too weary to take on his opposing full-back, Tarnat swung in a hopeful cross to the far post where Jon Macken rose to head home. Spurs players collapsed while City's went over to the small gathering of away fans, minus one who was doing a jig around a table in Hertfordshire. Typical City. Typical football. It was reassuring to know that in the modern world of new stadia, expensive, imported talent, and commercial might, comic book football could still co-exist. Thank you, Kevin Keegan. Thank you, Spurs. City were drawn against United at Old Trafford in the fifth round, and I was present to see the 4-2 defeat. It was the first time I had been back there since that first baptism.

In 2005, barely two years after saying goodbye to Maine Road, St Michaels's College in Leeds also closed its doors for the last time. Both institutions were built in the early part of the 20th century and both had played seminal roles in their communities and influenced the lives of many young men. Both had exposed me to a range of experiences that had helped to shape the person I became. In between the regret and painful recollections of my school there were happy memories. I was blessed to have met some truly great teachers and inspirational human beings who cared for me and every boy. I took part in some wonderful extra-curricular activities that stretched and grew me culturally, spiritually, and physically. At times, the most unexpected moments of kindness and compassion by school-mates both surprised and touched me. I just happened to be in a unique circumstance, place, and time when culture, attitudes, and actions occasionally conspired against me.

I happened to be visiting Leeds later that year and, on a whim, diverted my journey to drive past the old building. I had not planned to stop but, once there, I decided to park up outside the imposing wall. I got out of the car and peered through the chained gate. The building was intact, but the classrooms, laboratories, gymnasium, and corridors were empty and silenced of the cacophony of boys and masters. The playground was overgrown with weeds and the breeze blew an empty crisp packet across the eerily vacant space before resting up against the chain-link fence. I recalled the film *Forrest Gump* and a scene where the adult Jenny returns with Forrest to the Greenbow, Alabama house in which she grew up and, we are led to surmise, was abused. Seeking some sort of closure, she throws first her shoes and then any rock she can lay her hand on at the derelict house before collapsing on the ground. I looked around and there were no rocks. As Forrest observed, 'Sometimes there just aren't enough rocks.'

Like uncorked champagne, Kevin Keegan has a life span. When freshly opened he is full of contagious spark and fizz that energises players and supporters alike. It is a stimulating and heady experience while it lasts, but when the bubbles go, all that remains is the flat dullness of old, dry white wine. By 2004/05 the bubbles had gone. Mid-table mediocrity was not Keegan's thing, and he was losing his appetite for City and the game. There was no danger of relegation but neither was there any chance of challenging the top places. The team was drifting in the Premier League's calmer waters, largely beating the worse teams, and losing to the better ones without being able to effectively alter course. There had been the brief and welcome novelty of a foray into Europe and the UEFA Cup, albeit via the fair play system, but that had ended in a 'z'-strewn Polish town as forgettable as the football itself. Manchester businessman and lifelong supporter John Wardle had replaced David Bernstein as chairman after the prudent Bernstein had disagreed with Keegan over funds for new players. The board had supported Keegan as much as they could, but the money just was not there to make the next step. Keegan was falling out of love with football, and it showed on his face and in his demeanour. It was therefore no big surprise when he resigned in February. Stuart Pearce, who had been groomed for the role ever since his arrival, was the natural replacement.

The Pearce effect was surprisingly immediate, and the tempo and purpose of the team noticeably picked up. Shaun Wright-Phillips – SWP – was at his electrifying best by the time the final game came, a winner-takes-all against Middlesbrough with the prize of a UEFA Cup place. With

80 minutes gone and the score 1-1, City were piling on the pressure. Boro were well organised and it would need something special to break through, something innovative. Pearce made his move and went to his bench where striker Jon Macken, the hero of White Hart Lane, was sat. The rookie manager had other ideas and instructed reserve goalkeeper Nicky Weaver to get ready. Was David James injured? Weaver readied himself and the board went up. Number six, Claudio Reyna. Was Pearce taking off an outfield player to play with two goalkeepers?

The outlandish plan was soon revealed. Weaver went in goal and Pearce handed James a pre-prepared blue shirt with his number one on the back. It had all clearly been planned in advance. The 6ft 5in James would play the final minutes as striker. Macken slumped back on the bench, incredulous that his talents were being overlooked in favour of the goalkeeper-cum-centre-forward. James was big and disruptive, but he did also have all the outfield football skills of a drunken giraffe. He played little part in winning the last-minute penalty that Robbie Fowler subsequently missed. That was about as interesting as it got during Pearce's two years in charge. David James, the centre-forward.

For seasoned fans the mundane ordinariness now being served up was an unfamiliar and uncomfortable experience. Comic mediocrity had been the norm while feelings of triumph had admittedly been rare. Any success had been relative to the failures that had preceded it. Each win and each goal became a thing of importance and celebration. The expectation was so little that any crumb of victory was gratefully received. The camaraderie and sense of kinship were never stronger than in times of adversity. As the masochistic, self-deprecating but celebratory anthem went:

We never win at home and we never win away,
We lost last week, and we lost today,
We don't give a fuck cos we're all pissed up,
MCFC okay.

We sang it loud and proud. Other clubs' supporters used to talk about City fans and their perseverance on radio phone-ins. Every report lamenting another defeat that reaffirmed the scale of City's downfall would reference the 'loyal and long-suffering fans' in admiring tones. My sister Kathy even submitted an Occupational Psychology degree thesis on the spirit in adversity of Manchester City supporters. The evidence was largely based on my trials, tribulations, and tales of woe, often calling in at her South Yorkshire home on the way to and from matches, unloading my angst and frustration. But at this point we were neither good nor bad and what I hated even more than being bad was being average. We were on the poor side of average. Nobody talked about us any more. We were irrelevant. In this great show that was the Premier League, this great entertainment spectacle, we were neither the valiant hero nor, as had often better suited us, the tragi-comic victim. We were the faceless, characterless chorus line, making up the numbers and playing out our stuff in a modern municipal theatre. Stevenage Playhouse if you like. They say be careful what you wish for and I know that when I was stood on the terraces at York, getting pissed on both off and on the pitch, I would have jumped at the chance of

Premier League mid-table mediocrity. But now we had it, it just wasn't doing it for me.

It would be cruel to suggest that the most interesting and creative things to be seen on the pitch at this time were the bizarrely innovative grass patterns of City's imaginative head groundsman, who seemed to have developed an artistic penchant for presenting a new pitch design at every home game, but some weekends it felt like it was not far from the truth. The lack of any excitement was not all of Pearce's making. He was constrained financially, and the signings he made reflected that with a mixture of cut-price imports, loanees and over-the-hill Premier League veterans. In the meantime, the one beacon of hope, SWP, was sold off to Chelsea. It made sense financially, but it hurt. Pearce did complete one astute piece of business, signing up little-known Shrewsbury goalkeeper Joe Hart, and he gave a debut to an emerging youth team prospect in Micah Richards. The first lines of a much bigger story were being written but for now the plot was achingly predictable. There were a couple of FA Cup runs to the quarter-finals that gave momentary hope, only for the team to flounder at the hands of arguably smaller but seemingly more progressive clubs in West Ham and Blackburn. The most noteworthy thing I can recall is that from 1 January 2007 until the end of that season we did not score a single goal at home. That's entertainment!

Only John Wardle and a few City insiders know just how perilous the club's finances were in the summer of 2007. The modest transfer activity coupled with the fact that the stadium had received little or no investment since the move indicated that there was not much to go around. The new stadium needed no major money but a couple of scoreboards and a bit of signage on the outside that made it more 'City' than civic; more 'Manchester' than municipal would have been welcome. The absence of these were perhaps indicative of the lack of spare cash. Wardle was of the old school of football chairmen, a self-made local man, and a supporter; Roman Abramovich he was not. A dodgy oligarch of our own was exactly what was needed.

As had frequently happened, the cricket tour in July was the catalyst for the summer activity to kick into gear. There had been press conjecture about the club being for sale and former Thai prime minister Thaksin Shinawatra had been linked with more than one Premier League club in the recent past. The deal was concluded shortly after the season had withered on the vine and Pearce was promptly sacked. While not unhappy or surprised about the change, I was nevertheless disappointed for Pearce. He was that rare breed of player, respected and loved by most regardless of allegiance, refreshingly honest and forthright with his football and his emotions. The vein-bursting 'Psycho' image belied a deeper and more reflective interior. His autobiography was one of the most enjoyable football books I had read, and I would have loved to have seen him succeed. The numbers spoke for themselves, though, and just 13 goals at home in an entire season was not going to cut it with an ambitious new owner wanting to make a big impact.

His replacement was a further sign of the changing times. A foreign owner and then a foreign manager. I did not have particularly high regard for Sven-Göran Eriksson as England manager, despite the celebrated 5-1 win against Germany. I felt he relied too much on the same favoured players with the same rigid tactics and indulged the 'golden generation'. At times he seemed almost in awe of David Beckham's celebrity status. There was no denying, though, that his track record at club level was impressive. I was on my way to Whiteparish when he made his first media appearance as the new manager. He was the same old charming, genial Sven of a thousand England press conferences, and you could not help warming to him. Shinawatra came through with the money he had promised, and Sven got to work quickly. In a frenzy of activity, he completed most of his dealings in the last week of pre-season. The opener was against West Ham at Upton Park. Such was the haste of the acquisitions that for the first time since I was a boy, I turned up for a City game not recognising half the team. There was Richard Dunne, Micah Richards, and Stephen Ireland of course but I needed to look at the players' names on the shirts to know who else was playing. Bianchi up front, Elano, Petrov and Geovanni in midfield, Corluka and Garrido in the full-back slots. Eriksson had leveraged his deep knowledge and extensive networks in Europe's leagues to assemble his new squad, all paid for with Thai baht.

The precise source of this abundance of Thai baht was something of mystery to all and the arrival of Shinawatra created a novel dilemma for many fans. The investment was welcome but there was no hiding from the fact that the new owner did come with a certain amount of baggage. Corruption allegations had long followed him. The fortune he had amassed did seem to suggest the rapid accumulation of a whole lot of cash beyond his legitimate business and prime ministerial incomes. He was also a polarising figure in his native Thailand: adored by the working classes and despised by the middle and upper classes. There were not too many experts on south-east Asian politics in the stands of the stadium, so ignorance and silence became the default reaction of most. At the back of the mind it did not feel quite right, but what was the alternative? Stop supporting City? Like many others, I took the 'support the team but not the owner' position.

Shinawatra, the consummate politician, did his best to endear himself and with some success too. The investment helped, as did the early results. He was a regular attender at home games and laid on Thai street parties in the city centre. He quickly became known to all as 'Frank' (Sinatra/Shinawatra; yes, it is a bit of a stretch) and as the Thai authorities circled around his assets, seizing whatever they could from wherever it happened to be hidden, he was splendidly celebrated in song, a bastardisation of The Proclaimers classic, '500 Miles'.

Oh you can freeze 500 million,
And you can freeze 500 more,
Cos Frankie boy has got ten billion,
Underneath his bedroom floor,
Shinawatra, Shinawatra,
Shinawatra, Shinawatra,
Da da da dun diddle un diddle un diddle uh da.

While the new owner might have caused a few uneasy feelings, his manager was immediately welcomed. For a team that looked like it had been assembled five minutes before kick-off, City remarkably won the opening game at West Ham, then the next match, and the next one after that (against United). Sven was working his magic in a way he never did with England's 'golden generation'. The impressive first half of the season was largely built on home form – every match won up until Christmas – and the midfield goalscoring prowess of Elano and Petrov. In February 'the double' was completed at Old Trafford, the first since the 1970s. And then, a bit like with England, it all started to unravel.

Sven put it down to tiredness after the exertions of the first half of the season as the team's form dramatically declined. In the corridors of the club Shinawatra's behaviour was becoming increasingly erratic. A parting of the ways seemed inevitable long before the final-day debacle as City were humiliated 8-1 at Middlesbrough. It was only one goal short of being their heaviest-ever defeat. Sven remained popular with the fans and, apparently, with the players, even if the team's woeful performance at Middlesbrough did not indicate a ringing endorsement. Despite the 'Save our Sven' campaign, Shinawatra had seen enough, and the managerial merry-go-round cranked into life once more.

Given that Chelsea, also looking for a new manager, had been linked with Mark Hughes it was generally considered to be astute business by City to secure his services. Once able to look beyond his unfortunate connections with United, he did have an impressive managerial record with Wales and Blackburn Rovers. Treated with grave suspicion by fans who gave him the moniker 'Agent Hughes', his first two acts as manager, the low-key signings of the relatively obscure Pablo

Zabaleta and Vincent Kompany, did nothing to set pulses racing, but slowly, unknowingly it was happening.

As Agent Hughes moved in, I was set to move on. While the passion was as strong as ever, the mid-table sameness of it all was starting to become, in the vernacular of Alan Partridge, rather moribund. The new ground and my own relocation to Hertfordshire had also added over 60 minutes to the now six-hour return trip to home games. Coupled with the increasing propensity of Sky to change kick-off times it made getting to the games an increasingly arduous task. What was happening on the pitch was not a satisfactory payback. The season under Shinawatra and Sven had provided something of a novelty and a glimpse of a different future, but that had ultimately ended decidedly 'mid-table'.

Once back in the UK, it had been great to be closer to friends and family of course, but from a career and lifestyle point of view I wanted a new challenge. As the new season beckoned and Hughes made the short south-easterly journey along the A666, I would soon be heading on my own, somewhat longer, south-easterly journey on an A380. An opportunity had arisen, still with Diageo, to take up a post in Hong Kong managing innovation programmes across Asia Pacific. As with my USA move, I meticulously researched the implications of living in Asia and it did not take long to decide that I could cope with watching my football late on a Saturday night in the bar districts of Wan Chai or Lan Kwai Fong. Deciding to go to Hong Kong was big news, but the more significant event of that August was yet to come.

13

The Noisy Neighbour

I HEADED off to work at the Diageo office just behind Oxford Street. I often stayed down in London during the week, so I had only a short walk across the road from my hotel room. The first job of the day would be to drop an email to friends letting them know that I would shortly be departing for Hong Kong. I was habitually at my desk early, usually before 7am, and I switched on my laptop and grabbed a coffee while the computer booted up. Once it had come to life, and before I could start any meaningful business of the day, my custom was to check out the morning football news. It was transfer deadline day, 31 August, so any big last-minute moves were going to dominate the back pages. Expectations that we would be making any significant signings were low.

I was immediately taken aback by the banner headline across the screen: 'Manchester City Become the World's Richest Football Club.' I did a double take. During the night, with the Thai authorities closing in on his accumulated wealth, the cash-strapped Shinawatra had sold the club to Sheikh Mansour bin Zayed Al Nahyan, owner of the Abu

Dhabi United Group. As with Shinawatra 12 months earlier, I knew next to nothing of the Sheikh and his business interests. One thing was for certain, it did not matter how much money he had; with a name like that he would not be getting his own song.

My dominant feeling was one of intrigue and scepticism. I had heard a thousand tales of supposedly rich benefactors coming into clubs, promising the world and delivering little. Even our own had now gone by the wayside. Was he just going to be replaced with another transient owner passing through? I checked out a few other websites – *The Guardian*, *The Telegraph*, and the BBC were all leading with the story. Maybe I was jetting off to the other side of the world just as City were about to go supersonic themselves. My hopes (and to some extent fears) were confirmed in the evening. I sat in my hotel room, still logged on to the *Sporting Life* site and followed the live updates of the final, frantic hours and minutes of transfer deadline day.

The new owners were wasting no time in making their intentions known. The big signing of the day was going to be by United, who were on the brink of bringing in Dimitar Berbatov from Spurs. Rumours abounded that City were about to hijack the deal. Berbatov was on his way to Manchester, but nobody was quite sure which way his chauffeured limousine would turn when it left the airport and headed along Princess Parkway towards the city. Would it be United or City? That ultimately did not matter because on a Manchester-bound private jet from Madrid was Robinho. There was no question as to where the Brazilian superstar was heading; the £30m deal was sealed just before midnight. City had more than doubled their previous transfer record just like that. *'Fuck me, this is the real deal.'*

Robinho looked confused and tired at the hastily convened press conference. Only that morning he had spoken of his intention to move to London and now inadvertently said how pleased he was to have 'accepted a great offer from Chelsea' before being hastily corrected. Mark Hughes looked like he was in shock, pleased to have had such an unexpected windfall but also powerless, unable to influence the bizarre course of the day. He would now have to consider how he would integrate Robinho into his team structure. No doubt he also had half a mind on his own future, having been appointed by the previous owners only weeks earlier. In the Bluemoon internet chat room the fans were bouncing off the screen with excitement. Robinho had signed within the first 12 hours. God only knows what we could do in a whole month. Roll on the new year and shopping, not for bargains in the January sales, but in Europe's most exclusive boutiques.

I managed to delay my departure for Hong Kong long enough to see Robinho's hat-trick against Stoke. The new City were up and running. I took Greg, my eight-year-old nephew, to the game and a few days later I boarded my flight content that the next generation of the family would maintain the legacy in my absence. I also had mixed feelings. Eager to embrace my new life, I was also wrestling with the uncomfortable dilemma that I might just be walking away from a bigger adventure closer to home. If the initial actions of the new regime were anything to go by, then when I came home, whenever that might be, it would be to a quite different football club. I wanted City to be successful but at what cost, and how would I feel if they were successful and I was not there to be part of it? What would I be missing? Would a club that was so grounded in its community, had so moulded its identity on its flaws and been defined by its comic failings lose its sense of personality? For now, I did not need to worry. I was sure that the fans would ensure that City remained City. I just wanted to win something.

Watching football in Hong Kong was all I hoped it would be. It could never replace the feeling of being at a game, but the television coverage was in fact more widespread than I was accustomed to back in the UK with every game being shown live across the TV channels. Once I had managed to locate the button on my remote control that switched the commentary from Cantonese to English, I was soon listening to the familiar punditry of Peter Drury, Andy Townsend, and Alan Curbishley. Often, I would wander down from my apartment in the Mid-Levels of Hong Kong Island to Lockhart Road and the night district of Wan Chai to hang out with the mix of expats and locals, finding a bar that was showing City's game and acclimatising my taste buds to the local Tsingtao beer. Most of the major clubs that had permeated Asia had adopted their own bars – Arsenal, United, and Liverpool being the main players. Ours would come in due course.

The first half of the season felt like passing time, waiting impatiently for the January transfer window to arrive. With the addition of Robinho, Kompany and Zabaleta the squad had significantly more quality, but the Abu Dhabi cash bonanza had yet to really kick in. There was a familiar mid-table feeling as the transfer window beckoned. Robinho's signing had been a statement of intent made in the last minutes of August. The new owners had been adamant City had to sign somebody big, anybody big, on that seminal day to show they meant business. The actual identity of that person was less important. Agent Hughes now had his fixed views on whom he wanted. His plan was to build from what he knew and that was essentially the Premier League. He addressed obvious weaknesses, acquiring established domestic quality in Shay Given, Wayne Bridge, and Craig Bellamy. His one big move into the European leagues was as unglamorous as they come as he secured the services of the industrious Nigel de Jong.

Meanwhile, chief executive Garry Cook had other ideas. Shortly after the takeover, Cook had spoken about the direction the club needed to take. Global brand visibility was intrinsic to the Abu Dhabi strategy. The signing of the best, highest-profile footballers was a part of it. In articulating the strategy, Cook had famously stated, 'Richard Dunne does not sell shirts in Asia.' It might have been harsh on the long-serving captain, five times the club's player of the year, but it was also true. City's loyal support were learning to face some new, sometimes uncomfortable realities in this vastly different world. So, while the manager secured his relatively low-key transfer targets Cook went in pursuit of bigger names. Not one to curb his ambitions for self or for City, the CEO targeted the best and attempted to prise Brazilian superstar Kaká from AC Milan. His move was bold and audacious, and it nearly came off.

The snipers were quick to talk of the arrogance of new money and scattergun transfer policies, but Cook was adamant that City would not be subservient to the established footballing dynasties. The parsimonious sneering and sniping that came with the newly acquired wealth was already becoming apparent for City fans. More used to being patronised by a fondness that bordered on pity, we had not been accused of arrogance because we rarely had anything to be arrogant about. We'd had no cause to consider the merits or shortcomings of a strategy because there had never been a strategy to consider, or at least not one that generated any external interest. Cook's pursuit of Kaká and his refusal to back down, culminating in his 'Milan bottled it' claim, brought the first swathe of rebuke and criticism from Europe's footballing aristocracy and media alike. It would be the first of many. But where City really needed to do their talking was on the pitch, and that was not yet happening. The home form was good, but away from Manchester it was abject. Robinho's early season glitter faded and for a brief, fleeting moment there was a danger that the richest club in the world could be sucked into a relegation battle, the humiliation to end all humiliations. A strong finish saw the danger averted and attention turned again to the summer transfer market.

Agent Hughes was not to be swayed in his direction. He was still going with what he knew and did his shopping in the domestic market. While many fans were impatient for the transformational signing of a mega-name from Europe, the manager's upgrades were more incremental. Aston Villa's Gareth Barry had looked set for a move to Liverpool but at the last minute, swayed by the hope of trophies and possibly astronomical wages, was persuaded to join. Joleon Lescott followed from Everton and there was a double swoop to acquire Kolo Touré and Emanuel Adebayor from Arsenal. Towards the end of the previous season City had been defeated at Old Trafford. The second United goal, scored by the on-loan Carlos Tevez, had been celebrated with chants of 'Fergie, Fergie sign him up' from the Stretford End. Ferguson was not convinced and prevaricated. Cook pounced, and the deal was done. Tevez swapped United red for City blue. The first meaningful blow of the new era had been landed and Cook, a marketer at heart, was intent on exploiting it for all he could. A huge poster went up above Deansgate, Manchester's most prominent thoroughfare, bearing an image of Tevez, arms outstretched in messianic pose against a blue background, with the tagline 'Welcome to Manchester'. Ferguson, so long unchallenged in Manchester, testily responded to the provocation and accused City of being the 'noisy neighbours'. Things were hotting up. I watched on from Hong Kong, loving it but desperately longing to be part of it.

The eternal pre-season optimist, I waited for the opening game of 2009/10 with a greater sense of expectation than I could remember in a long time. Twelve months on from the takeover a very different-looking City took to the field at Blackburn and it took just three minutes for Adebayor to get the season going. The win was followed by three more against Wolves, Portsmouth, and impressively against Arsenal, and then Old Trafford beckoned, the noisy neighbours versus the self-proclaimed lords of the manor. The match was won 4-3 by United, Michael Owen's winner coming in the fifth minute of 'Fergie time'. The defeat hurt as much as any of the derby losses, but City had shown their quality and character, three times coming back from behind. The week before, my role had been moved from Hong Kong to Singapore. As Owen slid the ball under Shay Given, I introduced myself to my new neighbours with a cry of anguish that reverberated around the apartment block.

To expect so many new players to gel as a unit straight away was a big ask and the form of the first four games failed to sustain itself. October and November saw a run of seven successive draws. All the same, by the time that I travelled home for Christmas, there had only been that one defeat.

I arrived back in a cold London ahead of Spurs versus City. It would be my first game since Robinho's hat-trick at the start of the previous season, my longest period since 1975 without seeing them play. True to type, the unbeaten run came to an end by way of a 3-0 mauling, and, by Christmas, Agent Hughes would be on his way. Hughes had not been appointed by the new owners so there was always an uneasy question as to how long he might last. Any dip in form, or failure to meet expectations, would likely go against him. City were about to appoint their 14th manager since Alex Ferguson had taken control at United.

I managed to get myself a ticket for the Boxing Day game at home to Stoke. I had seen City play under a multitude of different managers but, without doubt, the new one was the suavest. Roberto Mancini walked out on to the City of Manchester Stadium pitch looking every bit the ice-cool Italian. He made a mass-produced, knitted blue-and-white scarf, a throwback to the 1970s, look as if it had been hand-selected from one of Milan's finest outfitters. He came with a proven pedigree as both a player and manager having recently won back-to-back Serie A titles with Internazionale.

While he was inheriting a side 'off the pace' in the Premier League, Mancini did have an early opportunity to capture both silverware and the hearts of fans by winning a League Cup semi-final against United. The first leg, at home, was taken 2-1, Tevez scoring both goals for the noisy neighbours. He scored again in the second leg and the tie was heading into extra time, City trailing 2-1, when Wayne Rooney scored a late clincher. For the second time in the season United had beaten City in injury time.

The League Cup would have been a bonus but the priority was the league and specifically qualifying for Europe. Cook, speaking on behalf of the owners, had made it known that ambition lay beyond domestic football and the first crucial step to achieving that was Champions League qualification. Steadily Mancini organised the team in his style, building from a solid defensive base. Heading into late March, fourth place was looking like a straight shoot-out between Spurs and City. With five games to go, United came across Manchester and scored an added-time winner for the third time in the season. All the money in the world could not buy that bit of luck, and it came down to the penultimate fixture of the season, the return against Spurs. Peter Crouch poked home the winner and Spurs were guaranteed fourth place. The glory that the new ownership had promised remained elusive, but progress was inexorably in the right direction. It hardly merited a mention that City had achieved their highest league position in 20 years.

Any concerns I had previously harboured about my eastern adventure meaning that I was disconnected from City and football had long since been discarded. My work took me across the diverse and fascinating Asia Pacific region from Australia through to India and everywhere in between. The interest in English football and the emerging force that Manchester City represented was manifest wherever I travelled. It became a great connection point with colleagues, suppliers, and customers regardless of language and cultural barriers. Of course, it was not without its challenges and not every hotel I stayed in when visiting China, Thailand, or South Korea showed the Premier League, but I had developed my coping mechanism. With many years' experience in the drinks industry, I had long since recognised the universal truth that every city of note in the world has an Irish bar, and that Irish bars generally show a lot of English football. Prior to any business trip to a city never visited before a call to the local Guinness sales manager would identify the appropriate location. Come kick-off time, I would invariably find myself, pint in hand, in front of a screen showing City. The commentary might not be English, and I was often the only City fan among a mixture of Asian and western United, Liverpool and Arsenal, supporters but at least I had City.

Back in Singapore, the local coverage was comprehensive with not just live games but also the Premier League's preview and review programmes. I soon discovered that Singaporeans also knew their football. I had joined the gym next to my One George Street office and the banter and repartee with the instructors, all of whom had their own proud (non-City) allegiances, was passionate, lively, and warm-spirited. They were also deeply knowledgeable. My personal trainer, Hairull, was an avid United fan who idolised Ryan Giggs. He would attempt to motivate me by winding me up about

City's lack of success and his thoughts on what United, and in particular Giggs, would do to City the next time they played each other. 'Giggs is going to kick your sorry asses man!' It usually succeeded as I would push through the pain barrier and increase the tempo and ferocity of my sparring in proportion to his provocation. My efforts to block out muscle burn would be aided by working through my encyclopaedic memory of past City games and speculating on the prospects for the forthcoming season and the expensively assembled squad as I struggled to complete my reps.

Back at home, Mancini had used his half season to astutely assess his personnel and their prospects. With money no object he knew that success – which meant Champions League qualification at the least – was a must. He made his moves in Europe and was not afraid to spend. Champions League winner Yaya Touré from Barcelona joined older brother Kolo. The emerging David Silva soon followed from Valencia and Alexander Kolarov from Lazio. His pet project, the enfant terrible Mario Balotelli, was bought from Inter. Closer to home, Joe Hart was recalled from an impressive loan spell at Birmingham to be his first-choice goalkeeper and Aston Villa were persuaded to part with James Milner. More crucial pieces of the jigsaw were steadily falling into place.

Hart immediately vindicated his manager's decision, saving City from defeat in the opening game at Spurs. Slowly a consistency of selection was emerging, and results followed. Mancini had his trusted lieutenants on the pitch: Kompany and Lescott at the back; Barry, Silva, and Touré in midfield; and the prolific goalscorer Tevez up front. Not always pretty but with the pragmatic Italian's focus on his defensive base, it was effective. A fleeting visit back home in October enabled me to see wins against Wigan and Chelsea, but by Boxing Day I found myself on the other side of the world, watching England's cricketers humiliate the Australians in Melbourne. I had taken advantage of the relatively short travelling distance from Singapore to join up with the Barmy Army for a week. City would remain in the top four all season and revenge was sweet as Champions League qualification was secured against Spurs. The place at Europe's top table was confirmed in the first week of May but by then minds and hopes were drifting towards north London and Wembley.

Despite the FA's best efforts to devalue the brand that is the FA Cup, my love for it has never diminished. My expectation that City might one day win it had taken a severe battering on the back of a multitude of ignominious exits. I had conditioned myself not to get too carried away until we were at least in the quarter-finals. Consequently, my excitement levels rarely rose above moderate. As the 'ticker' banner hanging in the Stretford End mockingly proclaimed, it had been 35 years since our last triumph of any sort, the League Cup that Paul Burns and I had held in 1976. The Premier League still felt like a stretch, but the FA Cup did, for once, feel within reach. Leicester were disposed of after a replay, and the same fate befell Notts County in the fourth round. Aston Villa then came to the Etihad (as the freshly rebranded City of Manchester Stadium was now known) and were comfortably dispatched. The quarter-final, at home to Reading, was the last of the four ties to be played. Stoke, Bolton, and United were already in the semi-finals. An hour before the Reading kick-off the draw was made. If they won,

City would play United in the semi-final. A tight, tense game was heading for extra time until Micah Richards, one of the few 'old City' to survive the transition, rose to thunderously head home a corner. It would indeed be a semi-final against United at Wembley.

A few months earlier a colleague had asked me if I had met Ryan. I looked across the office, to where she was pointing, and saw an earnest-looking financial analyst poring over an Excel spreadsheet. The prospect of meeting Ryan did not unduly excite me. 'No,' I replied. 'Should I have met Ryan?'

'I thought you might know him,' she responded, 'he's a Man City fan.'

I immediately dropped what I happened to be doing and walked over to introduce myself to this fine-looking titan of business. Ryan is 20 years younger than me, but we immediately bonded around our common interest and watched games together in the bars of Circular Road and Robertson Quay. He was, as far as I knew, Singapore's only other City fan.

The semi-final was at 5pm, midnight for us, so we decided to watch in my apartment. If we were to lose it would not be in the company of hundreds of the 'Singapore United' fans. Part of me was expecting the worst and the opening passages of play seemed to confirm my fears. United were attacking in waves. Berbatov and Scholes had chances. City were sitting deep and letting the red shirts dictate the game. It felt like a matter of time before the inevitable, all too familiar United win. Ryan and I were saying little; we did not need to, we had both been there before so many times. As half-time approached the scores were level but we were slowly growing into the game. Lescott went close and Balotelli, the antidote to any City inferiority complex, was starting to cause problems for the United defence.

The mood after the break was more upbeat. Suddenly blue shirts pushed further up the pitch and Yaya Touré prowled like a panther, waiting for a slip, one mistake. When it came, he pounced. Carrick misplaced his pass and Touré seized his moment, taking two long and languid strides and sliding the ball under Edwin van der Sar's body. As Wembley erupted into a crashing blue wave of noise, my fellow apartment block dwellers reached for their earplugs, the peace of their early hours' sleep interrupted. The noisy neighbours were making their presence felt in Singapore and at Wembley. With half an hour to go, City were now dominating, playing with control and patience. With minutes to go Paul Scholes imprinted his six-studded calling card on Zabaleta's thigh and was duly sent off. We knew it was won. City had faced up to United and this time, for once, it had been the enemy who had blinked.

With Stoke winning the other semi it felt like a trophy was at last within touching distance. The only question was how to get a ticket. Wembley might be 7,000 miles away, but I simply had to be there. My solution lay in the form of an old friend. My ex-Nacanco colleague, Sunday morning team-mate and football watching companion, Nick, was now working for the Reading owner John Madjeski. As Reading had been in the quarter-final the Berkshire club had exercised their option to take an allocation of tickets. Fortunately for me they were in the City end. Nick came through with the goods and my credit card came through with the flights.

I would spend nearly as much time in the air as I would on UK soil.

Thirteen hours is a long time to spend in economy class. Fortunately, the generous travel expenses policy of my employers meant that it did not happen too often. In between the sporadic, interrupted sleep, there was a lot of thinking time. The exciting realisation of what might be about to happen, and the chilling fear of what defeat might feel like. There were the memories of past FA Cup finals and the chance that this modern City might be about to write another chapter in the competition's great history. There were also reflections on my own relationship with City. It was one that had been defined by everything but success. If we won tomorrow (or was it today?) would it be different?

The beautiful May morning could not have been finer as I made my way into London, meeting Nick and some friends – Stoke supporters – before heading out to the 'new' Wembley. The banter was good on the tube. The followers of two old-fashioned clubs enjoying a day in the sun, literally and metaphorically. Underneath the camaraderie, the jokes and the singing, both sets of fans were nervous. Wembley Central was a mass of club colours, red, white, and blue. Outside the station a man about my age held up a placard, plaintively begging for help. It read 'City fan of 30 years desperate for a ticket'. For a moment I wondered if I should feel guilty that I had obtained my ticket through the back door, leveraging a friend and corporate connections, and then jetting in from Singapore for what would be only my third game of the season. I quickly dismissed the notion of any lingering guilt. I had served my time and was no 'johnny-come-lately' glory hunter. In the darkest hours at Lincoln, York, and Bournemouth I had been there. I deserved today and was going to enjoy every moment of it.

While it might have been disastrously over budget and timeline, the FA had ended up with a fine new Wembley Stadium. My last visit had been in the final days of the old ground and the new version was a considerable upgrade. A thoroughly modern arena for a thoroughly modern City. I located my seat and noticed that the new structure had no place for the old stanchions that had supported me in my despair as City trailed Gillingham in the play-off final. Part of me was expecting to, once again, need support at some point during the afternoon.

Before I knew it the game was under way. I cannot honestly say that I enjoyed much of it. For once City were expected to win. With the money spent and squad assembled City were the bookmakers' favourites. Stoke, as underdogs, were the nation's favourites and it felt like the country wanted nothing other than a Stoke win. The media could then roll out the tired old stories about City's overpriced and overpaid stars. To cap it all, United had been crowned as Premier League champions earlier in the afternoon. If we lost, comparisons would be made, and they would not be favourable ones. There had been many end-of-season games that had far more at stake: Luton, Liverpool, Gillingham, to name a few. Games that decided relegation or promotion. Today, win or lose, City would still be the richest club in the world, still be in the Premier League and still be in the Champions League. Yet it felt like so much more was at stake. A win would be viewed by anyone other than City fans as the minimum. A defeat would open up the door to ridicule, derision, and a psychological hangover that might well carry through to next season. Hell, this is the FA Cup Final; I should be enjoying myself.

Recollections of the result will stand the test of time far longer than the game itself. City had chances, mainly from long range, but had to rely on Joe Hart thwarting Stoke's Kenwyne Jones midway through the second half. It proved decisive as minutes later Yaya Touré lashed home a loose ball in the Stoke penalty area for the game's only goal. Cue 'The Poznan', thousands of City fans turning their backs on the pitch, arms around each other's shoulders, jumping up and down with glee. Thirty-five years after that League Cup triumph, City had at last won something. I felt relief more than triumph. The expectation was that this had to be the start of a new chapter rather than the end of an old one. In the two biggest games of the season City's skill and character had prevailed. Tevez climbed up those steps to collect the famous old trophy. Countless times I had watched with envy as captains from many supposedly smaller and less celebrated clubs had made that same walk and proudly lifted the FA Cup. Today was City's turn and I wanted more of it.

Forty-eight hours and 14,000 air miles after departing Singapore, I returned happy and tired. All in all, it had been a most rewarding trip.

14

Fantasia

I HAD often wondered how I would feel when City finally won something of note. Consequently, it was a question that had been pondered for nearly as long as the one about 'the meaning of life'. Would it diminish my appetite for further glory, or would a first taste of success simply feed the desire for more? Before my plane had landed back in Singapore I knew the answer. The FA Cup was a welcome triumph, but dreams were now replaced by expectations, and those expectations went beyond the cups. I was greedy for more, and the Premier League was the one that mattered. It was the one that would bring global recognition but, most of all, it was United's trophy, their family crest. City had to be top dogs in Manchester before anything else. After the cup win, the Stretford End ticker banner had been replaced by one that said 44 Years' referencing the last time we had won the old First Division. They knew it and we knew it. Until we won the Premier League, until we had one to go with their 12, the banner, and all it represented, would stay.

Three years of Abu Dhabi-funded profligacy had ensured that most of the building blocks were in place. Mancini knew who his summer targets were and acted decisively. I did not know a lot about Sergio Agüero apart from vague memories of him playing in the 2010 World Cup, and the endless references to his father-in-law being Diego Maradona. I backed Mancini's judgment. His previous signings, especially Yaya, Silva, Balotelli, and Milner had all proved to be good business and the prospect of an Agüero/Tevez partnership was reason enough to feel excited.

The FA Cup win meant another trip to Wembley and the Community Shield. It was like waiting for a bus. None in years and then three in five months. The jokes about needing a map to find the way there were now well and truly redundant. The same could not be said for the capacity to self-destruct, and a 2-0 lead against United was surrendered in the second half. The respective post-mortems and celebrations were understated. Managers, players, and fans across the city all knew that more important matters lay ahead.

There are good debuts and there are spectacular debuts. I had also witnessed many bad debuts. Sergio Agüero's was spectacularly good. He was introduced as a substitute in the opener against Swansea with City leading 1-0. As soon as Agüero touched the ball the crowd in the Etihad responded. Short, fast, strong, and with a low centre of gravity, he looked made for the Premier League. He scored the second goal, made the third, and slammed home the fourth from 25 yards. I watched it at 3am while lying in bed. 'He'll do,' I thought, as I turned over to dream sweet dreams of Premier League glory.

November approached and the season had been pretty much perfect to date. Edin Džeko had scored four in a 5-1 win at Spurs and Agüero a hat-trick on his full home debut. Balotelli was also contributing big goals in big wins. Behind it all was David Silva, the creator-in-chief. Dancing between the lines, head up, ball at his feet, he would spot the pass, see the run and glide past his marker. The best football seen in most supporters' lifetime was taking City to the top of the Premier League. An impressive 22 points out of a possible 24 had been amassed in the first eight games, with 27 goals scored. It was 'fantasia' football, as if choreographed in the magical world of an animator's imagination and palette, and this fan in Asia was loving it – for now.

There was just one dark cloud: City's debut season in the Champions League had not gone quite as intended. After a disappointing 1-1 draw at home to Napoli there was a 2-0 defeat at Bayern Munich, but what happened on the City bench in Germany rather than the pitch would have bigger implications for the season ahead. The Agüero/Tevez partnership had never quite taken off. Tevez had returned from pre-season nursing an injury and he was no longer an automatic pick due to Džeko's impressive start to the season. This did not help his already testy relationship with Mancini and neither did the manager's decision to name Tevez as a substitute in Munich. Trailing 2-0 and with time running out, Mancini called for Tevez to prepare himself. Whether or not the Argentine did refuse to warm up is disputed by both parties but suffice to say words were exchanged. Tevez stayed on the bench and at the post-match press conference Mancini vowed that Tevez's City days were no more. Tevez reciprocated by taking himself off on the longest unauthorised round of golf back in Argentina, but with the goals flying in from all angles his absence was not a major concern, for now. The first derby of the league season loomed large and all knew that the result would be crucial. The title looked increasingly likely to be won and lost in Manchester. City were leading but only just, and United were second. A derby win would extend the margin to five points.

Years of marathon training with a body more suited to darts than long-distance running had finally taken its toll. I had undergone surgery on both my knees in the week prior to the game so, with my mobility restricted, I decided to watch it in my apartment along with Ryan and crack open the Tiger beer. It might have been the Tiger, or it could have been City's performance, but at some time in the late hours the crutches went flying across the floor and I miraculously rediscovered the power to walk. To walk, jump, and dance like never before. As Džeko thumped the sixth goal into the United net, and ran off to celebrate with the City fans high up in the Old Trafford away end, Ryan and I embraced. We could finally start to believe. Five points and a ten-goal swing in goal difference that had to count for an extra point. The title was ours to lose, even before November. In the post-match euphoria, I did not heed Alex Ferguson's prophetic words as he lamented that 'it could all come down to goal difference'.

I missed Dad's 80th birthday celebration because of the knee operation, but that did not stop me recording a video message, wearing my City shirt, the background walls adorned in 'United 1 City 6' posters hastily created on

PowerPoint. He had no particular interest in the match, other than through myself and what it meant to me, but I knew the sight of his 45-year-old youngest son still getting so excited about a football match from 7,000 miles away would amuse (and exasperate) him. I had also acquired a couple of United supporting nephews and nieces so I knew that they would also see it. Somehow the 'embracing victory with humility' lesson had passed me by when growing up.

Life in Singapore was good, a great experience in a wonderful and friendly, if expensive, city. The ideal hub from which to explore south-east Asia. As an independent nation, the nation state of Singapore is just eight months older than I am. Through vision, consistency of leadership, and boldness of execution, it had forged itself into a powerhouse success story. Not a bit like Manchester City then. I lived in Singapore for seven years and it was there that I later met Yvonne, the wonderful lady who would become my wife. Naturally, we often return to Singapore. Many people who have heard great things about the place ask me what the best aspects of life in this small, vibrant country are. I think about the efficiency and cleanliness. I think about the dynamic economy, the standard of living for all, and excellence of government. I salivate when I think about the food not only in Singapore but also its accessibility to the neighbouring countries and their cuisines. My heart warms when I think about the unconditionally welcoming people.

But I keep coming back to one thing, diversity. I have lived in countries that make bold claims about diversity and make great efforts to encourage diversity but ultimately hunker back to distinct ethnic enclaves. Lee Kuan Yew, the founding father of modern Singapore, is a much revered and sometimes controversial figure. He was often accused of interfering too much in people's lives and he was unapologetic about this. He had a vision and he wanted to see it through. One part of his vision was that Singaporeans should be proud of their ethnicity and heritage, but they should be still prouder one-nation Singaporeans. His public housing policy reflected this, insisting on quotas of residents from the different ethnicities (Chinese, Malay, Indian, etc.) within each housing development. Consequently, while areas like Little India, China Town, and Arab Street celebrate race and culture, and provide great tourist and dining venues, there are no residential areas that are exclusive to one. I could walk one mile from my apartment and pass Buddhist, Hindu, and Sikh temples; mosques, churches, and synagogues and think nothing of it. Now *that* is diversity. In Singapore I counted as my close friends people from multiple denominations and countries. My small professional team of 19 encompassed 16 different nationalities. The boy who had been ashamed and embarrassed to be called a 'Paki lover' had come to Asia as a man to embrace and be embraced by all nations. It felt wonderful.

The one thing that Singapore did not have, which I missed profoundly, was seasons: the meteorological kind and the footballing kind. Being virtually on the equator the weather is pleasingly predictable, between 29 and 32 degrees with 30 minutes of tropical rain at 3.15pm every day! I did, however, miss the sense of renewal and the passage of time that each new season brings. And of course, I missed the football seasons and could not help but feel some ambivalence about my location each time I sat down and watched City play some of the best football I had never seen. The al fresco viewing and balmy evenings quenched by shared five-litre iced towers of cold Tiger beer, made up for it a little. Despite the sight of the shivering masses in the stands of the Etihad I could not pretend that I was not missing it terribly, but I would not have to wait long; Christmas was coming, and I planned to get my fair share of the festive fun before this season had run its course.

I arrived back home ten days early. Undefeated and at the top of the league, I managed to get hold of a ticket for City's match at Stamford Bridge. We were in the Chelsea end but that was okay. I was going with another colleague, Ed, a fellow Blue, and we had enough about us to know how to disguise our allegiances. The wet Monday night rain sparkled in the bright lights of the London buses and bounced off the shining black roads. The traffic meant that the queues were long around the ground. We needed to collect our tickets and then stand in line to gain entry, security checks now commonplace. We finally got in and ran up to the top of the West Stand stairs as the match was kicking off. Ed had to visit the toilet so I told him that I would find the seats. I hurried through the concourse just in time to see Mario Balotelli roll the ball into the empty Chelsea net; 1-0 and not yet a minute played. City dominated and should have increased the lead, but Chelsea grew into the game and levelled before half-time. Roared on by the passionate night crowd, warming up the cold London night, Chelsea attacked. When Lescott was adjudged to have handled in the area, Lampard slammed home the penalty and the Chelsea fans all around us celebrated like they had won the Premier League, FA Cup, and Grand National all in one. I remarked to Ed that I had waited all season just to see City's first defeat. He reminded me that, unlike himself, I had at least seen the goal. It felt like scant consolation.

Come Sunday, back in Manchester, I met Chris, my brother-in-law, and nephews Greg and Joe outside the Etihad. All around the ground was the evidence that the Abu Dhabi money had not just been spent on improving the squad but also on enhancing the matchday experience. The pre-game entertainment in the newly formed City Square was attracting big crowds with its mixture of local bands and ex-players appearing on stage. Inside the ground the new scoreboards showed videos of past glories as well as constant replays of the 6-1 derby win from just a few weeks earlier. My initial concern in the frantic hours following the takeover, that it would result in City losing identity and sense of community, had been misplaced. Could we find our winning ways again?

Arsenal at home felt like the ideal game. I told my nephews that the sign of a good team is how it responds after a defeat and City confirmed my status as 'all-knowing uncle' as they responded with a 1-0 win. Three days later I returned to the Etihad. My brother Alban had risen to an executive position at famed Bolton-based bakers Warburtons. I was able to take advantage of his Manchester flat and, more importantly, the VIP suite tickets that his employers had acquired. From the hedonistic opulence of the Etihad directors' box, I enjoyed a splendid view of a more routine 3-0 victory against Stoke, accompanied by 'tournedos a boeuf'. I had never before regarded 3-0 wins as routine, but neither was I accustomed to washing down my victories with freeflow glasses of Chateauneuf de Pape so who was I to complain. I could get used to both.

By hook or by crook I obtained a ticket for the Boxing Day game at West Brom, but I would have to fly back to Singapore the next day. Try as they might City could not break the opposition down. For the first time all season they failed to score and had to settle for a 0-0 draw. I ushered in 2012 back in Singapore, foregoing the fireworks and celebrations to sit in front of the television and watch City succumb to an injury-time winner at Sunderland. The lead was now down to just two points and worse was to follow. The FA Cup is no respecter of circumstance and as fate would have it the third-round draw once more brought together City and United, this time at the Etihad. For the first time in so many derby fixtures we would be the favourites. As the whistle blew for half-time City were losing 3-0 and a man down, Vincent Kompany having been harshly sent off. The glorious memories of the 6-1 were becoming a thing of the distant past as Ryan and I seethed at the perceived injustice of the decision. But this group was made of strong stuff and pulled back two goals. United were desperately hanging on against the ten men. Mancini wasted no time in pointing out the strength and significance of the second-half performance. City went out of the cup but the mind games, so often and astutely deployed across the other side of Manchester, had started.

Mumbai; Sunday, 11 March 2012

A business trip meant that I needed to be in Mumbai. City were to play at Swansea and United were at home to West

Brom, with the gap now just one point. I loved visiting India. In many ways it reminded me of my first-ever encounter with football. The country was a complete assault on the senses at every level. The feeling of community was evident everywhere, as was the obsession with their sport, albeit a different one.

Earlier that day, after celebrating Mass, I had wandered aimlessly around the vicinity of my hotel and come across the Oval Maiden, an area of public land in the midst of the sprawling city. It was the Hackney Marshes of cricket. On a piece of grass that was the size of maybe six football pitches there must have been 50 separate cricket matches taking place. Boundaries, physical and metaphorical, overlapped each other and to the unfamiliar eye distinguishing which fielder belonged to which team was an impossibility. I did not need to know as the ones who were playing evidently did, and amid the chaos in front of me there was also a great sense of order, respect, and civility. I sat and watched the multiple games for most of the morning, marvelling at the universal appeal of sport across cultures and countries and its power to connect people regardless of race, status, or wealth. My accommodation was not far away, the Oberoi Hotel, scene of a horrendous terrorist attack that had taken place a few years earlier, and a reminder of the ever-existent darker side of life. The contrast could not have been greater.

Conscious of the action taking place in Swansea in the early evening, I had checked out the location of the nearest Irish bar but as the Oberoi had the cable feed from South Wales it was not needed. City never hit their straps and it took a Joe Hart penalty save to keep them in the game until in the dying minutes when Swansea scored the only goal. Meanwhile, United had defeated West Brom. Having led the league since October, we were now no longer on top and it was painful to look at the table. The camera showed scenes of a fan in tears as if all was lost. It was far from the case but nevertheless my stomach had started to tighten.

Singapore; Sunday, 8 April 2012

March had not been a good month. It started with the Swansea defeat and, desperate to reinvigorate the struggling forward line, Mancini had swallowed his pride and brought the exiled Tevez back in from the cold. It briefly had the desired effect with the Argentine creating a winning goal against Chelsea. But a further two precious points were dropped at Stoke and City's 100 per cent home record had also been fractured by Sunderland in a 3-3 draw. It could have been worse as two goals in the last five minutes had rescued a barely deserved point. United were now efficiently churning out wins and led by five points.

To maintain touching distance, City had to win at Arsenal, a feat not accomplished since the 1970s. They played like a team lacking the belief that they could win either the match or the league. It almost came as a mercy when Mikel Arteta fired home to give Arsenal the victory their better football had merited. With minutes to go Balotelli, reverting to his erratic self, lunged into a tackle, and was sent off for the third time in the season. I switched off the TV and went to bed before the final whistle had even sounded. City were now eight points behind United with six games to go. I was beginning to accept that the title dream was ebbing away and there was little that could be done to revive it. I needed to be up early and on a flight to China the next morning.

Chengdu; Tuesday, 11 April 2012

I felt tired and frustrated. I had spent the whole day presenting to business colleagues at a Chinese White Spirits factory in Sichuan province. My command of Mandarin was basic, so I was speaking through an interpreter, which made it harder work for both my audience and me. Some of them had responded by resting their heads on the table and falling asleep. It had been one of those weeks.

Taking a cue from my Chinese colleagues I decided that I needed a good night's rest and, even though we were playing West Brom, resolved to sleep through the night in my hotel bed. I would habitually record the midweek games to watch the following morning but, on most occasions, I would also lie in bed and watch them live. I did not plan it, but some sort of extrasensory perception would naturally wake me up around kick-off time and once awake there would be no return to slumber, try as I might. The Sheraton in Chengdu did not have the game on the room TV. At some point in the 21st century I had upgraded my small pocket transistor radio for an iPad so was able to follow the various (non-government censored) websites, but with the fate of the season just about decided I intended to sleep through.

I am a light sleeper and at about half past four my phone buzzed. I wiped the sleep away and read a text from Ryan, 'Have you seen the score?' I reached for my tablet on the bedside table. City had rediscovered their goalscoring touch and were leading 3-0.

'A game too late for that,' I replied.

'The United score,' was his intriguing response.

I scrolled down the page. United were losing to bottom-placed Wigan. Maybe there was just a glimmer of hope. If the scores stayed the same the gap would be five points, significant but United had still to come across town to the Etihad. City scored an immaterial fourth that I hardly noticed as my concentration was now fixed on the update from Wigan, desperately waiting for the bold letters 'FT' to appear next to the score. After a few more minutes it was confirmed. Three hours later I walked into the Chengdu boardroom with an extra spring in my step, energy restored; there would be no falling asleep during my presentation.

Singapore; Saturday, 14 April 2012

Before the Arsenal game, we had been five points behind United and the outcome of the last two matches had not changed that. In fact, now, with two fewer fixtures remaining, City were worse off. But it did not feel like that as two significant things had occurred. The goals had started to flow again and United, whose form since Christmas had been imperious, had demonstrated they could be beaten. There was a shift in the momentum, not a big one, but just enough to give hope.

From Singapore it looked like a beautiful spring day for the lunchtime kick-off at Norwich. City, with the same spring in their step, responded to the feel-good weather with a feel-good win. Tevez and Agüero scored five goals between them, at last dovetailing into the deadly partnership we had been hoping to see all season. Tevez celebrated his redemptive hat-trick in front of the fans with a mock golf swing, an ironic homage to his impromptu leave of absence. The more pompous in the media described it as disrespectful and insulting. I, for one, did not care.

United were now two points ahead with a game in hand. For the first time in weeks, they would be playing with a little more pressure, self-inflicted through the Wigan loss, but also the sky blue revival would surely not have gone unnoticed across the city. Within a few hours the optimism of the preceding four days was dampened as United restored the five-point gap, winning against Aston Villa.

Ho Chi Minh City; Sunday, 22 April 2012

As if Singapore life was not pleasant enough, I had taken myself off to Vietnam for a short holiday: three days in Ho Chi Minh and then some quiet time on the beach island of Phu Quoc. I arrived at my hotel on the Saturday afternoon, and I went straight up to my room to check out the TV. No sports channel and therefore no Premier League. Before I could relax, I needed to know exactly where I would watch the following day's game at Wolves. I dumped my bags without unpacking and went into the city. The hotel concierge had given me the name of a few sports bars. Not altogether convinced that he knew what I was talking about, I needed to check them out for myself so I wandered out, map in hand. The first place on the list did not exist and the second one was an Aussie bar that was only going to show Australian rules football and rugby league. The third was run by an American and screened mainly US sports, but the owner assured me the Premier League games would be shown. Priority number one accomplished, I could now start to kick back and enjoy myself.

I spent most of Sunday exploring the wonderful place that is Ho Chi Minh. This city and the City that dominated my thoughts shared a common theme – one of a troubled past and an optimistic future. While fully enjoying the sights and the culture, my mind turned to the coming evening as the sultry day wore on. First up was United at home to Everton – not easy but a match they should win. Immediately following, City would play a Wolves side heading towards the relegation trap door. I got back to the hotel to follow the United game on my laptop. Everton had a brief glimmer of hope as they equalised Rooney's opener but from the minute-by-minute updates United were creating the better chances. They soon exerted this authority and established a 3-1 lead. Everton were not going down without a fight but 3-1 quickly became 4-2.

The exertions of the hot day and the couple of beers that had wetted my lips took their toll and I drifted off. I could only have been asleep for a few minutes as when I awoke the match was playing out its final moments. I roused the laptop from its own evening slumber to confirm the inevitable United win but in the short time that I had been comatose, Everton had scored twice. The score was now 4-4. I needed confirmation that this was not a mistake; United did not have a habit of conceding two-goal leads at Old Trafford. I sent a text to Ryan and for the second time in ten days my eyes were fixed to the screen waiting for the updates from a United game. Ferdinand went close, as did Rooney, but United dropped the points. With three games to go the dream was back on. I got up, enthusiastically lathered myself in the shower and skipped jauntily to the sports bar.

My new American friend was as good as his word and the Wolves game was about to be screened. The players would surely know the result from Old Trafford, and it could almost be sensed in the way they started off. The carefree swagger of the previous two matches had been replaced by a tension befitting the dramatically increased stakes. Fortunately, the desperately poor home side were unable to take advantage of the early nerves and, once Agüero had converted Clichy's clever through ball, the result was never in doubt. I relaxed, ordered another beer and got stuck into my chicken wings and Vietnamese spring rolls. Samir Nasri secured the precious points in the last minute and once more the destiny of the title was back in City's hands. The vastly superior goal difference would see to that. With the next game being against United, victory was undeniably in their hands too. Three points the difference and three games to go.

The days following the weekend action were slow ones. Without the distraction of work to keep my mind busy I lay by the hotel pool in Pho Quoc thinking of little other than the United game, playing out every scenario in my head. My poolside reading matter was Paul Lake's brilliant autobiography and I wondered if he too was counting down the days. Lake, the truest of Blues and Mancunian through and through, surely would be. No doubt wishing he could have been part of it, but all the same beseeching victory for those who, from all corners of the footballing world, now stood in his place and pulled on the shirt.

Singapore; Monday, 30 April 2012

I returned to Singapore and the weekend hung around interminably. I took a passing interest in the Premier League games being played elsewhere but everyone, not just me, was waiting for Monday night. The internet, the newspapers, and Mio TV (the Singapore football channel) were full of it. The biggest game in Premier League history, they kept telling the world. City had started off their Premier League journey with Sky's first *Monday Night Football* broadcast. The atmosphere at Maine Road that evening had been a new and unfamiliar one with parachutists descending on to the Moss Side turf and dancing girls at half-time. The off-pitch entertainment had seemed to be more important to Sky than the football as the fledging league tried to launch itself with power and impact. Twenty years later no hype was needed. The only thing that mattered would be what happened on the pitch.

The kick-off time was 4am in Singapore, so I snatched a few hours of sleep before Ryan came round. Both sides were pretty much at full strength so there could be no excuses. Mancini went with the same attacking line-up that had served him so well for the last three games. United announced their team and the tone for the evening was set. With the three-point cushion, Ferguson could have gone for the win that would have almost certainly been the killer blow but chose to opt for a more cautious approach, selecting defensive midfielder Park Ji-sung. The initiative had been handed to City before a ball had been kicked. The Etihad never looked better and 'Blue Moon' had never been sung with more passion as the overhead cameras zoomed in on the floodlit stadium. From Singapore I longed to be there with every beat of my heart.

The action played out as the team selection had suggested it might. City had the bulk of the possession but turning that into chances was proving to be challenging. It appeared that Ferguson and United would happily take the draw, content that four points from their remaining two games would give them the title. Any chances created would need to be taken and the most likely route was looking like a set piece. Seconds before half-time, Silva swung in a corner and captain Kompany, City's most consistent performer over the season, leapt to power an unstoppable header past keeper David de Gea. Kompany ran off to the East Stand to celebrate, the iconic image of a great leader at his peak. We briefly let out a cheer to be heard in Manchester, quickly hushed, remembering the ungodly hour.

A goal up, City could approach the second half differently. Unable to suddenly change gears United hardly created a chance of note. As the tension on the pitch and in the stands increased, so it did on the bench. Ferguson and Mancini exchanged words and very nearly blows as the subtlety of mind games were replaced by the visceral passion of the moment. Mancini would not be intimidated like so many before. The City players were serenaded home through the Manchester night to choruses of 'Blue Moon' and the job was done.

The crowd dared to dream and the cameras honed in on the executive boxes. Long-time fan and one-time drinking companion Noel Gallagher, the man who had modelled the doomed Kappa kit as City plumbed their nadir of the Second

Division, was in rapture, banging on the glass window. Underneath the excitement and the joy in his face you could sense he longed to be out there among the crowd. For the moment being a fan trumped being a rock 'n' roll superstar. More recent recruit Diego Maradona, the father-in-law of Sergio Agüero, was there with his daughter, delighting in the family success if not totally appreciating the significance of the moment for those who had waited so long. Maradona cheering at the Etihad? This was starting to feel unreal.

Mio showed the league table, which confirmed what all City fans needed to see before we could believe it. In four games City had turned over an eight-point deficit and were now back on top, albeit on goal difference. Win both of our remaining games and we would be champions. It needed saying again. If City won their last two games, we would be champions. The pragmatic Mancini refused to get carried away. The cool Italian could switch between Latin passion and ice-cold realism in a heartbeat. He also had the measure of Ferguson and was not going to drop his guard at this late stage. United remained the favourites, he insisted, as their final two games were easier than City's. The next match, at Newcastle, was by no means an easy task, but QPR at home looked like a formality. United had Swansea at home and then a trip to Sunderland. Whoever wished to be champions would need to win both their games. I showered and headed to work, the adrenalin coursing through my veins compensating for any sleep deprivation.

Kuala Lumpur and Singapore; Sunday, 6 May 2012
Nearly 30 years had passed since Saint and I first met in our Sunderland student flat. Much had changed in the

ensuing time, not least the globalisation of football and ease of world travel. One thing that had remained steadfast was our enduring friendship. While Saint had continued to live in the Sunderland area, he had risen through the ranks of his profession, bringing an astute commercial brain to the halls of academia as business development director at Northumbria University. He was required in Kuala Lumpur to meet with the local faculty and discuss the delivery of franchised courses. When he told me that he was coming I had no hesitation in making the hour-long flight from Singapore to join him for the weekend.

I lay by the hotel pool as Saint concluded his business, meeting him for sundowners and then beers late into the night as we watched Chelsea win the FA Cup. It seemed like a lifetime ago, and not just one year, since City had been celebrating their breakthrough victory at Wembley. Right now, the FA Cup, the trophy cherished for so long, seemed 'small beer' compared with what could be accomplished in a week's time. Expectations had been irrecoverably altered.

The next morning, thick-headed and devoid of the inspiration to think for ourselves we hopped on a city tour bus to see the sights of Kuala Lumpur. We politely observed the contrasting architectural styles of the city, a mixture of colonial and Asian, and paid lip service to the historical commentary while savouring the time we had together. We reflected on the journeys we had both travelled in life: the constancy of our friendship, the good fortune that we had both been blessed with in terms of friends and family, and the unpredictable nature of fate that had taken us from our student flat in Sunderland to an open-top bus in

Kuala Lumpur. It was a special time spent with a dear and loyal friend.

Much as I valued every moment, my mind inevitably drifted elsewhere as the bus neared completion of its loop around the city. Flights between Kuala Lumpur and Singapore are frequent and reliable, but I did not want to take any chances and had booked myself on one that would get me back home with plenty of time to spare. I said my goodbyes to Saint in the early afternoon and headed to the airport. To my relief my flight was on time and Singapore Airlines duly delivered me back home in a timely fashion.

Newcastle, having a surprisingly good season, were challenging for a Champions League place. A win would be no formality. St James' Park, a wonderful modern stadium, had changed massively since my first trip there in the mid 1980s, but it had retained its character. It still dominated the Newcastle skyline, its location in the heart of the city centre serving as a focal point. A formidable place for opposition fans and players to visit, especially when Newcastle were doing well. The away supporters were positioned in the highest of upper tiers almost invisible and inaudible to their team at pitch level. All City's players would hear and see would be the black-and-white ranks massed in the Gallowgate and Leazes stands. This would be a tough penultimate obstacle to overcome, but if they prevailed the finishing line would finally be in sight.

Much to my approval, Mancini kept faith with the same 11 that had prevailed against United, and the match followed a similar pattern with City dominant in possession but chances at a premium. As each one came and went – Gareth Barry's rare shot on goal and Agüero's scuffed prod – the tension became more pronounced. United were playing Swansea straight afterwards and I could picture their fans in the Old Trafford concourse bars, nursing their beers, watching the game and willing Newcastle to win every tackle and thwart every City attack. Half-time came and went, and the match resumed, the tempo much the same. The 70-minute mark quickly passed. Precious time was ebbing away. Mancini sat on the bench, pondered his tactics and contemplated his next move. I rose from my seat and sought inspiration. How could I help things? A desperate situation called for a desperate solution and there was only one thing that came to mind.

In 2005, England's cricketers had won the Ashes in what was one of the most thrilling and absorbing sporting contests. After 24 days of high-octane Test cricket the outcome went down to the last afternoon of the last match. But that was so nearly not the case. Had Australia not lost the second Test at Edgbaston by just two runs then they would have likely crushed England in the series. History records they did not and on that long, agonising Sunday morning Michael Kasprowicz gloved the ball to England wicketkeeper Geraint Jones, Freddie Flintoff famously consoled Brett Lee and a nation found belief in a new set of heroes.

I had woken up on that distant Sunday morning in 2005 full of confidence. England, after all, only needed two wickets and Australia needed around 100 more runs. It should all have been done and dusted in the first couple of overs. It wasn't, and with every streaky edge that went for four, every scrambled single, and every appeal denied, the optimism and confidence slowly dissolved. With the target down to about

20 runs I stood up and started walking around my dining room table. I felt a lot more comfortable on my feet; it got the blood circulating and relieved the tension. I decided I would continue to walk until the Australia innings was over, win or lose. The total continued to rise and the target came down, into single figures and then below five, one lucky shot away from victory, or more significantly England's defeat. I continued to walk around the table. Fast bowler Steve Harmison steamed in for one final effort, Kasprowicz obliged, and delirium followed. Oddly, my dining room table never got a mention in any of the post-match analysis, but I was convinced that cricketing destiny had been shaped by an 8ft by 3ft slab of oak and my jittery walk to victory.

That same slab of table was behind me in my Singapore apartment, shipped via Hong Kong, all the way from Hertfordshire. I looked at it and wondered. Could it once more come to the rescue? I started walking and immediately felt more relaxed. Seven paces towards the balcony with my back to the television then a turn at the top and retrace my steps towards the living area and the screen. As I got to the end, Mancini was preparing to make a substitution. I turned round and I could see it was Nigel de Jong, that most defensive of midfielders, replacing the creative Samir Nasri in a must-win game. The manager's genius, as de Jong settled in front of the back four, was to allow Yaya Touré to venture forward. I continued to pace my well-trodden path.

Touré, all guile, strength, and composure, started to affect the game much further up the pitch. Agüero laid the ball beautifully into his path and from 20 yards he serenely placed the ball into the bottom corner of the net. I took a deep breath and carried on walking around the table. To stop now was to risk all. Newcastle, still fighting for their own Champions League ambitions, duly responded but City showed their resolve and determination. When Touré scored the second goal in injury time I leant over the table and kissed it. The best £700 I ever spent.

I envisioned the collective groan that must have gone up around the crowded Old Trafford bars and concourses as United's last real hope had surely been extinguished. Mancini was his usual cautious, conservative self in the interview afterwards, but the joyful tears of City legend Mike Summerbee sat in the stands were more telling. Next week we would be at home against a QPR side that had the worst away record in the division and had struggled at the bottom end of the table all season. One short, agonisingly long week away from glory and redemption.

15

Staggering

THE ELEVATOR doors closed. There was no turning back.

The taxi ride from Newton Circus to Singapore's Robertson's Quay takes about 15 minutes. It felt fitting that I travelled alone. After all, I had not lived in Manchester since the age of nine so the vast majority of my journeys to watch City, be they to Maine Road, the Etihad, or stadia scattered across England had been solo ventures. I never, in my wildest dreams, imagined that my footballing odyssey would all come to a climax in Singapore. Still, I was experienced enough in the ways of both Manchester City and the traveller to appreciate that the chaos of both had brought me to this point and place. In the words of Jerry Maguire, 'If this is where it has to happen, then this is where it has to happen,' and Singapore had better be ready for it.

I got to the The Chamber, a popular expat haunt. The open-air concourse in front of the bar was almost devoid of customers, but full of plastic seats and tables positioned at every possible angle to see the multiple screens. The proprietors were planning for a big night. A few of the seats

were occupied by F1 enthusiasts taking in the latest episode
of Bernie Ecclestone's money-go-round. I found my reserved
table and settled in for the night, impatient for my friends
to arrive and occupy the vacant space around me. I needed
conversation and company to calm my nervous energy.

Steadily the place filled, as the Tiger towers started
to empty, and the expectant buzz grew. Katie and Gav, a
colleague and her husband, arrived with some friends. They
had lived in Chengdu (of the soporific presentation), and Gav,
a Glasgow Rangers fanatic, had established his own football
team there. Chris, another long-standing colleague and a
die-hard Evertonian, arrived with his girlfriend Gillian. Back
and forth all year we had debated the merit of City's success
in the context of the financial investment. In another world
it could have been Everton who had benefitted from the Abu
Dhabi riches and City could have been languishing in mid-
table. Chris had constantly bemoaned the randomness of it
all. 'All you have done is win a lottery,' he would frequently
poke me. A part of him was jealous and a part of him was also
pleased, recognising that City, like Everton, were a football
club with real tradition and loyal, long-suffering supporters.
The money could take none of that away. For me, if not for
my football club, he was begrudgingly happy. With minutes
to go before kick-off, Ryan finally arrived. He had been away
for the weekend but made the dash back to Singapore. He
simply had to be with a fellow City fan.

Mancini's final team selection was probably his easiest.
He chose the same 11 that had been victorious in the last
five games. A sixth win and we would be champions, and
only QPR stood between City and glory. QPR would fight

their own battle like cornered tigers for those last points they needed to avoid relegation. They were now managed by Agent Hughes, still smarting from his shabby dismissal by City, and captained by ex-City player Joey Barton, a man who would love nothing more than to piss on his former employers' big parade.

My story had started to become real against QPR. That trip to Maine Road courtesy of Joe Corrigan's letter and the discounted season ticket I subsequently saw advertised in the matchday programme. The humiliation of relegation in 1998 had been against QPR with Jamie Pollock's farcical own goal. City's first Premier League game, Paul Lake's ill-fated comeback, had been against QPR. Whatever the next 90 minutes would bring, QPR were going to have another defining role in my story.

I looked up from the conversation and Robertson Quay was now full to capacity. The vast majority were red-shirted, Singaporeans and Koreans, hoping that City could fail one last, spectacular time. As ever, there was also a presence of westerners, most with no particular allegiance, but nonetheless a significant interest in the outcome of the evening's proceedings. I viewed them with suspicion, trying to assess their motivation for being present. Happy gatecrashers at my party or tricoteuse at my guillotine? As far as I knew, Ryan and I were the only two City fans among the eagerly expectant throng.

Finally, Captain Kompany and his sky-blue team appeared in the Etihad tunnel. To a man they looked serious and tense, focussed on the task in hand. Was it a portent of steely determination to get the job done or did it betoken stage fright? The next two hours would reveal all. As I had once so proudly done in a stadium and age that now seemed aeons away, Kompany led his charges on to the Etihad pitch. The turf was scattered with blue and white ticker tape. It reminded me of one of my first football memories, the 1978 World Cup in Argentina. Could it be that City's Argentinian contingent would play a pivotal role tonight? I felt the first pangs of jealousy as I saw the faces in the crowd, so many of them of my generation, so many shared memories between us. As the teams lined up for the kick-off, I closed my eyes and tried to imagine that first life-changing moment. The noise, the feel, the smell and, most of all, the sight of that greenest of grasses. On this stage for my life's drama, the final act was about to start. My brief escape from the moment was abruptly interrupted by a 'What the fuck?!' from Ryan.

I opened my eyes, looked up and instantly raised him to, 'Shitting hell!'

The controller of the large screen in front of us had switched its feed from the Etihad to Sunderland's Stadium of Light and before our eyes were the ignoble figures of Ferguson and Rooney. After a few polite but unerringly strong words in the proprietor's ear, the channel was switched back to the Etihad and United were relegated to a small monitor situated below the main screen. I sat down, my heartbeat slowly calming to something like 50 per cent above normal. I had my seat, I had my friends, I had my beer, and I had my City. I leant back, breathed deeply and relaxed, confident that the night ahead would now be one of uninterrupted and triumphant bliss.

There is a certain inevitability that the match will start off slowly. QPR, in all probability needing only a draw, are never going to throw caution to the wind. City, who must assume that only a win will suffice, dominate the possession but there is little to show for it. While the score remains goalless at the Stadium of Light, I am relatively relaxed. Elsewhere, Stoke make the evening's first significant move as news comes that John Walters has scored against Bolton. QPR's position is strengthened and as things stand even a defeat will see the London club safe. Now there is less imperative for them to go seeking a goal and abandon their strategy of defend at all costs.

City probe and prod, Silva dances between the lines, Tevez and Agüero make darting runs into space, Zabaleta and Gaël Clichy advance from full-back to create the extra man on the flanks. Hart is a lone spectator in goal. Still QPR resist. The crowd at Robertson Quay watch enthralled. The various permutations and how they are playing out are more engrossing than the action itself. Below the big screen, the smaller monitor is showing the United game. I look at it, not wishing to tempt fate, but unable to resist a furtive glance. *That's fine, United are drawing, we are still top.*

I know that both games staying goalless for an extended period is unlikely. It will also result in the most agonising of evenings as one slip, one lucky goal for or against, could change everything. There is no need for me to keep glancing at the screen. If United do score the place will surely erupt. Regardless, I look again. Valencia swings a cross into the Sunderland penalty area. Rooney ghosts around the back of the static defence. His bald, round head meets the ball and the net bulges. Singapore celebrates. Ryan and I look at each other. This is not the script we had anticipated or hoped for, but neither is it the time for doubt; there is over an hour to play. No need to panic – yet. Within seconds the news of the goal filters through to the Etihad stands. Initial angst among the expectant fans is quickly replaced by a rallying cry, a call to action for the players. The Robertson Quay gallery whoops as the revised league table appears on the screen and shows United in first place. As things stand, they will be champions.

City visibly respond to the crowd reaction with more urgency and pace. Yaya Touré moves into those forward areas where he has been so effective so often. He carries the ball forward and Zabaleta makes one of his trademark runs. This time, instead of going outside to send in a cross, he comes inside Touré. Yaya reads him and feeds him. Zaba runs on to the ball and shoots. It is not a clean shot, but it is powerful enough to bend the hand of goalkeeper Paddy Kenny and slowly, achingly it loops into the net. Zabaleta, the 'Coeur de Lion', who has not scored all season, wheels away to the corner flag in celebration. City have regained their grip on the trophy. Robertson Quay groans as Ryan and I celebrate. Refusing to be deterred by the glowering faces around us, we dance our merry dance before remembering the defining character of the team we are supporting. We quickly sit down. Across the plaza and the adjacent bars we can hear a few more cheers, possibly from City supporters but more likely from the Liverpool, Arsenal, and the 'anyone but United' brigade. I sit back and take a satisfied sip of my beer. The revised league table is again displayed on the screen returning matters to their rightful order. The previous version seems like a brief, bad, nightmare.

I pat Ryan on the back. 'We'll be all right now, mate.'

Significantly, Bolton have just scored, not once but twice at Stoke. They are above QPR and it means that the London team will now have to throw more men forward in pursuit of the point they need. That will surely open up more space for City to exploit. The stars are all aligning. Distracted by the moment, I do not notice the injured Yaya Touré limping off the pitch and out of the game on the cusp of half-time.

I have had nearly as many half-time pees as I have seen football matches. That is a lot. Not too many of them stick around in the memory all that long. At home, when watching the match on television, it is generally a solitary and hurried affair, the aim to get it over and done with it before the adverts are finished. At the ground it is a much more sociable occasion as a result of the inevitable bottleneck caused by dozens of men discharging themselves of several hours of pre-match drinking. The match analysis there takes a different form, largely depending upon the previous 45 minutes, and characterised by the darkest of gallows humour. There is the knowing acceptance of what has just happened and is likely to happen after half-time. At away games it is usually prefixed by a sigh and an 'all the fucking way just to watch this shower of shit'. Occasionally there has been the happy surprise of an unexpectedly good first half, but more often there is outrage at a perceived injustice courtesy of a match official. The unerringly consistent thread throughout is an unshakeable belief in the certainty that City are bound to fuck it up in the second half. To have ideas other than this would be sacrilege; tantamount to invoking the darkest of spirits. Blind optimism is an unwelcome guest in this environment. And yet I remember this pee for the sense of giddiness. My worst pre-match fears had all but been dispelled. A few jugs of Tiger followed by Zaba's goal had seen to that. There were now just 45 tantalising minutes between City and glory. The way the first half had flown by I felt, against all my better instincts, irrationally confident. I weave my merry way back through the tables and chairs with a hop and a skip to re-join my party. I even join in with some 'normal' conversation. Above the Singapore Park Hotel that stands in the plaza I can see a clear sky and, if not a blue moon, then certainly a bright one. I do not see that behind me, above my shoulder and moving ominously towards me, are dark clouds.

The game restarts, and then it all happens. A speculative ball played towards QPR's Djibril Cissé looks just that, a pass hit with more hope than expectation. Joleon Lescott is alongside Kompany and there should be no danger. Lescott has been a solid and reliable performer all season but in the big games he often has one mistake in him. Twelve months ago, in the FA Cup Final, Kenwyne Jones had outmuscled him and ran into a one-on-one contest with Joe Hart. Luckily for City and Lescott, Hart had prevailed. On a pitch measuring around 10,000 square metres, football is so often decided by centimetres. Maybe the swirling wind holds the ball up in the air but Lescott's positioning is marginally out. He is too far under the hanging ball to make proper contact and it skids off his head, backwards and into the path of the advancing Cissé. This time our goalkeeper is unable to come to the rescue as the striker advances before lashing a ferocious drive past Hart and into the net. The Quay erupts with shock and joy. Forty-eight minutes on the clock. Our ascendancy has lasted for just nine minutes. 'Plenty of time left,' I reassuringly tell Ryan. 'We'll be fine.' I wonder if he is seeing the same fear in my eyes that I can see in his.

The response from the broadcasters is immediate. United first on 89 points and City back in second on 87; the screen confirms it all. The response from City is less immediate. They are faltering, momentarily shocked into paralysis and self-doubt. Passes are now going astray, shots are scuffed and the runs of Silva, Nasri, and Agüero that have been so penetrative all season are all now leading down blind alleys, each one guarded by multiple sentries. Intervention is needed and I don't care where it comes from.

Like most others, I do not see what happens when Carlos Tevez falls to the ground holding his face. The fact that Joey Barton is in the immediate vicinity is enough. He must go. The multitude of television angles do not reveal anything conclusive, but referee Mike Reed's suspicions warrant a consultation with his assistant. From the moment he starts walking towards Barton it is obvious that the red card is coming out.

Barton is not for leaving the scene with a whimper. His parting act is to kick out at Agüero and to stick his face into Kompany's with a hope of forcing a reaction that might then even up the numbers. The City players resist, and the pantomime villain belligerently departs stage left as the boos and hisses rain down. All that is now needed is a bit of calm and City, with one more man, can resume normal service.

As it happens, normal service is starting to become a challenge for Singapore's broadcaster, Mio TV. The pictures on the big screen start to freeze. The feed buffers intermittently and then kicks back into action. In many ways it is matching City's stuttering performance. Every few seconds surges of activity and forward momentum are being brought to a frustrating halt. Repeated again and again. It has been nearly 20 minutes since Cissé's equaliser and we have hardly made an impression on the QPR goal despite the numerical advantage. Ryan and I keep telling each other it will come. The television feed has now sorted itself out just in time for us to see uninterrupted coverage of QPR making a rare break down the left wing. Kompany thinks he can intercept the attack, but he mistimes his tackle and is now out of position. The cross comes into the City area and a red-shirted QPR striker arrives late on to the penalty spot and connects perfectly. I feel physically sick as the ball nestles in the back of the net.

There is not so much a cheer that goes up at the Quay as an intake of breath and a chortle of disbelief. Not even the United fans had anticipated this. Not in their wildest dreams. Nothing is said or needs to be said between Ryan and me. All the bravado is a distant memory and we both know that words of faux confidence and self-delusional reassurance will be just that. We are almost benignly accepting the inevitably of it. The glory football of the past 18 months had just been a fantastic dream and we are now waking up to the cold reality of our footballing fates.

Still, while there is time there is hope. There is also precedent – Gillingham in the play-off final and more recently Spurs in the FA Cup.

321

I break the silence, 'Shit, shit!' It is all that I can think of, the rest is up to the players. The table comes up on the screen but we all know what it will tell us. United are now ahead by three points. Just 20 minutes left and two goals required. Beneath the cold numbers lay deeper, darker emotions.

On the sidelines Mancini is now out of his seat. The man with ice in his veins has long since lost his composure. On his haunches, then on his feet, kicking every ball and diving into every tackle. He makes his final changes of the long season as he withdraws Tevez and Barry and sends on Balotelli and Džeko. There is no great tactical insight behind it, just a desperate throw of the dice. The grandma-style scarf worn around his neck with such style all season is increasingly starting to resemble a hangman's noose, strangling the last vestiges of rational thought and sureness of purpose.

In Singapore, away from the disintegration at the Etihad, Mio TV has also long since lost all sureness of purpose. The broadcast glitches have returned to the screens around Robertson Quay and the pictures are now as frozen as City's performance. Once more they buffer and then freeze, the audio commentary carries on oblivious to the plight of the viewers. Ryan, with the impatience and optimism of youth on his side, wanders off to find a bar with the feed intact. I am resigned to venting my anger at the static screen in front of me. We are choking and I am unable to witness what is happening. I slump in my seat, perversely frustrated that I cannot see that what I least wish to see. It puts me in mind of the Woody Allen joke about two ladies lunching in a restaurant.

First lady: 'Oh the food is just terrible in here.'

Second lady: 'Yes and such small portions as well.'

By contrast, from Sunderland both the pictures and United's progress continue uninterrupted. One goal to the good for the last hour, they are in cruise control. I have long since resigned myself to the certainty of their victory. There will be no helping hand from Sunderland or indeed anywhere. We must score two goals and time is running out.

I sit, despondent, in a white plastic chair, miles from home, surrounded by red United shirts, and contemplate how it has all come to this. Through the countless disappointments and humiliations, I have often asked why I manically follow a group of men I do not know kicking a football around just because that disparate group happen to wear the same shirt. If this means so much to me, then what does it say about the rest of my life? Sure, family, friends, and work all matter from both an emotional and a practical sense but nothing other than football has ever affected my feelings so often and so intensely. Time and time again I have questioned it all and time and time again the answer is the same: it is because I have always believed that a day would come when all the hurt, the expense, the emotional investment will be rewarded. But at the end of the rainbow there is no crock of gold. Fairytales do not, after all, come true. Yes, City had been there for me when I most needed them in my past, but I had paid back that debt many times over. It was time for some reciprocity and that time was supposed to be right here, right now.

What is, or what is not, happening on the stop-start screen is becoming more of an irrelevance as I descend into my dark place. I look up with forlorn hope as the stuttering picture kicks into life only to see Balotelli head straight at the goalkeeper from four yards.

In the past I have been able to move beyond all the disappointments, but I am not sure if I will be able to get past this one. If I do, it means coming back for more and right now I am not sure if I can take that. My mind keeps going back to the 6-1 win at Old Trafford and how great it felt to be associated with City that day. I think of the video I had made for Dad's 80th birthday with 6-1 posters all around the apartment. I had scoured every newspaper online and downloaded every podcast, taking in report after report that glorified the performance. I had watched the replay of the last few minutes so many times that I knew each word of the commentary. 'It couldn't be six could it? It is you know.' Blow it today and those memories would be meaningless. Worse than that, they would just serve as a permanent reminder of the humiliation that was now unfolding. I keep coming back to the same question: 'Why does it mean so much to me? Why do I let it mean so much to me?' I had always assumed that I would grow out of it. If I had done the things that normal people do like have a wife and family then maybe I would have. But here I am, stuck with this millstone around my neck.

'Why does it mean so much to me?'

I have no answer other than that it does.

I do not care or notice that the TV glitches have sorted themselves out. The final minutes of normal time creep upon us and the cameras are now more interested in the emotional drama unfolding in the stands at the Etihad. The world is an unwelcome voyeur on my football family's private grief.

More schadenfreude than sympathy. Among the crowd are a thousand desperate faces I can relate to. There are the traumatised ones, paralysed with shock as they look upon the car crash laid before them, powerless to do anything about it. There are the angry ones venting their frustration on scarfs, seats, and loved ones, desperate to expend that pent-up energy they have brought to the Etihad in expectation of celebration. The camera zooms in on what looks like three generations of the same family. They have hollow haunted faces. They are staring into nothing, saying nothing. The ghosts of City past, City present, and City yet to come. The bewitched, the belligerent, and the bewildered. In each one of their faces, I see my own and I can look in the mirror no longer. It is time for me to leave.

My friends, witnessing my anguish, have long since given up on any conversation. As if I had just told them that I have a terminal illness they make a few attempts, first at reassurance and then condolence, but we all know the outcome and there can be no words that will ease the pain. Not right now.

The clock ticks past 90 minutes. Zabaleta goes down the right wing for what seems like the 100th time and wins another corner. I look around at the United fans getting ready to celebrate and reach into my shorts to pull out a handful of $10 bills that are as crumpled as my dreams. I hand them to Chris, sat next to me.

'That's for the beer, mate. I'm not hanging about to see the end of this crap.'

It feels like a coward's way out, but I am past caring.

The corner swung over by Silva is the same as the numerous corners that had preceded it. I wait to see the same predictable outcome, the ball scrambled away by a QPR defender. Edin Džeko sees it differently and slips his marker for the first time. From six yards he cannot miss, and the force of his header is too much for the goalkeeper and those protecting the line. Its innate simplicity contrasts with the complication of all the preceding huff and puff; 2-2 and there are just three minutes of added time to go. One goal needed. I do not let myself get too excited, recognising that the situation remains desperate. I am, however, sure that we will get one last chance in those precious last three minutes. But can we take it? I decide to hang on just a while longer.

Robertson Quay's reaction is mixture of gasped excitement and muffled horror. The rollercoaster has just made its long, slow climb and is teetering on the summit. The uncontrollable plunge towards its final climatic descent is about to start. My knuckles whiten as I take a tight grip of the arms of my chair.

City regain possession straight from the kick-off. The renewed energy of the Etihad roar can be heard, and the cameras now show the contorted, animated faces in the stands. Invigorated by fresh belief, they are imploring their heroes to one last herculean effort. Training routines and tactics boards are all irrelevant as ten desperate sky-blue shirts swarm forwards. The ball is kicked upfield again and runs out of play on the halfway line for a QPR throw-in.

'One more chance. I know we will get one more chance.'

I lean back in the seat then immediately rock forward again, my head in my hands. And then, where's Ryan? I have not seen him since he went off to search for a bar with an uninterrupted TV feed. I look around. Maybe he has found

one. Maybe he has gone home. The distinct, isolated cheer
that goes up from the QPR supporters in the south end of the
Etihad can be heard on TV. News has come through from
Stoke and their fans are starting to celebrate. A 2-2 draw at
the Britannia Stadium means Bolton are relegated. Safety and
joy for QPR. As things stand the 2-2 score at the Etihad will
be despair for City.

'One more chance, just one.'

The throw-in is taken into the City half and Lescott easily
wins the ball back. It seems like days ago that his error had let
QPR into the game. De Jong takes control and looks ahead to
see all the blue shirts camped around the opposition penalty
area. Resisting the temptation to launch a long ball in among
the crowded bodies he moves forward into the swathes of
vacant grass. An inset appearing on the screen shows that the
final whistle has gone at Sunderland. As expected, United
have won and their players are now impatiently waiting for
the Etihad result before celebrating in front of their travelling
supporters. De Jong moves forward.

'One more chance.'

Agüero breaks ranks from the masses and comes short to
receive the ball on the edge of the area. He turns and with
no other option among the touch-tight marking he plays it
into the feet of Balotelli, his back to goal. I do not notice
Agüero continue his run into the space on the right. I do
see Balotelli use his strength to hold the ball up against the
pressure of his defender. Falling back, he feeds the ball out
to the blue shirt to his side. The diminutive figure moves
forward into the penalty area. Is it Samir Nasri? Is it David
Silva? I plaintively appeal for a penalty in anticipation of the

327

nearest QPR defender fouling him, but the blue shirt evades his lunge.

'Just one more chance.'

He shoots. For a second there is the most perfect stillness as the ripple of the net slowly makes its way to Singapore. I do not react immediately, doubting what I have seen. When I do, I am snapped out of my frozen stupor by the image of Agüero running away, bare-chested, whirling his blue shirt above his head in delirium. The boy from the *villa miseria* in Buenos Aires celebrating like he has lived in Burnage all his life. Just another boy, like me, 7,000 miles from home. Kompany and Balotelli grab him and wrestle him to the floor. Joe Hart, for so much of the game a lonely spectator races around his penalty area as the Etihad erupts, a volcano of emotions. I get out of my seat, stunned and staggering.

'No. No. No!'

I look around at the other screens across the plaza and despite what I can see on each one I am in glorious denial. Robertson Quay lets out its final collective gasp, the incredible nature of what we have all witnessed momentarily transcending any partisanship. From the various bars around me come pockets of cheers. I am engulfed by my friends who seconds earlier were witnessing my desolation. They are not so much pleased for City as they are for me. I try to compose myself for the remaining 30 seconds. Surely not even City can cock it up from here.

The whistle goes and the crowd swarm on to the pitch. The beautiful, glimmering carpet that first drew me to the game dissolves into a mass of blue-and-white humanity within seconds. I am embraced again, this time by strangers who have observed my agony and ecstasy from afar and want to feel a small part of it. They congratulate me as if I have scored the winning goal myself.

I look around again. 'Ryan, Where's Ryan? Ryan?'

Like Sylvester Stallone desperately searching for Adrian at the end of the first *Rocky* film I am swaying, punch-drunk, looking for my soul mate, the one person in Singapore who will truly know how this feels. From nowhere he appears, a vision of exhaustion, elation, and trauma. From his seat at a bar across the plaza, he had embarked on an Agüero-style run down to the Singapore River. We have our homoerotic moment as we hold each other like two survivors of a shipwreck, washed up on safe shores.

'We did it, mate, we fucking did it!'

From the ladies around us there is a group 'aaahh' and, I am told, the hint of a tear.

The rest is a bit of a blur. Robertson Quay quickly emptied as the United fans and neutrals headed home to get ready for the working week that would commence in a few hours. The remaining City fans and neutrals partied together as the champagne corks popped and Vincent Kompany raised the Premier League trophy aloft.

For most of my UK-based friends watching on Sky, Martin Tyler's 'AGUERROOOOO! ... I swear you will never see anything like this again' remains the indelible soundtrack to the goal. For international viewers, Peter Drury brilliantly delivered his own verdict, 'Agüero! ... staggering, just staggering ... where does football go from here?' I did not hear the words at the time, drowned out by the noise around me and my own delirium. I have heard them many, many times since on replays, souvenir DVDs, YouTube clips, and promotional trailers for the Premier League.

I departed Roberson Quay in the early hours of that May Monday morning, staggering to the taxi rank that I so nearly sought as my premature refuge. I collapsed into the back of the cab and asked myself,' Where do I go from here?' I now had what I most wanted. Was it really the end of the journey?

I switched on my phone and immediately the emails and text messages came flooding through. They were from family and friends, old and new. Some from people who I had not heard from for years. The early ones were commiserative, the later ones triumphant and congratulatory. The Whippet, a long-standing friend from cricket tours, simply wrote, 'That is the most ridiculous thing I have ever seen.' I sunk back in my seat; I was tired beyond belief but I knew it would be hours before I got any sleep.

Epilogue

THE ELEVATOR doors opened, and I stepped back into the sanctuary of my apartment. The white walls provided a much-needed calm. A sanitorium-like serenity. I poured myself a glass of whisky, sat on the balcony, and tried to make sense of it all. To sift through the tangled wreckage of what I had just witnessed. Not just the match but everything it entailed, past and present.

Exhausted, and emotionally spent, I was incapable of rational analysis. I thought of the past, the life-forming moments that forged my bond with City. The happy ones such as holding the League Cup and becoming a Junior Blue, as well as the painful ones when City represented an escape from the troubles of my school life. I thought of the oh so many painful defeats. I thought of the people along the way. My family, especially my brother David, Nanna and Gangan, Paul, Saint, Nick, Peter Jones, Joe Corrigan, and the many wonderful people that football had brought me closer to. I even thought about my class-mates from St Michael's and wondered if any of them had been thinking of me as that goal went in. I thought of the victims of Bradford and

Hillsborough, who I had never met but with whom I shared a common bond.

Eventually, I started to think about the next season and then it clicked. It was never about what *had* happened but about what *might* happen. The only thing that has ever scared me about dying is that City will play their next match and I will not know the score. Ever since I could remember it had been the constant in my life, the light on the horizon. At the times of greatest darkness and greatness joy there would always be the next game to look forward to. The bullies, the struggles, the triumphs, and the travels had never been able to take that away. The words 'feeling blue' have had so many different meanings for me and tonight described a new and unique emotion. But I also knew that in a few days, once the euphoria had settled and the internet had moved on to the next story, I too would move on and the most important thing would be the next match, followed by the one after. If, ultimately, that was all it was about, just always having something to look forward to, then I could live with that.

Content, I leant back and sipped my whisky. Below me, sat outside the street café some locals were savouring the last embers of their shisha pipes. I breathed in and tried to catch a waft of the spicy aroma drifting up in my direction. I felt a smoky sweetness on the back of my throat that took me back to a never-to-be-forgotten time and place. Balkan Sobranie. Always, always Balkan Sobranie.

Acknowledgements

THIS BOOK could not have been written without the help and support of many people. Some with knowledge of the enterprise, others unknowingly.

My publisher Jane Camillin of Pitch Publishing showed great belief in this project and she and her team of Duncan Olner, Laura Wolfe and Gareth Davis helped me through the challenges of being a first time author, with professionalism and expertise. Thalia Suzuma and Justyn Barnes shared their insight and gave authentic feedback that turned my confused ramblings into a coherent story. Peter Drury, who was present at this story's climax and moment of inspiration gave me encouragement and, in the midst of a frantic football schedule, found the time to craft a brilliant foreword.

To recognise all the friends and colleagues who have helped me navigate the choppy waters of life's journey would be a book in itself. They are very many and that journey was so much more fun for knowing you. Nick, Colin, Stuart, Chris T, Adrian, Paul E, Chris A, Whippet, Mark … you know who you are and thank you.

Ryan, we will always have our Aguero moment!

Paul B, this book would be nothing without you and your family. Who knows what dark direction my life would have taken if not for a playground conversation some 45 years ago.

Saint, you and Helen have been my rock for so many years. Your steadfast friendship has been a great joy in my life. May it continue for many more years to come.

My family are central to my story and continue to be so. To my siblings, Elizabeth, Kathy, Rachel, Alban and David you have always been there for me in your different ways. You lived with much of this, indulged my obsession, and grounded me in reality. Your support of me telling my story has been a great source of strength. David, much of this story evokes painful memories, you have been generous and understanding in corroborating it and encouraging me to tell it. To my many nieces and nephews, thank you for being you. You inspire, amuse, and energise me even if you do have some strange tastes in music, clothes, and football teams.

During the writing of this book both my parents, Michael and Anne, passed away. The lives they lived were rich, generous, and full of love. They raised a family in a vibrant and energetic home and encouraged passionate interests and the freedom to express oneself through any medium. I hope the book is fitting to their memory. They were the epitome of love, life and belonging (but maybe not football) and are dearly missed.

My wife, Yvonne, does not feature in this story as we met after its conclusion. Nevertheless you are present on every page and in every thought and action. Your patience, understanding and superb attention to detail as I burdened you with this project is truly appreciated. More than that you have been my companion, support and soul mate on the last six years of our crazy worldwide adventures together. My love and admiration for you is the point at which I am finally lost for words ... but I could not end without acknowledging the many supporters and players of Manchester City Football Club, past and present. What can I say? It has been a blast, hasn't it?

Also available at all good book stores

9781909626553

9781909178717

9781908051646

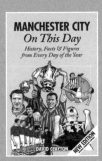

9781908051004

9781785314995

9781801501149

9781801500586

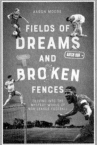

9781801501002

9781801500470